ABOUT THE AUTHOR

Oliver Lindsay is a soldier. After being Adjutant
of the Guards Depot, passing through the Staff
College and holding a Staff appointment, he was
stationed in Hong Kong with the 2nd Bn
Grenadier Guards, which gave him the opportunity to meet many who had been captured by
the Japanese.

His next posting was to National Defence
Headquarters, Ottawa, where he discussed Hong
Kong's war years with many Canadians who were
there. This inspired his first book, *The Lasting
Honour: The Fall of Hong Kong 1941*, also
available in Sphere Books, and the present
volume.

Lieutenant-Colonel Oliver Lindsay is the fifth
generation of a family which has served the British
Army with distinction since 1794. He is now a
member of the Defence Policy Staff in the
Ministry of Defence.

Also by Oliver Lindsay in Sphere Books:

THE LASTING HONOUR

At the Going Down of the Sun

Hong Kong and South-East Asia 1941–1945

OLIVER LINDSAY

They shall grow not old, as we that are left grow old:
Age shall not weary them, nor the years condemn,
At the going down of the sun and in the morning
We will remember them.

Poems for the Fallen, Laurence Binyon

The emblem of our flag is the Rising Sun and the fame of
the 'Land of the Rising Sun' will shine forever as brightly as
the Rising Sun itself through the brave and indomitable
actions of the Japanese who are sincere advocates of peace.

Japanese propaganda leaflet, 1941

SPHERE BOOKS LIMITED
30-32 Gray's Inn Road, London WC1X 8JL

First published in Great Britain by Hamish Hamilton Ltd 1981
Copyright © Oliver Lindsay 1981
Published by Sphere Books Ltd 1982
Map drawn by Denys Baker

Set in Lasercomp Times

Printed and bound in Great Britain by
©ollins, Glasgow

For Victoria, Mark and Fiona

CONTENTS

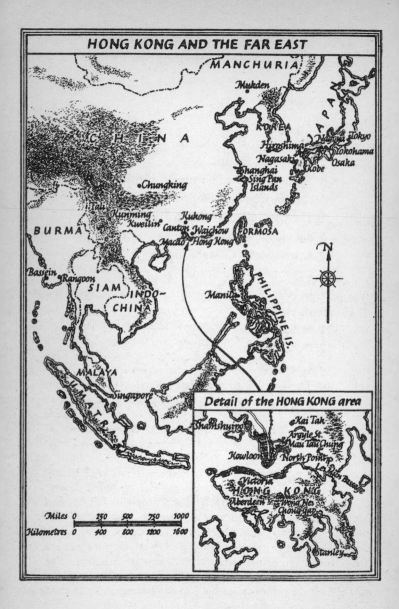

HONG KONG AND THE FAR EAST

MANCHURIA

Mukden

C H I N A

KOREA
Hiroshima
Nagasaki
Kobe
Osaka
Nagoya Tokyo
Yokohama

JAPAN

Chungking

Shanghai
Sing Pan
Islands

Tali
Kunming
Kweilin
BURMA

Kukong
Canton Waichow
Macao Hong Kong

FORMOSA

Bassein
Rangoon
SIAM
INDO-
CHINA

Manila

PHILIPPINE IS.

N

MALAYA

Singapore

SUMATRA

Detail of the HONG KONG area

Shamshuipo

Kai Tak
Argyle St.
Mau Tau Chung
North Point
Lei Yue Mun

Kowloon

Victoria
HONG KONG
Aberdeen
Wong Nei
Chong Gap

Stanley

Miles   0   250   500   750   1000
Kilometres 0   400   800   1200 1600

Hong Kong. Christmas Day, 1941. Sir Mark Young, the Governor and Commander-in-Chief, could distinctly hear from Government House the chatter of Japanese machine-guns now barely a mile away to the east. Apart from one platoon of the Middlesex Regiment and some scattered outposts of the 2/14 Punjab Battalion, scarcely any troops remained between the enemy and the undefended centre of Victoria, the capital of the Island. The few exhausted soldiers in Government House, and Fortress Headquarters nearby, would soon be involved in bloody hand-to-hand fighting. Once this occurred, all possibility of controlling the shattered forces would cease.

Major-General C. M. Maltby, MC, commanding the allied forces in Hong Kong, urged the Governor by telephone to surrender, for he knew that further resistance was futile. Sir Mark briefly consulted his Colonial Secretary and Attorney-General who were in the room with him. His glance fell on Winston Churchill's signal on the desk before him: '. . . You guard a vital link long famous in world civilisation between the Far East and Europe . . . Every day your resistance brings nearer our certain victory.' Sir Mark believed as a matter of principle that the defenders should fight to the last man. He ordered General Maltby to fight on.

Since the summer of 1941 the Japanese flag, the Rising Sun, had reigned over a vast empire which included Korea, Manchuria, Formosa (Taiwan) and much of China. But Japan was greedy for further conquests, and in July the Japanese marched into southern Indo-China (Vietnam), thereby placing her armed forces within striking distance of areas and trade routes vital to Britain and America. The British, American and Dutch Governments responded by cutting off all oil supplies to Japan. Faced by economic collapse, or loss of face by withdrawing from some of her conquered territories, Japan resorted to war.

On 8 December the Japanese attacked at Pearl Harbor, Hong Kong, and Malaya.

An American radar unit at Pearl Harbor had detected the approach of aircraft, and close to the Island an American warship had sunk a Japanese submarine. Nevertheless the alarm was not raised and no special precautions were taken. Surprise, the essence of the Japanese plans, was complete and the Americans received a catastrophic blow which crippled the Pacific fleet.

Hong Kong, on the other hand, was ostensibly ready for war. The 12,000 British, Canadian, Indian and Chinese troops were in their defensive positions and ships at battle stations. At 5 a.m. on 8 December, General Maltby ordered the blowing up of the bridges at the frontier – four hours before the Japanese 38th Division, virtually equivalent in infantry to the defenders, attacked across the border on the mainland.

This Division consisted of highly trained soldiers with a wealth of battle experience from fighting in China. Their artillery was greatly reinforced beyond the normal establishment. By contrast the British forces consisted mainly of units hitherto employed on garrison duties, indifferently equipped, lacking experience of warfare and even of battle training, and hastily formed into extempore formations.[1] These deficiencies, together with total lack of air support and inadequate sea power, made the defeat of Hong Kong a foregone conclusion.

By 12 December, the Japanese had broken through the mainland defences held by 2nd Battalion Royal Scots, 2/14 Punjabis and 5/7 Rajputs[2]. These Battalions were withdrawn to Hong Kong Island to join two newly arrived Canadian Battalions, the Winnipeg Grenadiers and the Royal Rifles of Canada, and 1st Battalion Middlesex Regiment. These units were supported by locally-enlisted men of the Hong Kong Volunteer Defence Corps, two Regiments of Coast Artillery and one Anti-Aircraft Artillery, a Regiment of the Hong Kong and Singapore

Royal Artillery, Signallers and Engineers. The five obsolete RAF aircraft were predictably destroyed on the ground by Japanese bombers which also caused considerable damage to the ships of the Royal Navy.

For six days Japanese artillery from Kowloon peninsula systematically destroyed the allied defences on the Island's north shore, while Japanese aircraft leisurely bombed allied positions. Meanwhile Japanese ships to the south steamed out of range of the coastal batteries, which suggested that an attack might come anywhere. General Maltby, unable to determine where the attack might fall, kept his troops in company positions so scattered that they were barely under battalion command.

Each day was a terrible ordeal for the Chinese civilians who were bombed and machine-gunned indiscriminately. Chinese fifth columnists attacked isolated allied posts, although the Chinese Secret Triad societies had executed over four hundred Japanese sympathisers.

At 7 p.m. on 18 December six Japanese battalions attacked the island's north-east coastline from the mainland. They stormed past the Rajput out-posts and gained possession of the commanding heights where the reservoirs were located, after which the island was indefensible. Within fifteen hours Brigadier J. K. Lawson, MC, commanding the Western Brigade at Wong Nei Chong Gap had been killed and his Headquarters overrun. Following the collapse of a very gallant but hopeless stand by a small party of the Winnipeg Grenadiers, the Japanese drove a wedge right across the island. The survivors of the Eastern Brigade, commanded by Brigadier C. Wallis, withdrew to Stanley peninsula from where they were unable to break out. The Japanese fought with great ferocity and they handled their numerous mortars with commendable skill and devastating effect.

By 2.30 p.m., 25 December, communications with Brigadier Wallis at Stanley had been lost. The troops holding the west of Hong Kong Island were being heavily shelled and repeatedly dive-bombed. The Commanding Officer of the Middlesex Battalion reported that the line was breaking, and the area held by the Battalion Headquarters of the Royal Scots was believed to have fallen. 'This loss was as serious as it was unexpected,' wrote Sir Mark Young later. 'The Japanese could now occupy the whole of the district where the European women and children were collected in houses. They were already being shelled and some houses were on fire. We were in the final pocket and this loss opened another seam.'[3]

Sir Mark telephoned his Naval Commander. 'I told him again,' remembers Commodore A. C. Collinson, RN, 'that we could probably only hold out for about two hours, and that the risk of the Japanese butchering the civilian population did not warrant further resistance.'

'Our troops were overwhelmed both in numbers and by artillery,' noted the Fortress Headquarters duty officer in the last entry in the war diary, 'besides being completely defenceless from the air. At 3.15 p.m. on Christmas Day, General Maltby advised the Governor that no further military resistance could be of any avail. At 3.25, the General advised all Commanding Officers to surrender, it being abundantly clear that any further resistance meant the useless slaughter of the remaining Hong Kong garrison.'[4]

'To all of His Majesty's Forces in Hong Kong the time has come to advance against the enemy. The eyes of the Empire are upon you, be strong, be resolute and do your duty' – so read Sir Mark Young's signal on 19 December 1941. However, it caused some confusion for the Royal Navy, which had been ordered on the same day to scuttle all ships in Aberdeen harbour with the exception of two river gunboats, *Cicala* and *Robin*, and the Motor Torpedo Boats.

During the eighteen days of fighting, the destroyer *Thracian* and the gun-boats lay off-shore bombarding the Japanese positions, while the MTBs in addition to night patrols attacked ferry boats, re-supplied army units and generally created problems in General Sakai's open flanks – the sea.

On 19 December a determined daylight attack on the Japanese ferrying craft near Devil's Peak by the second Motor Torpedo Flotilla ended in disaster. Six MTBs in pairs led by Lieutenant R. R. W. Ashby, HKRNVR, sped forward with machine-guns blazing. Several Japanese troop-carrying craft were sunk, but surprise was quickly lost and, within minutes, two MTBs were sunk and two others were damaged.

Two days later, *Cicala* had been sunk and the dive-bombing of *Robin* caused some damage. MTB 10 was riddled by shell splinters, but miraculously the only fatal casualty was one live duck, designated for Christmas lunch, which was killed by a splinter earlier than intended.

As the inevitable defeat in Hong Kong approached, the MTBs prepared stores and arms for a possible escape. Lieutenant-Commander G. H. Gandy, RN, was given emphatic orders that he must be prepared, on receipt of the order 'Go', to take on board in the MTB flotilla three secret service men, F. W. Kendal and his two assistants, McEwan and Tallan. 'Emphasis was put on secrecy and there was to be as little discussion as practicable, even with my own officers,' Gandy wrote later. 'The escape plan was all pretty nebulous to me, barring landing with packs, arms and tinned food somewhere on the Chinese mainland, and occupying two derelict mines as a last resort.'[1]

Kendal, a Canadian, had led Force 'Z', an irregular sabotage group under the command of the Secret Operations Executive in Singapore. Their plans, to disrupt Japanese communications from two almost inaccessible caves beyond Kowloon, had gone awry. Little had been accomplished due to the speed of the enemy advance. Kendal had been about to brief a Company Commander on the forward defensive line on 9 December when a Japanese attack captured the position. He evaded the Japanese, but was unable to get back to the caves and so went instead to Hong Kong.

Kendal told Lieutenant-Commander Gandy that there was no chance of a successful escape until he had made plans with Admiral Chan Chak who had established a mission in Hong Kong based on Victoria. The Admiral was a flamboyant and ruthless character, with a prominent, pugnacious jaw. He had lost a leg in a naval action against the Japanese on the Yangstze River. The mission's second-in-command, Major-General S. K. Yee, represented the Chinese Secret Service. During the fighting for Hong Kong both these officers assisted the British with counter-espionage measures and in the liquidation of Chinese fifth-columnists.

The British had promised Chiang Kai-shek to do their utmost to ensure that the Admiral and General Yee would not be captured by the Japanese, and so plans were made for the MTBs to carry them from Aberdeen to China before Hong Kong fell.

By the afternoon of Christmas Day, however, chaos reigned. Aberdeen harbour was under heavy artillery fire from the Japanese batteries close by, and movement was vulnerable. The five remaining MTBs moved to the west of Aberdeen Island which sheltered them from the artillery bombardment. Although Gandy had Kendal and his group on board, there was no sign of the Chinese officers.

'At 3.15 p.m. I received the signal from Naval Headquarters: "Go",' noted Gandy. 'As I had no news of the two important Chinese officers, and our movement by daylight would be obvious to the enemy, I decided to disobey the orders and wait.' At 3.35 p.m. he signalled back: 'Propose go after dark. Must pick up two Chinese from Aberdeen. Will enter after dark.' The uncompromising reply came back from Lieutenant-Commander J. H. Yorath, RN, in Fortress Headquarters: 'Go all boats.'

While it might be acceptable in war for ships' captains to disregard their orders in order to speed towards the sound of gunfire, it was unheard of for a commander to prejudice the safety of his ships to save two Chinese, however distinguished.

As the signals to the MTBs were difficult to transmit and no ships could leave Hong Kong when the surrender had become effective, Lieutenant-Commander Yorath was ordered to find the MTBs and order them to leave immediately. He therefore ran from Fortress Headquarters to his house, which had received several direct hits, and collected his hired car. He then drove to Aberdeen where he found no MTBs, but he guessed they might be sheltering beyond the island.

Yorath found a ship's lifeboat alongside a ferry and he persuaded a marine Chief Engineer, N. Halliday, to help him row out to Aberdeen Island. Shelling from four Japanese guns forced them to return to the shore for shelter. They then followed the coast to the west and, straining at the oars, they dashed across to the island. Yorath landed and climbed up the rocks from where he could see the MTBs. He contacted Gandy and ordered him to sea. The orders were now sufficiently emphatic to demand compliance.

Yet Kendal on Gandy's MTB was insisting that Admiral Chan Chak still in Hong Kong must be saved. He argued that Chiang Kai-shek would lose trust in Britain if his two officers were captured by the enemy. Their torture and death would inevitably follow.

7

Gandy's dilemma was acute, particularly as he had sent a further signal at 4.55 p.m. telling Admiral Chan Chak and General Yee to meet him at 7 p.m. The reply from Victoria had been received at 6.30 p.m.: 'Not approved, proceed immediately with Kendal.'

An hour earlier, Admiral Chan Chak, General Yee and the Admiral's henchman Henry Szue, dressed in ordinary Chinese clothes, were driving around the coast in an old Austin car with a canvas top, looking for the MTBs. They had been joined by two staff officers from Fortress Headquarters – Captains Freddie Guest and Peter MacMillan, an Old Etonian in the Royal Artillery who was the son of a bishop.

As this conspicuous group approached the enemy road blocks, Henry Szue yelled in Japanese with such enthusiasm: 'Banzai! Long live the Emperor,' that only desultory shots were fired after them.

At Aberdeen harbour they were joined by thirteen others – an RAF Squadron Leader, a British Superintendent of the Indian Police named Bill Robinson, a Staff Officer from Delhi; two others ostensibly from the Ministry of Information, named MacDougall and Ross, a Norwegian, several Merchant Navy seamen and a few Chinese. They found a small ship which they loaded with food, water and petrol. Filled with optimism, they chugged at six knots down the south-east channel from Aberdeen, straight into the arcs of fire of the Japanese batteries.

The calm of the lovely cool evening was broken by shells which slammed into the water close by. Heavy machine-gun and rifle fire riddled the frail craft.

Admiral Chan Chak told Henry Szue to pray to God on his behalf and announced that he would be baptised as a Christian should he survive. When the engine caught fire the Admiral unstrapped his false leg, which was full of money, gave his lifebelt to a Chinese who could not swim, and jumped with eleven others into the water. The bullets continued to fall like hailstones around them; the Admiral was hit in the wrist and MacDougall in the back. Nevertheless they swam on, through a shoal of giant jelly fish, for almost an hour before reaching Aberdeen Island. The Japanese in their battery had watched the swimmers through binoculars and started to shell the beach as the forlorn party staggered ashore.

The British and Chinese split up and made for the far side of the island, and their relief can be imagined when they saw a single MTB in the sea beyond. They took off their shirts and waved frantically. However the MTB crew mistook them for Japanese, and machine-gun fire hit the rocks above their heads. The MTB then weighed anchor and moved tantalisingly further out to sea. It was a sickening sight, and several were on the verge of tears with frustration. They discussed what they should do. More swimming seemed out of the question, but an RNVR Cadet, Holger Christiansen, swam out to the MTB.

Lieutenant-Commander Gandy recalls that as Christiansen was dragged on board: 'He gasped out what sounded like – "there are ten Japs after me." Lewis guns were accordingly trained on floundering figures in the water behind him until it was realised that Christiansen had meant, not ten Japs but ten chaps of the escaping party who had followed him.'

Three other MTBs were ordered to join Gandy and pick up the swimmers. However, one MTB's engine could only be started by being towed at speed across the bay, although this inevitably brought them into view of the Japanese batteries.

As the shelling resumed, Gandy was shocked to discover that Admiral Chan Chak had not swum out from the Island. 'Here at last was talk of Kendal's key figure, so essential to our escape,' Gandy wrote later. 'But where was the Admiral and what should I do with these unarmed swimmers expecting a ride? Of course I must take them, but what were their credentials? For instance the Ministry of Information was a rather low priority Government Department. I had no idea they were from Military Intelligence.'

Henry Szue said he could find the Admiral whom he had left in a cave, and so he was sent off in a skiff with the most reliable rating, Able Seaman A. L. Downey. They returned as it became dark to report that, although the Admiral had only one leg and a bullet still in his wrist, he had left the cave and could not be found.

Superintendent Robinson and Lieutenant-Commander Yorath volunteered to persevere and search for him. Yorath's boatmanship proved excellent, and they were both soon clambering over the rocks, whistling loudly, hoping that the Admiral would hear them.

A stone came rolling down the steep hill just as they were despairing of finding him. 'The Admiral was practically at the top, although it was a difficult climb,' Yorath wrote later. 'I think he must have gone up there to die – Chinese like having their graves on hillsides. We lugged him down and got him in the boat. He must have suffered agonies. As we rowed back, he sat facing me in the stern and crossed himself which rather surprised me.'

The Admiral had his wound dressed in Lieutenant-Commander Gandy's cabin. He put on the Commander's naval cap and radiated confidence.

At 9.15 p.m. the five MTBs sped at twenty knots in a long, single column out into the China Sea. The hero of the occasion was undoubtedly Gandy. 'He showed commendable discretion,' records the official Royal Navy despatch, 'in not precipitately obeying the order to "go at once". Had Admiral Chan and General Yee fallen into Japanese hands owing to our neglect to contrive their escape, it would have been not only deplorable but shameful.'

Gandy asked Admiral Chan Chak what course they should set. 'Make for Peng Chau Island in Mirs Bay, and there we will get valuable information,' he replied. The nearest friendly territory, Singapore, was far beyond the range of the MTBs, whereas Mirs Bay, to the north-east of Hong Kong, was controlled by Chinese guerrilla forces which should prove friendly.

The MTBs sailed in extended single line past the sullen, sinister coast line of Stanley peninsula, where Brigadier Wallis at that moment was contemplating the miserable prospects of surrendering. Glimmering fires could be seen on shore and the noise of muffled explosions reached the MTB crews.

Suddenly a Japanese destroyer appeared on the horizon. Its searchlight probed the darkness and several red rockets glimmered across the China Sea.

Unbeknown to the MTBs, the destroyer had found another small Royal Navy group on board a diesel launch, C410, which carried the senior Naval officer still afloat, Commander H. M. Montague, RN. This launch had been used to carry ammunition to Stanley on Christmas Eve, but she had run aground in Aberdeen Channel. Commander Montague had refloated her at high water and they, too, were sailing for Mirs Bay. 'We were greatly alarmed when the Japanese searchlight found us,' he recalls. 'We turned directly away to the south-west and presently the light was switched off. It is possible that our yellow funnel looked like a sail and the destroyer thought we were only a sampan.'[2]

The MTBs, meanwhile, had anchored close to the island of Peng Chau. Kendal, Captain Guest and Superintendent Robinson were rowed ashore with orders to kidnap the Chinese headman and bring him to the Admiral. On reaching a small fisherman's hut, they rapped sharply on the door. It slowly opened and the Chinese put his head out. He was immediately grabbed and taken triumphantly back to the MTBs where Admiral Chan Chak filled him with copious quantities of Royal Navy rum and interrogated him upon the Japanese patrols.

The headman was extremely co-operative and knew of the Chinese guerrilla resistance movement, which Hong Kong had been financing. He arranged for his fishermen to be put aboard as pilots, and at 2 a.m. the MTBs moved off in close formation and at slow speed to a small bay at Nam-O.

As the MTBs approached the bay, the crews saw a mysterious craft with a funnel. The Lewis guns were hurriedly trained upon it, but a stream of coarse British oaths drifted across the calm water. The strange ship was Commander Montague's C410 which had run aground once more. Fortuitously he had chosen the same escape route.

The Commander decided that the ships should be scuttled and that they should escape on foot by trekking 1200 miles across China. Sampans were put alongside each ship and the unloading of blankets, oil skins, provisions, rifles and ammunition was completed at dawn on 26 December. Scuttling the ships proved more difficult. Under protest from the villagers who wanted the wrecks, they were taken out to deeper water and holes were knocked in the decks and below the water line. The villagers were most friendly and produced condensed milk and hot water for a meal on shore.

Admiral Chan Chak organised a small escort from the guerrilla bands and villagers to carry him and the wounded MacDougall in sedan chairs along the narrow hillside paths. It was a lovely fresh morning, but the sailors were saddened at the loss of their ships and apprehensive of the long walk ahead in enemy territory.

The British numbered sixty-two, and were dressed in oddments from the naval stores. Most wore khaki trousers, white naval sweaters, steel helmets or naval caps. Each man carried a rifle or pistol and two heavy haversacks filled largely with food.

Admiral Chan Chak looked splendid in Lieutenant-Commander Gandy's naval cap, set at a jaunty Beatty angle. Gandy resigned himself to an uncomfortable steel helmet for months to follow.

The villagers cheered enthusiastically as the party moved off at 6 a.m., in a long straggling single file. The naval ratings were told that they were not going far on the first day, but the paths gradually grew steeper. On reaching a high ridge everyone looked back at the shimmering bay, and to their dismay, they saw several of the scuttled MTBs were not completely submerged.

If the Japanese saw the wrecks too, the presence of the Royal Navy would be discovered and the villagers slaughtered for which the surplus naval stores left for them on the beach would be no compensation.

Commander Montague and Admiral Chan Chak decided that movement by day was too risky and so they hid in a tree-covered valley close to a small village, Kow Tit – the name inevitably inviting ribald jokes. At 5.30 p.m. they continued along a pretty coastal path, following the shore before striking north into the interior of China.

The guerrillas accompanying them were wearing faded blue clothes and also carried grey blankets. At one of the ten-minute halts, Gandy asked a young guerrilla girl what her parents thought of her present role. 'I belong to the New China, but they do not,' she replied. Several guerrillas suggested a pistol shooting competition at a crow obligingly perched on a tree two hundred yards away. 'I took aim very carefully and squeezed the trigger,' recalls the Commander. 'Puff! No explosion, only laughter from the guerrillas. My ammunition was faulty, having deteriorated with age. Mortifying of course, but perhaps just as well, because there were no more hints from the Chinese that their forces needed modern arms.'

The party marched fourteen miles to the guerrilla Headquarters at Wang Nih Hui where everyone slept fully clothed on straw. At 8 a.m., on 27 December, they set off again after an excellent breakfast of tinned sausages and cocoa. The countryside was fascinating. Tidy paddy fields and sugar cane plantations had been planted alongside graceful bamboo trees. However evidence of the war was never far away. Several of the villages had been bombed with incendiary devices which left them in charred ruins.

Gradually the mountain path became steeper as the day became hotter. Several ratings abandoned their personal possessions and a young RNVR Lieutenant with a weak heart collapsed. Fortunately coolies, including girls in their teens, carried the naval stores in baskets on each side of a bamboo shoulder bar. They added the stragglers' rifles and ammunition to their loads.

That evening they approached the Tah Shui-Shao road which was used by Japanese patrols and convoys. Captain Guest and several guerrillas went ahead to the road to plan its crossing. 'We watched Japs in trucks go by with field guns. Then I heard our men coming up in the darkness behind us,' he wrote later. 'They were making the devil of a noise. A Jap motor-cycle and side-car came along and stopped almost opposite to where I was lying. A Jap officer got out and looked up and down the road. Could I get them both with my pistol? I wondered. Just then another motor-cyclist arrived from the other direction and they all departed together. The noise of their engines fading in the distance was one of the sweetest sounds I ever heard.'[3]

After marching forty-seven miles, they reached San Hui which lay within the territory of the Chinese Regular Forces. 'There we had an elaborate meal of rice, pork and tea,' recalls Gandy. 'I made the mistake of taking food from a dish of water-lily roots and felt extremely ill for the next two hours. However, by 28 December, we were all well-rested and fell in, in as orderly a manner as possible now that the eyes of the Chinese soldiers were upon us. After more marching we were put up in a dormitory of a Chinese military barracks which had a stage at one end, but no beds. My last recollection before sleeping was seeing Kendal playing the finger guessing game with Chinese generals for "Yum Sing" ("bottoms up" drinks). My next impression was a rude awakening when I fell off my bench.'

29 December was a beautiful day, and half the party left for Waichow, twenty-four miles away. The remainder, suffering from stomach upsets and footsore, were promised bicycles. 'This seemed a splendid idea,' Gandy remembers, 'until we found the road was a frightful track and the bicycles were manned by pedalling coolies to take us pillion on the carriers. It seemed almost quicker to carry the coolies there, though conventionally "infra dig". The pace was slow; there were too many stops at chasms and broken bridges to make riding anything but a succession of walks and wobbly rides.'

The bicyclists eventually caught up with the walking party on the outskirts of Waichow. There they saw part of the Chinese army returning, they were told, from a tardy attempt to relieve Hong Kong. A lone Japanese aircraft flew high above them.

A ceremonial entry to Waichow was arranged, for it was the first occasion that the Chinese there had ever seen the

Royal Navy. The White Ensign and Chinese flags were carried side by side at the head of the parade as the travel weary remnants of the 2nd MTB Flotilla marched past the Chief Magistrate. He led them through the bombed streets to a small ex-German missionary hospital which was staffed by very professional Chinese nurses. The local army general entertained them to a vast Chinese banquet of chicken, duck, sucking pig and other meats, all of which was gobbled down with chopsticks or a small china spoon. One of Lieutenant-Commander Yorath's remaining possessions, a spoon taken from the Hong Kong Club, came in useful.

On 30 December everyone paraded for a formal photograph. Most felt rather scruffy as razors were unobtainable and no two men were dressed alike. Admiral Chan Chak sat between Commander Montague and the Chinese District Commander, with the Chinese flag and White Ensign draped over their knees.

After the first photograph had been taken, gongs and bells suddenly clanged to warn them of an imminent air raid. Two Japanese planes leisurely circled the sky dropping no bombs. Having ruined many Chinese cities earlier in the war, they now found it more effective merely to be seen, thereby disrupting Chinese activities.

A service in the small German church followed, with Chinese in the pews on one side and Europeans on the other. 'The pulpit was first occupied by a Chinese official whose pep-talk we did not understand,' wrote Gandy. 'He called for the Chinese National Anthem for which we all stood up, and hummed the tune. Commander Montague spoke next and expressed our thanks to the Chinese for their kindness and generosity, despite the Japanese who had bombed much of their fine city. "However, it will be rebuilt," he said, "once the barbarians are defeated; Chinese and British alike are now joined in the common task of defeating the aggressor." We then all lustily sang "God Save the King", one verse only, our memories not being up to standard.' The musical accompaniment was provided by naval ratings blowing through combs wrapped in toilet paper.

Everyone was surprised to see a tall, unmistakably British

Colonel mysteriously dressed in a padded grey Chinese coat which reached his ankles. It transpired that he was Lieutenant-Colonel Chauvin who was with the Military Mission to China. The Colonel arranged with the Chinese for everyone to travel along the East River to Leung Chuen – almost two hundred miles to the north-east. Boats had to be chartered to carry the party.

The Japanese were not the only enemy; the river was notorious for pirates who preyed upon small traders and well-laden barges, such as were conveying the escapers.

Four river craft, normally used for carrying rice, were produced. They were each of similar build, about seventy feet in length and covered by a canopy. Two were propeller-driven with a six-cylinder lorry engine aft, supplied by gas from charcoal. These two boats towed the other two, fifteen passengers being carried in each. The crews were Chinese and the captains signalled to the primitive boiler-room by pulling a string which agitated a bunch of rushes; the number of swishing, rustling noises indicated the power required.

They set off on 31 December against the current, travelling east at little more than two knots. Clean straw was provided for a little warmth against the bitterly cold nights. And so, as passengers, the MTB crews travelled blindly through the last night of 1941.

On 1 January it was apparent that the little group was in trouble, for one engine was continuously breaking down, which necessitated frequent stops. Although the river was fairly wide it was very shallow, making navigation difficult and the boats went aground frequently.

Admiral Chan Chak decided that progress was too slow and so one barge was abandoned, the passengers having to cram on to the junk which had pulled it. The countryside was wild and beautiful, and the villages were picturesque, though on closer inspection they consisted largely of poky, unhygienic streets.

At Leung Chuen the party met Colonel Owen Hughes who had left Hong Kong on the last aircraft. He produced five large trucks which carried them over the mountain passes. As daylight was fading they crossed two deep ravines and arrived at Namwah, a remote Buddhist monastery. After passing between two vast, brightly-coloured statues, they were shown three mummies of previous Abbots, one of which was reputed to be over a thousand years old. The three figures were the colour of mahogany and sat in glass cases wearing faded robes; their features were bloated and hideous, at least in part due to the number of layers of varnish which disfigured them.

The behaviour and mannerisms of the monks fascinated the sailors. They wore flowing saffron robes, had shaven heads, and several spoke a strange English learnt entirely from the Bible. The monks carried dainty fans with which they covered their faces whenever they passed a woman, whom they were not permitted to glance upon.

On 7 January the party reached Kukong where bad news awaited them. The Japanese had found their scuttled MTBs which were being raised for the Japanese navy. Furthermore the villagers who had helped them had been severely punished.

The international news was disastrous; Manila had fallen and the British were withdrawing fast in Malaya. 'Tokyo Rose' was aware of the escape of the Royal Navy party and in her propaganda broadcasts she was prophesying their doom. At Kukong plans were made for the party's next move. Their destination was Rangoon – the fall of the capital of Burma still seemed inconceivable, and a Chinese army was said to be advancing into Burma to save the allies. On 16 January the party split up. Admiral Chan Chak remained in hospital to have the bullet removed from his wrist and treatment for an ulcer. He was very ill and needed blood transfusions.

Commander Montague and most of the army flew on to Chungking to provide the first account of the surrender of Hong Kong and report on the lessons learnt in the defeat. Lieutenant-Commander Gandy was given 14,000 Chinese dollars by Owen Hughes to enable the Royal Navy party to continue their journey by rail. 'As each dollar was worth only about one penny, this sum was more bulky than

17

valuable,' he recalled. 'The best I could do was wrap it in a towel and sleep on it at night.'

On their last day in Kukong the sailors played a seven-a-side football match against the Chinese YMCA team, but the Navy were soundly beaten, 8–0, excuses being that the ground, ball and their opponents were too small.

After the match the Governor of the Province gave them a great reception, which was slightly marred when the hungry mariners wolfed all the rice served at the end of the meal. Etiquette demanded that the rice should only be toyed with, to show that the host had provided more than could be eaten.

For the following five days the party, now numbering fifty, travelled across China by train to Kam Shing Kong. There, on 21 January, they hired four trucks, 80,000 Chinese dollars having been borrowed at Liuchow from the Adjutant-General, IV Chinese Army, for this purpose.

Unfortunately, Lieutenant Ashby fell seriously ill with typhoid and a temperature of 104°. Gandy tried to encourage him while they waited for an ambulance. 'I told him that I would surely recommend him for the Distinguished Service Cross for his daylight MTB attack on the Japanese in Hong Kong. I added that, as he well knew, I was a procrastinator about reports, unless reminded; I expected him to do the reminding in this case, and that was an order. I believe that my remarks did a lot of good. He survived and received the medal in due course.'

Petrol was prohibitively expensive in the hinterland and drivers switched off their engines to coast down out of gear to save fuel. This proved dangerous, particularly as some of the trucks had defective brakes. Several minor accidents resulted, and four sailors were left in various hospitals.

On 1 February 1942, the party left Kunming in Red Cross lorries, for the six hundred mile journey to the frontier of Burma. They passed the lake and village of Tali, jokingly referred to as being on the roof of the world. Temples and pagodas nestled amongst the snow-covered peaks. The scenery made a marked impression on the sailors: 'We saw three Tibetan men accompanied by a good-looking girl who was selling charcoal and firewood,' one recorded. 'She wore silver bangles and had a wonderful peach-like complexion. Was she Persian, or from a lost tribe of Israel? As tongue-tied strangers in their mysterious land, we merely wondered.'

A week later the party entered Burma. At Wanting the British officers of the Burma Frontier Force gave them a warm welcome, although nobody had been expecting them. The news of the war was worse; the fall of Singapore was imminent and the Japanese in Malaya were now advancing north on unexpected coastal routes towards Rangoon.

It seemed inappropriate that the healthy combatants of the Royal Navy should travel in Chinese Red Cross lorries, and so trucks were obtained instead. After the discomfort of their ride, the last stage of the journey was a pleasant two-day trip southward by train through Mandalay to Rangoon.

The number of officers in the party was reduced by eight. Two had been left in hospital, three Merchant Navy officers had joined their shipping companies and three others had earlier been ordered to report to Chungking to work in the Embassy. The chances of those left reaching England seemed remote despite the rigours of their momentous journey, for the Commander-in-Chief East Indies signalled that the Hong Kong survivors were to be retained for the battle for Rangoon. Meanwhile they were to plan the defence of Bassein – a port ninety miles to the west.

Lieutenant-Commander Gandy reached Bassein in time to see Japanese bombers leisurely circling in the clear blue sky, just as they had in Hong Kong and Malaya. Bombs thudded down on to the airfield, destroying the runway and the ancient RAF transport planes. 'A few bombs fell in the native town causing panic and a few fires,' he recalls. 'I saw no ambulance, no regular fire engine, only a solitary old Burmese driving an iron-wheeled, steam driven, incredibly Victorian machine with a pump. He drove it slowly backwards up to a burning store so that he could always go forwards for a quick getaway. But he had no hoses and no assistants; he was just an old man with a sense of duty and a useless machine.' This scene seemed symbolic of Britain's lack of preparation for war throughout the Far East.

Gandy and a few officers and officials who were termed the Bassein Defence Advisory Committee decided to return by boat to Rangoon, since the lack of preparations for the defence of Bassein made further planning futile. They sailed down the Burmese canals, past burning rice mills and natives in canoes which were full of looted rice bags.

As the Japanese drew nearer, the Naval party from Hong Kong became increasingly frustrated, and bewildered as to what might happen to them.

On 23 February the vital bridge at Sittang, less than ninety miles to the east of Rangoon, had been destroyed to prevent its imminent capture, although much of Major-General J. G. Smyth's 17 Division was still on the far bank amidst the Japanese.

The previous day John Curtin, the Prime Minister of Australia, had telegraphed Winston Churchill refusing to agree to the diversion to Burma of 7 Australian Division – the only significant force which could affect the eventual outcome. Curtin wisely believed that moving the Division to this theatre was not a reasonable hazard of war in the light of earlier Australian losses in Greece and Malaya, superior Japanese sea and air power in the Bay of Bengal and the grave effect on Australian morale. The loss of part of 17 Division and the refusal to divert the Australian Division changed the whole situation in Burma.

However the Naval survivors from Hong Kong were at last rejoicing at their good fortune, for on 23 February they sailed for India. To their profound relief they watched the Burmese coast gradually fade over the horizon, but their joy was short-lived. On the following morning their ship was ordered to return to Rangoon forthwith – they were wanted for the defence of Burma after all. They returned to find that law and order had broken down; mental homes and prisons had been thrown open releasing criminals and lunatics, and looting of shops and houses was in progress.

General Sir Harold Alexander arrived in Rangoon on 5 March and assumed command. He saw that the situation had deteriorated so rapidly that there were only two courses open; to concentrate his forces and go on the offensive, or to accept defeat and abandon Rangoon. Although he had had no opportunity to assess the calibre of the Japanese or the state of his own forces, he was not prepared to leave Rangoon without first trying to restore the position. Meanwhile inadequately-trained reinforcements were reaching Burma from India. Too little was arriving too late, as had been the case in Hong Kong.

Late on 6 March, General Alexander changed his mind and decided to abandon Rangoon. On the following day the Hong Kong Naval party boarded a requisitioned Danish ship, *Heinrich Jessen*, which had escaped from Hong Kong and Singapore and was the last merchant ship to leave Rangoon. The weary passengers on the ships leaving harbour saw a strange spectacle: 'A heavy pall of smoke hung over the town,' recorded one. 'The electric power station was ablaze, there were fires at the wharf where the port warehouses were blackened skeletons; the cranes, part destroyed by dynamite, leant over at a drunken angle . . . not a sign of human life was to be seen . . . when it was almost dark, the flames, topped by dense black smoke rising thousands of feet into the air from the oil refineries presented an awe-inspiring sight, and as the night fell the whole sky was lurid with the glare of that inferno.'[4]

On 8 March the Japanese 21st Regiment entered Rangoon, to find to its surprise that the city was unoccupied and deserted. A vital Japanese road-block hemming in the British forces had moved elsewhere, thereby enabling the units to escape, and dispute the control of Burma for another ten weeks.

The *Heinrich Jessen* reached Calcutta on 12 March, largely due to the success of the RAF and American air squadrons which had inflicted heavy loss on the Japanese air forces, thereby making the evacuation possible.

By now the survivors of the Hong Kong flotilla had been reduced to three officers and twenty-eight ratings, for several had been left with Rangoon demolition parties, and others had joined gun crews for armed merchant ships. They sailed from Bombay on 26 March, with survivors from HMS *Repulse* and *Prince of Wales*. At Durban they were made responsible for over 500 Italian prisoners of war who seemed equally anxious to reach England safely.

Almost five months to the day after evading the Japanese in Hong Kong, the remnants of 2nd MTB Flotilla numbering thirty-one reached Glasgow, thereby completing a remarkable journey through the corridors of war. Tragically, one young officer, Sub-Lieutenant Brewer, who later reached England via a different route, had come too far; he was killed in a motor accident on the A1 road at the start of his leave.

Commander Montague, in his official report to the Admiralty, particularly commended Admiral Chan Chak's most noble example of fortitude and cheerfulness, and he had nothing but praise for the generous hospitality of the Chinese villagers throughout the journey.

'I had known most of the Naval officers a long time, and they all performed their duties to the high expectation I had of them,' the Commander concluded. 'The conduct and bearing of the men was altogether admirable, and they fully maintained the reputation of His Majesty's Service. By God's mercy we were preserved.'

During their escape the thoughts of the sailors strayed frequently to the plight of the prisoners of war and civilians captured in Hong Kong. As they read in the newspapers of the atrocities committed by the Japanese in the Colony, many recalled their last glimpse of what they considered to be the dark, sullen, unfriendly coast line of Stanley peninsula, during the allies' most humiliating disaster in the Colony's long, proud history.

The sun shone brightly on Boxing Day 1941, in Hong Kong – the first day of the Colony's capture.

At Stanley Fort on the southern peninsula of the island, the weary soldiers formed long, shuffling queues to throw their rifles, gas masks and helmets on to the appropriate heap. Some men joked hilariously, but most remained in a stupor of dejection.

'Discipline had vanished,' recalled Private R. J. Wright, a Company Clerk of the Middlesex Battalion. 'We encountered our superiors only when it was unavoidable; they had lost the respect and authority conferred by rank and uniform. We scrounged, looted and stole, ignoring the respect we owed to each other. We fought and argued over trivial matters and behaved like untutored and inexperienced children.'

The most unwelcome task which faced everyone was the burial of their dead. Armed with picks and shovels, burial parties fanned out in pairs. The dead bodies stank overpoweringly. They were ugly; the faces blue and the skin purple, with maggots attacking the open wounds. Private Wright found the body of one of his officers, Captain West, amidst six others. 'He had been among the most popular of officers who inspired that confidence which binds an officer to his men with unbreakable bonds of loyalty,' wrote Private Wright later.

An officer obtained permission from a Japanese sergeant to bury these dead together in one grave. 'We felt that Captain West would have wished this, as we knew his men would have followed him to the end of the earth. They had been together throughout the battle for Hong Kong.'

They dug the graves in the garden of a bungalow where the lawn was like velvet, and the hedges were alive with colour. They laid the bodies side by side as the sun was sinking behind the mountains. 'It angered me to see how ignorant we were that none of us knew the funeral service,' recalls Private Wright. 'We eyed each other uncomfortably. Then, in the gathering twilight, a tall, gaunt, bearded soldier quoted those moving lines written by Rupert Brooke which every member of the British Legion knows by heart:

> 'If I should die, think only this of me:
> That there's some corner of a foreign field . . .

'We remained with bowed heads long after the last words had been borne away with the breeze. The Japanese sergeant had gathered flowers during the recital and had spread them over the bodies. Then we restored the earth.'

The burial parties were the first to meet the Japanese after the surrender. Sergeant C. B. J. Stewart and Captain J. A. Lomax were wrapping dead bodies in blankets and lowering them into trenches when two armed Japanese approached them. 'I beckoned them over, although the Captain wasn't keen on any contact,' recalls the Sergeant. 'They approached cautiously, but their suspicion soon melted. They showed us photographs of their families and we compared weapons, for there were plenty of ours lying about. The Japanese expressed sorrow over our task and indicated that they, too, had many dead whom they were dragging into large fires.'

That night four men of Private Wright's Battalion died in hospital. They were laid in a sandbank which had been the children's playground, and little wooden crosses were erected to mark the graves. After the war, their bodies were dug up and laid to rest in cemeteries which have been kept beautifully ever since by the War Graves Commission.

On 29 December the 2200 prisoners of war gathered at Stanley Fort were told that they would all march, including the wounded and sick, to a camp the following day.

When the Japanese entered the Fort the allies paraded. Among them was a Free Frenchman, C. Arnulphy, who had fought with the Volunteers. He was thoroughly perplexed when the Japanese arrival was greeted by three ironical cheers from the prisoners since this was the first they had seen of the Japanese other than courteous officers who were complimentary of the allies' fighting.

Brigadier Wallis made a short speech to the prisoners warning them about the adversities ahead, and after three rousing cheers for the King, they set off in a long column towards Stanley village. The day was oppressively hot and the Chinese villagers jeered, threw stones and cursed the soldiers. Japanese flags and bunting fluttered at most doors and windows. The only welcome sight was solemn groups of Japanese who were still burning their dead. The ashes were placed in small, wooden boxes bound in white cloth.

The prisoners carried all that they owned, which was very little as most clothing and equipment had been lost in battle. However, some Canadians were fortunate for they passed concrete shelters which they had last occupied on 19 December. Before withdrawing from the area, they had locked part of their equipment behind steel doors to prevent looting. They now re-entered the shelters and collected clothing and blankets. In one shelter they found Rifleman A. Pryce who had locked himself in on 19 December after being bayoneted and left for dead. The Rifleman had survived for ten days on rum, the only nourishment available in the shelter. He was in a terrible physical condition and was not expected to live, but he eventually recovered and survived the war.

At 2 p.m., after a march of about twelve miles, they arrived at North Point refugee camp which was much too small to accommodate everyone. The camp had been built for Chinese refugees in 1937. Since then it had been looted and fixtures stolen. During the fighting some of the huts had been destroyed, the windows broken and most of the roofs perforated by shell fragments. The Japanese had used the camp as stables for their mules and horses, and the huts were filthy. The prisoners entered the barbed-wire gates, beyond which they were to endure starvation, maltreatment and even, in some cases, torture. As a surly Japanese sentry counted them through, another handed Private Wright a piece of chocolate and smiled. 'I was never more surprised or pleased. How can anyone understand these people?' he wondered.

The task of collecting the allied wounded on the hillsides fell upon a remarkable Australian doctor – Lieutenant-Colonel L. T. Ride, who had fought in France in the First World War and held the post of Dean of the Medical Faculty in Hong Kong Hospital. He had commanded the Volunteer Field Ambulance during the Japanese invasion.

'All Colonel Ride's leisure for the past few years had been given freely to public service designed to prepare the Colony against the Japanese attack, which he saw as inevitable,' read a British report in May 1942. 'He set himself the highest standard of citizenship and patriotism; apathy, wishful-thinking and inefficency he regarded with bitter and out-spoken contempt. If our Colonies were populated with Rides we would run an Empire which would be the marvel of the age.'[1]

On the afternoon of Christmas Day, while Sir Mark Young had been debating whether to surrender, Colonel Ride noted that the Japanese deliberately shelled the War Memorial and Matilda hospitals, whereas hitherto the enemy had restricted their artillery and bombing to military targets.

Colonel Ride considered this change significant, 'for it indicates that the Japanese fight according to the rules of warfare only so long as it suits them,' he wrote a few months later. 'The argument so often heard in the prison camp that "when things settle down they will treat us better" was therefore fallacious, and a mere expression of a pious but doomed hope. The Japanese reverted to type by shelling the hospitals when they knew we were absolutely at their mercy and completely cut off from world opinion.'[2]

The Japanese authorities in Victoria were not interested in the collection of allied wounded, and permission was not given to look for them until 29 December. 'We found no wounded, but the dead that we found explained why,' Colonel Ride reported to General Maltby. 'We counted over fifty bodies of officers and men of the Navy, Army and

Air Force, most of them having had their hands and feet tied had then been murdered by sword thrust or bayonet stabs in the back, by rifle bullet or butt. I interviewed the Japanese authorities but permission was refused to bury the dead. I was told: "Tomorrow you go to another place and there perhaps you can ask again. Anyhow you need not worry about your dead because no member of the Imperial Japanese Army would ever desecrate the body of a British soldier." Rather ironical after what I had seen just a few hours before!'

Colonel Ride asked whether medical supplies could be taken with them to the camp but he was again told that the Japanese Army would look after all their needs. Knowing better, his medical staff loaded medical supplies and equipment on an ambulance, but at 6 a.m. on 30 December three armed Japanese came into the hospital and drove the ambulance away.

During this period the Japanese confiscated any vehicle they wished and chaos reigned in the narrow streets, as the Japanese soldiers of varying proficiency in driving were travelling or stalling in all directions. It was then almost as dangerous to be on the roads as during the hostilities. Organised looting by the Japanese was universal. One party, accompanied by an officer, smashed open the drawers in the University medical department and took away all the microscopes and instruments.

While the survivors from Stanley were marching to North Point camp, the remaining 7000 prisoners of war assembled at 7.15 a.m. on 30 December in Victoria. This was the last opportunity for civilian friends to say goodbye to each other.

At 1 p.m. they moved off towards the ferry to cross to Kowloon. No transport was provided for General Maltby, who was made to carry his own haversack and suitcase; the Japanese wished to heap every indignity upon him in front of the Chinese who lined the roads. General Maltby marched in front, straight as a ramrod; the Chinese stood silent and apathetic.

On landing at the Kowloon wharf several Japanese who could not speak English gathered the prisoners in groups of

500 and marched them off haphazardly past the Peninsula Hotel. It soon became evident that the guards did not know the way. After being led aimlessly round the streets of Kowloon, the prisoners heard references to Shamshuipo Camp, and so they guided the guards there.

As the prisoners staggered under their heavy loads an elderly Chinese coolie, pulling a rickshaw, ran alongside General Maltby and carried his kit, quite oblivious to the shouts of rage from the guards. He was eventually tipped twenty-five dollars, rather than the customary twenty-five cents.

The state of the camp was similar to that at North Point. There were no windows or doors left in any of the huts, and all furniture, beds, blankets, taps, basins, baths and cooking utensils had been removed, and most of the woodwork in the huts ruthlessly ripped off by looters. Some buildings had been destroyed, others partly burned; rubbish, broken glass, tiles and bricks lay around in utter confusion. The few remaining latrine buckets were soon filled to overflowing. A dozen dysentery patients were found lying on the floor.

At sundown the heat of the afternoon gave place to the cold of a bleak, windy Hong Kong December evening. Men frantically pulled damaged buildings to pieces to get material to block up empty windows and doors.

At a meeting of the senior British officers the following day, it was explained that the Japanese were not going to help them, so plans were drawn up for each service to do what it could.

Colonel Ride earmarked buildings for hospitals and allocated Medical Officers, but he realised that all this was almost valueless because of the complete lack of medical equipment and supplies. Colonel Ride explained the problems to the Japanese Medical Officer, Major Joh. 'Throughout all our dealings with this individual, one cannot call him a man, he was overbearing, arrogant, insultingly rude, unco-operative and procrastinating to an almost unbelievable extreme – an utter disgrace to any army and to any profession,' wrote Colonel Ride. 'To all our requests he either turned a deaf ear or grunted "tomorrow".'

The Colonel gave Major Joh a list of the medical equipment required. The list was returned to him since Major Joh wanted it printed in block capitals. This was done, but it was returned again with the demand that it should now be written in German. Eight days later Ride knew nothing had been done, for he saw another Japanese officer take the list from his pocket when he was hunting for a scrap of paper on which to make some notes.

On 31 December, an inadequate amount of uncooked rice reached the camp. It was the first food that they had received, and it was necessary to supplement it with what could be bought through the fence from the Chinese outside.

On 2 January 1942, Major Joh visited the camp accompanied by a medical Major-General from Canton. He was shown the sick in the hospital lying on the concrete floor of a bleak, open room. Colonel Ride explained that they had been given no medicines or equipment, to which the General said through the interpreter: 'Why don't you ask for them?' When Colonel Ride replied that every request received the promise of 'tomorrow', Major Joh flushed and shouted to the interpreter to shut up.

'When I referred to the Geneva Convention,' wrote Colonel Ride, 'Major Joh broke into English saying: "British doctors in the Philippines have turned machine-guns on our men, pop-pop-pop; you will stay here." In vain did we explain that there were no British doctors in the Philippines. We again asked when would he send us the medicines, and he replied "tomorrow, may be morning, may be afternoon." With that he jumped into his car and I never saw him again.'

Colonel Ride persuaded another Japanese officer to let him visit the Argyle Street prisoner of war camp. There he found about 1200 prisoners of whom many were Indians.

The conditions in the Indian hospitals were dreadful. About a hundred dysentery cases lay on the cold concrete floors of the windowless, doorless rooms in an old recreation building. 'They lay where they happened to fall when they were helped in,' wrote Colonel Ride shortly afterwards. 'Those who were too weak to move passed their frequent motions where they lay. Those who could move crawled outside, but without supervision they relieved themselves anywhere on the ground. Pools of blood, mucus and pus lay everywhere, and what was not sucked up by the swarms of eager flies, soaked into the ground.'

Colonel Ride told General Maltby that he was convinced that this treatment by the Japanese was deliberate and that when the warmer weather came it would be impossible to stop the spread of dysentery with the primitive facilities at their disposal; the meagre diet of rice would so weaken men that they would fall an easy prey to any epidemic. Cholera, which was endemic in Kowloon, would certainly slay those whom dysentery had failed to kill.

'I was convinced,' recalls Colonel Ride, 'that the only thing that could possibly save the lives of the prisoners of war was for someone to escape and either force the Japanese to alter their policy by pressure from without, or to smuggle vaccines and medicines into the camps from China . . . General Maltby did not have much faith in my plans . . . I decided I must attempt to leave the camp on the following night.'

Colonel Ride's name will occur again frequently in this story, for he did almost more than any other to maintain Britain's and Hong Kong's prestige in China during the grim years that followed. He survived the war and was later knighted for his services to Hong Kong.

During the eighteen days of the Japanese invasion, the Chinese in Hong Kong kept their heads and showed great courage, although refugees from China frightened them with stories of the starvation, disease and death which they could expect from the ruthless Japanese.

Public food kitchens had fed several thousands per hour of the very poor, and long queues formed for the free rice, despite the bombing. However, the food control system was inefficient and many starved.

'On my first trip through the poor quarters of the

Wanchai, during the bombardment,' recalls one Chinese, 'I saw cartload after cartload of dead bodies which surprisingly did not stink. I thought I had better look. Examining the legs protruding from the rear of one of the carts, I found that the soles of the feet were all anaemic white, nothing but skin and bones, unmistakable victims of starvation.'[3]

Extensive damage had inevitably been done to property, and the homeless had to crowd in where they could. Many remained all day in the air-raid shelters.

Water had been cut off on 20 December and supplies had to be drawn from wells; lavatories could not be flushed and a repulsive stench pervaded most buildings. Refrigerated food went bad after 21 December when electricity and gas were cut off.

The air raid precaution schemes and the Police Force largely disintegrated during the battle, although the Ambulance, Rescue and Demolition services remained efficient, as did the Fire Service.

Towards the end of the fighting malaria, cholera, typhoid and diarrhoea broke out as the Sanitary Department had ceased to function; the coolies and anti-malarial squads had refused to work by day as the streets were unsafe. During the pitch-dark nights putrefying bodies were dragged hastily into large pits for burial. Hurricane lamps drew immediate fire from Japanese snipers and the coolies had to work in silence and complete darkness.

When the shock of the British surrender had passed, the Chinese adapted with sullen acquiescence to the new conditions. Neither the British nor the Japanese were in control during the following few days and looting took place on a massive scale. The Japanese tried to stop the pillaging by tying looters to trees by their necks in groups, and leaving them to strangle. Others had their hands pierced by bayonets and were thrown into the sea with their hands threaded together by rope.

The cheap, ill-fitting khaki Japanese uniforms made their soldiers look unimpressive at close quarters, but their long infantry bayonets compensated for their short stumpy figures. The officers carried large, clumsy Samurai swords.

On 28 December the Japanese held an impressive Victory Parade. Two thousand men marched through Victoria led by the Divisional Commander, Lieutenant-General Sano, who rode a white horse. The Chinese were encouraged to line the route which they did with little enthusiasm.

The Europeans were forbidden to look down at the parade on pain of being shot. However, a Canadian found himself not only overlooking the Japanese, but also with a unique opportunity of killing General Sano and his officers. H. L. White had emigrated to Canada twenty-one years before and had become an office clerk and Hudson Bay Company salesman before being commissioned into the Winnipeg Grenadiers. Captain White was in a room twenty feet above the street down which General Sano was approaching. 'A Sergeant came up to me, white as a sheet,' he recalls. '"What shall I do with these, Captain White?" the Sergeant asked. He had two live grenades in his hands! Imagine my consternation and excitement. There were Japanese Military Police and sentries all around. God help all of us if they saw the grenades. I went into the lavatory and hid them in the water cistern. I was sure trembling, I can tell you.'

During the victory celebrations, the Japanese had difficulty controlling their soldiery, and a number of Chinese girls were raped. A few days later Colonel Eguchi, the Chief Medical Officer of the Japanese Army in Hong Kong, called upon an influential Chinese surgeon, Doctor Li Shu-fan. 'Colonel Eguchi was a short man of about forty-two,' wrote the doctor later. 'He had a small Hitler-type moustache and wore a uniform weighed down with decorations, neat white gloves and a huge, unwieldy sword.' The Colonel was accompanied by Doctor R. K. Valentine, the former medical officer to the Volunteers who had not yet been imprisoned. As Colonel Eguchi started to apologise stiffly for being able to speak only Japanese and German, Doctor Valentine whispered to Li Shu-fan, 'I say, if you have any whisky, bring it out. They all like it, you know.' Li Shu-fan was amused to notice that the translation of the Colonel's name on his visiting card meant 'river mouth'.

Over a bottle of Johnny Walker Black Label, Colonel Eguchi quickly relaxed, and smiled occasionally, showing a small dimple. He suddenly came to the point: 'I want five hundred girls. Where can I get them?' he asked.

Li Shu-fan explained that Britain had signed the Geneva Convention one of the provisions of which forbade white slave traffic, and no 'business houses' had been allowed, although a number of clandestine brothels existed in the Wanchai. 'Why don't you send a wire to your Japanese Government in Canton asking for an immediate shipment of five hundred prostitutes?' asked Li Shu-fan. Colonel Eguchi thought this was a splendid idea, until it occurred to him that the General in Canton would have contempt for anyone who had captured Hong Kong and could find no prostitutes there. Colonel Eguchi decided to rope off the Wanchai district, and hundreds of geisha girls were later imported from Japan, with prostitutes from neighbouring ports for the occupation troops. An amusement area was constructed, with houses lavishly decorated as Japanese pavilions and palaces; Rising Sun flags made the streets resemble Japan itself.

As Colonel Eguchi was departing, Li Shu-fan explained how Japanese soldiers prowled around the hospital looking for nurses. The Colonel immediately produced from his car the Japanese posters which announced that the hospital was under the protection of the Imperial Army seal. The posters were quickly put at the entrance and on the main hospital building and were a great success. 'Whenever the Japanese came prowling at night,' the Doctor wrote later, 'our three Indian watchmen, promising to take them to nurses, would lead them to the posters, press a flashlight button – and there the Imperial warning confronted their eyes. With one look the soldiers would whirl round and get off the hospital grounds as fast as their bandy legs could take them.'

The Japanese seemed in no hurry to re-establish law and order, possibly because the chaos harmed the Chinese civilians more than the Japanese military, and the Government in Tokyo had not yet decided whether Hong Kong was to be governed on the same basis as their other 'colonies' of Korea and Formosa. Meanwhile prominent members of the Chinese community were arrested and the Japanese administration began to plan to reduce the Chinese population immediately, for they were determined that useless mouths should not be fed. Nor was there any intention of looking after the old and weak Chinese in Japan's Greater East Asia Co-prosperity Sphere.

Japan had not formulated plans to deal with enemy civilians, and the treatment of the internees in Manila, Borneo, Shanghai, Singapore and Hong Kong depended on the individual Japanese in charge, and not upon control from Tokyo.

On Sunday, 4 January 1942, ten days after the surrender, the Japanese interned most of the British, European, American and Dutch civilians. About 2500 were crowded into a dozen insanitary Chinese boarding-houses, taking with them whatever belongings they could carry by hand. This 'accommodation' was chosen by the Japanese with a view to destroying what little remained of British 'face' or prestige. The rations issued consisted of $8\frac{1}{2}$ ozs of rice per head per day – a spartan diet for those accustomed to European food.[5] The Japanese barred the majority of Chinese and Eurasian wives from accompanying their husbands into captivity, presumably because they did not wish to feed more than necessary in internment. The Portuguese wives were equally excluded as Japan was not at war with Portugal although a company of the Volunteers had consisted of Portuguese who had chosen to fight with the British.

Some internees had been told that they were not prisoners but were in Japanese custody for their own safety; they were to be sent to the Peninsula Hotel, regarded by most as the best in the Colony, where they would be well taken care of. 'We arrived in Kowloon on barges,' recalled one American woman. 'When we got there, they put us on trucks and we were driven round for hours for the amusement of the Chinese. They then drove us to the Peninsula Hotel where we started to disembark, but we ended up at the Kowloon

Hotel, which was nothing more than a brothel. Then a Japanese spokesman told us that we were prisoners, that we were in a concentration camp and that they would give us some food for which we must pay, and that if we did not obey the Military Police we would be shot. Everyone was crushed and frightened.

'We were made to bow low to the Japanese whenever they came into our rooms, which they did at any time of day or night. We were given only hot water and badly cooked rice twice a day, but luckily we could buy tinned food at exorbitant prices from the Chinese boys in the hotel.'[6]

Eventually a Japanese soldier confided to one internee that they were going to a proper camp. 'All things there will be good,' he promised. 'Food will be plentiful and conditions will be pleasant. I hope that you appreciate this kindness from the Imperial Japanese Army. As you know, the soldiers of Nippon are always kind to women.'

The internees wondered, with justification, what fresh horrors lay ahead of them.

In early January 1942, the Japanese decided that the internees should be concentrated in a single camp rather than in overcrowded and unhygienic hotels.

Sir Atholl MacGregor, the former Chief Justice, suggested that the Peak, where the more wealthy and influential British lived, was a suitable place for an internment camp, since it was healthy and isolated. However the Japanese were not prepared to be looked down upon – mentally or physically.

Doctor P. S. Selwyn-Clarke, the former Director of Medical Services, had a better proposal. He had not been interned because the Japanese felt that he alone could prevent a serious outbreak of infectious disease such as cholera.

The Doctor urged the Japanese to put the internment camp on Stanley Peninsula as there were numerous buildings there, and it would be more suitable for children. The Japanese agreed, but decided that the internees should be bottled up on the peninsula away from most of the houses.

In the middle of January, Doctor Selwyn-Clarke visited Stanley with a few British, American and Dutch internees to clean up the worst of the debris, which had resulted from wholesale looting. 'Good work was done by the advance parties,' he wrote later, 'but the time was too short and I fear that a small section behaved rather selfishly and, after completing the work, staked out claims in buildings which had been earmarked for families and elderly people.'

The internees started being moved to Stanley from the hotels on 21 January. Among the first to arrive was Mary Goodban, an Auxiliary Nurse, whose husband, the headmaster of the Diocesan Boys School, was imprisoned with the Volunteers. Their first baby, Nicholas, had been born at Queen Mary Hospital, with the help of a Chinese doctor who had been up all night tending the wounded, two days before the surrender 'amidst the most deafening roar of shells and planes strafing positions close by,' she remembers. 'It sounded as though they were saluting his arrival, the poor little scrap. The surrender was a black moment, but we were sure our enslavement couldn't be for more than a few months. I thought there would be a wholesale massacre and torture of Europeans and each uneventful day that passed was a relief.

'When we moved to Stanley a nurse gave me a basket-cradle for Nicholas. An armed Japanese soldier watched impassively as I attempted to breast-feed my baby. The dusty journey in a truck was tedious and bumpy, with frequent stops and searches. Our arrival was chaotic and unorganised. With the help of friends, we somehow got through the first night without light and with very little food or water, on the crowded floor – an ordeal for a hungry baby who hardly stopped crying all night. The source of his food supply was already beginning to fail as a result of the turmoil, and for him this was the beginning of ten weeks of slow starvation which would have been fatal but for the timely arrival of Red Cross supplies of powdered milk – thanks to the efforts of Doctor Selwyn-Clarke.'

Another Auxiliary Nurse, Mrs Topsy Man, had been employed before the war by the Colonial Office to teach European children physical education. Her husband, Captain C. M. M. Man, of the Middlesex Regiment, had been able to telephone her almost each day during the fighting. She had always made a particular point of looking after the wounded of her husband's Battalion in the Queen Mary Hospital. One day she found that one of her patients, Corporal Collier, who had been severely wounded in the hand, had vanished. She met him many years later at a Regimental reunion and asked him why he had gone. 'Well,' he replied, 'I 'ad one good 'and, 'adn't I? – so I nipped off to join our men. We 'ad a bit of fightin' still to do.'

Mrs Man remembers waiting for the Japanese to arrive: 'I shivered in my camp bed, listening for the sound of marching feet, but eventually we were all so scared we instinctively clung together in what had become our "commonroom", rather than be caught anywhere alone. When the Japanese arrived, I thought how ludicrous they looked – some so small, that their mighty swords trailed on the ground. They behaved with civility to us; one Japanese soldier even entertained us with a sort of cabaret act for he was an excellent tap-dancer. However, when they moved on, life took on a more sinister aspect. One day I had a visit from our former cook, Ah Yung, who had become very much part of the family. He had been badly wounded in the thigh and his wife and children killed. I gave him food and money, and sadly watched him limp away. He promised to come back, but I never saw him again.

'The first night of our internment in Stanley will always be a nightmare. Four of us were given a cold, grey cell with no beds or furniture. We huddled together and couldn't sleep, so we talked long into the night about our husbands and wedding days, and how wonderful life would be when we were released. I thought to myself, "we can't live like this – we will die".'

The internees spent the first day in Stanley burying the dead, cleaning up the filth and dirt left by looters, and patching windows and roofs with whatever makeshift materials they could find.

'Teamwork counted for most,' wrote one internee. 'Those who produced the best teamwork built the best camps and provided themselves with the best food. The American community was small enough to function as a single entity and it set the pace, while the British community was initially divided by class, race, occupation and prejudice. There was, for example, an area for the police, another for the married couples and single women, and a third for the "Peak Residents". The teamwork of these groups was good, bad and indifferent in that order. I shall never forget the portly matron who watched a gang of Americans building a store and who was so impressed that she remarked to a friend: "Isn't it fortunate that the Americans have so many members of the working class in their camp?"'[1]

38

The internal organisation of the camp became divided into three autonomous groups – 2325 British, 290 Americans and 60 Dutch. Each group had their own quarters and committees, which had control over such matters as billeting, assignment of duties on work details, sanitation, medical clinics and education.

'The public spirit in the British camp seems to be terrible by contrast to the vigorous action of the American community who seem to be standing the strain very much better,' wrote a British Brigadier in the Directorate of Military Intelligence in India in July 1942, after interviewing escapers. 'This may be partly explained by the Americans not having any Government officials among them. The Americans worked out a plan in advance of taking over the camp which took into account the needs of their communities as a whole, while the British, whose task it was to prepare for a number ten times larger, relapsed into planless individual scrounging and staking out rooms for themselves and their friends. The permanent result of these preliminary differences was the great variation of conditions among the communities which became one of the most painful features of camp life.'[2]

William Hunt was a wealthy and influential American who gave the leadership to his compatriots which was so badly needed throughout the camp. Although many objections were made to his autocratic method of operating, he achieved much, whereas the British community suffered from lack of decisive leadership until the newly-arrived Colonial Secretary, F. C. Gimson, arrived in Stanley and his authority was accepted.

After the surrender of Hong Kong the Governor had been imprisoned and held incommunicado in a place unknown to the allies. His responsibilities therefore fell on a stranger to Hong Kong, Mr Gimson, who had arrived in Hong Kong from Ceylon on the day before the Japanese invasion. During the fighting he had little time to acquaint himself with the political and social aspects of life in the colony.

After the surrender 'there was no precedent for guidance as to the attitude to be adopted by a Colonial Government on occupation by a hostile and victorious army,' he wrote later. 'No communication was received from the Japanese as to the future mode of administration.'[3] Mr Gimson was advised by the Attorney-General, C. G. Alabaster, that the civil Government, despite the defeat and enemy occupation, could continue to function and safeguard the welfare of the civil population in accordance with International Law.

Mr Gimson believed it imperative to maintain the Government in being, and issued orders that no official should take instructions from the Japanese except through him. He started by writing 'in a language scarcely diplomatic', protesting at the squalid and inhuman conditions in which the internees had to live in the Chinese 'hotels'. The letter resulted in his immediate arrest and imprisonment. 'If I had used similar language on later occasions, my fate would probably have been death,' he noted. However the Japanese Consular staff in Hong Kong secured his release thirty-six hours later. The Consular staff tried to alleviate the hardships imposed by the Japanese army and Military Police, partly because they had all been well-treated when interned by the British after war had broken out. Unfortunately they had little influence over the military.

Mr Gimson found that he was able to achieve very little as he could not contact the Chinese leaders; the Indian and Portuguese communities preferred to negotiate direct with the Japanese, and the Japanese regarded him with great suspicion.

The Colonial Secretary was not interned at Stanley until almost three months after the others. On arrival he was dismayed to discover that the former Hong Kong Government was regarded most unfavourably for failing to have made better preparation for the Japanese attack and for refusing to surrender once resistance seemed futile. 'There was in Hong Kong from the outbreak of hostilities a demand voiced in influential quarters that Hong Kong should be declared an "open city",' he wrote later. 'Exactly what this implied, I never discovered, but the idea seemed so unrealistic that I could only conclude its full complications were never explained. However, the view was widely held.

'My appeal for loyalty to the Government of Hong Kong was not well-received. Distinction was drawn between loyalty to the Crown and to the Colonial regime – a distinction the Japanese would not understand.'

As the British internees had little respect for their government's officials, for reasons about to be explained, they excluded them from those chosen to administer the camp.

'The first impulse that ran through the camp would, on a larger social scale, have been called revolutionary,' wrote one internee. 'On every side, by almost every mouth, the former leading men of the Colony were bitterly denounced. They were held to blame for what had happened in Hong Kong. Along the camp roadway, where people gathered to gossip, one heard the same angry talk of the Government servants' complacency, stupidity and shortsightedness.'

In addition, the internees believed that bribery and corruption had been rife in Government departments before the war. The full extent of the pre-war corruption in Hong Kong had only dawned on the former Governor, Sir Geoffrey Northcote, on 8 September 1941, after his official goodbye and on the day he was sailing for England. P. E. F. Cressall, the Chairman of Hong Kong's anti-graft Commission, told Sir Geoffrey on his ship just before sailing of many incriminating facts.

'Several Government officers,' wrote the former Governor immediately to the Colonial Office, 'are under the gravest suspicion of having taken bribes or presents . . . I feel sure that in Downing Street you will agree that these stables should be swept as clean as possible . . . I fear that the other disturbing outcome from the anti-graft Commission report is going to be the revelation of serious laxity in the control of Government expenditure, at any rate on defence works . . . All this leaves me with a nasty taste in my mouth on my departure hence, and I feel somewhat culpable myself.'[4]

Two months later, the new Governor, Sir Mark Young, wrote to Whitehall to report the setting up of another Commission of Inquiry to probe generally into the existence of corruption in the Public Service, although Sir Mark felt 'that the number of black sheep is greatly exaggerated in the public mind.' There was evidence that some Government officials had opened accounts at small Chinese banks in the names of Chinese nominees; several had invested considerable sums of money although on low salaries, and finally many had bought and sold shares in local undertakings through dubious exchange brokers, although prohibited from doing so by Colonial Regulations. Judging by newspaper reports, corruption has remained a feature of Hong Kong during the post war years despite energetic steps to stamp it out.

As a result of the lack of respect for government officials, Mr Gimson was unable initially to impose his authority on the camp, and the administrative talents of the interned officials were ignored. Mr Gimson's conciliatory role was therefore made much more difficult.

'The disrepute in which the former Hong Kong Government was held had unfortunate repercussions in the general outlook of internees towards any policy wider than domestic issues,' Mr Gimson wrote later. 'Yet to counter the unjustified criticism would have been of no avail.'

The British Community Council administered the camp with the help of a vast number of committees. 'When several are gathered together, if they be Englishmen, one of the first things that enters their heads is to form a committee,' recorded one cynical internee.

Mr Gimson felt that the Council should not operate independently of him, as he was the King's Representative and the highest-ranking Government official in Hong Kong. He was finally invited to co-operate in an ill-defined position as a partner to the Chairman, for whom he had little respect.

This awkward relationship with the Council gradually subsided, which was fortunate for more serious issues were later to arise. 'The anti-Government feeling which developed to treasonable proportions has, since Mr Gimson's arrival, abated due in part to the inability of the ruling groups to improve conditions, but due mainly to his presence,' recorded one American. 'Gimson is a man of firm character; he has a good mind and great patience.'[5]

Mr Gimson found that, as one would expect in such circumstances, all was far from well in the camp: 'The maintenance of discipline was closely linked to the prevalence of high morale,' he wrote later. 'The shock of defeat and the disgust with the past, together with the forebodings as to the future, reduced morale to the lowest ebb.' Discipline was hard to maintain although only one case was tried by Sir Atholl MacGregor, the Chief Justice. A policeman was found to be buying goods looted from a store. The Chief Justice sentenced him to four months imprisonment. He was kept under guard in his quarters and only allowed out for exercise.

All schemes for the pooling of cash and personal food stores were opposed by Sir Atholl on the ground that the whole principle of private property was involved and 'endless litigations' would arise in the future. The Americans were more sensible and pooled many of their resources. Individuals also received loans to be repaid by the community if and when possible. Standard Oil and General Motors each advanced $1000 and William Hunt, the autocratic American community leader, $3000. All this money helped the Americans buy supplementary rations.

These internees had one advantage over many civilians imprisoned in other parts of the Far East. The camp at Stanley lay alongside a pretty bay, and 'the green trees, flowers, wide spaces, warm sky and friendly sea were things to feed our souls, if not our bodies,' recorded another American, 'and it is better to have that than nothing.' A healthier site for the camp could not have been chosen.

The accommodation consisted partly of the residential quarters of the former European, Indian and Chinese prison officers and their families. Other buildings included those used before the war as a sanatorium, hospital and canteen which had all formed part of the Hong Kong prison. A former school, St Stephen's College, and staff bungalows also lay within the camp.

There were sufficient teachers to educate all the children

who adapted quicker than their parents to internment. Many children forgot what 'outside' was like and it seemed to them a kind of fairy land, full of abundance. One child saw a horse and assumed it was a big dog, while another asked what a river was – a big gutter? In a class of fifteen, only one could remember a sheep and trains; post offices and villages were completely forgotten. School started with prayers and a hymn, but Roman Catholics refused to let their children participate until a compromise was reached whereby the children were separated for religious instruction. Teachers received two extra biscuits each day. The children's education may not have suffered unduly and, after liberation, five of the older ones entered British universities.

Men and women were not separated into two camps as happened in some other territories occupied by the Japanese. Morale may thus have been enhanced though morals were jeopardised. The Japanese did not take advantage of the women in the camp, 'though I regret to record there were some of the latter who were only too ready to receive the attentions of the former,' noted Mr Gimson.[6]

Religion played an important part in camp life. There were twenty different denominations represented. The majority of the internees were Anglicans, and there were 400 Roman Catholics. They and the Christian Scientists held separate services. The thin pages of the prayer books were found to be excellent for cigarette paper which was unobtainable, and guards had to be posted during services to see that the pages were not torn out.

The internees faced one insurmountable problem – a starvation diet which led to malnutrition and discord.

As the years of internment dragged by, conditions became harsher and a growing moral and physical deterioration was evident. The main preoccupation was food, which started as being inadequate and became ever increasingly so, as the allied blockades sunk Japanese shipping, and guerrillas in China prevented foodstuffs coming from the mainland. Welcome parcels of food were received by some internees due to the courageous generosity of some Chinese, Indians and Portuguese still living in Hong Kong who were not interned as the Japanese wanted their co-operation. 'No expression of gratitude can do justice to their magnificent gesture of humanitarian friendship,' recalls one internee. 'It is a debt which can never be paid. Recipients were warned time and again not to acknowledge receipt of these parcels for fear of betrayal of the senders to the Japanese. These warnings went unheeded and many local benefactors unnecessarily suffered.'

Those who had worked for large business firms before the war maintained good credit ratings even though they were interned. But less than ten per cent received parcels, while one man was sent so many he got a hernia carrying them up the hill to his room.

The official rations fixed by the Japanese were barely a cup full of rice per day per person plus a very small quantity of salt and flour.

Doctor Selwyn-Clarke promised, on behalf of the British Government, to purchase additional rations from the Japanese. These amounted, in theory, to one ounce of meat or fish and one ounce of green vegetables per internee per day. However sacks of rice invariably contained less than the alleged amount, possibly because Chinese supervisors helped themselves before delivery. When the food was weighed, no allowance was made for bones in the meat or for fish heads and tails. On one occasion a block with 700 people received an allowance of meat said to weigh sixty-five pounds, but it amounted to only fifteen pounds of actual flesh. The ration for a bungalow of fifty people amounted one day to a buffalo shank from which they could obtain no meat at all. The fish ration was frequently red mullet which often went bad before delivery. The only other fish delivered was conger eel.

Some internees put the lowering of morale down to the constant hunger, whereas others attributed its deeper roots 'to the unsatisfactory social conditions of pre-war Hong Kong. Most conspicuous was the almost total absence of anti-Japanese feeling,' one internee wrote later. 'Parents had no objection to their children playing with Japanese

45

soldiers and officers. On the contrary, they encouraged them to do so in the hope of obtaining small gifts such as sugar.' The entire camp was shocked into an awareness of their attitude by an incident which occurred when the Japanese army was removing stocks of food from godowns nearby.

Chinese coolies who normally did the work went on strike when they were paid not in money but with a can of bully beef and a can of condensed milk. The Japanese therefore asked the internees to provide the working parties instead. The first men detailed went reluctantly, but when they were paid with the cans turned down by the coolies, there was a great rush of eager volunteers. By the second day there were so many volunteers that the American detail refused to compete and retired in disgust, while the camp was treated to the scene of Japanese soldiers having to hold back with their rifles a crowd of would-be workers. The Japanese amused themselves by rolling cans of treacle down the hillside and watching the internees scramble for them. On the third day the Chinese coolies decided that avoiding starvation was more important than the principle of receiving no cash wages, and so they came back to work under the supervision of their grinning Japanese guards.

After this episode there was a definite reaction and morale began to improve. 'The initial effect of the fall of Singapore and other reverses wore off, and people began to reconcile themselves to the fact of a long war', recalls one internee. Many people buoyed themselves up with hopes of repatriation, and few seriously believed that they would be left in Stanley through the summer months of 1942.

From the outset, the internees demanded repatriation, and many found Mr Gimson's reluctance to endorse the principle of repatriation quite incomprehensible. For this reason some residents in Hong Kong today, almost forty years later, have mixed feelings about him.

Mr Gimson felt that the British internees were British subjects on British territory, therefore they had no claim to transfer from one section of the Empire to another, particularly when no allied ship could be spared, and the number of internees would scarcely equal that of the casualties of a large air raid in England. He believed that repatriation would weaken the case for Britain retaining Hong Kong as a Colony after the war.

Many internees bitterly denounced this attitude, arguing that their residence in the Colony was temporary; they were citizens of the United Kingdom and so had no allegiance to the Hong Kong Government. Repatriation, they maintained, was their right, particularly in view of the hardships they were suffering. They believed that a neutral ship was readily available and it was only due to Mr Gimson's failure to acquaint the British Government with their plight that repatriation was not forthcoming. Some felt that they faced certain death by slow starvation in the Colony, as opposed to being supported on arrival in England in the standard of life to which they had been accustomed in Hong Kong.

Mr Gimson, after the war, felt that he had been unduly influenced by his previous service in Ceylon, where everyone had been British subjects, as a result of which there had been no distinction between European and Asian. 'I failed,' he wrote later, 'to appreciate Hong Kong's position in relation to other settlements of the British in China where the obligations to the local welfare were not closely recognised. I fear that the rejection of my arguments increased my adherence to them, and cultivated a strain of obstinacy which jeopardised a balanced judgement. Unfortunately repatriation persisted throughout the internment as a *cause célèbre*, and any reason I adduced, to justify the actions of the British Government, involved criticism of my leadership, which fostered an air of antagonism of which I was acutely conscious, and which tended to isolate me from public opinion in the camp.'

While some internees may have doubted the suitability of Mr Gimson to represent the camp, although he was the senior Government official and the King's Representative, the Japanese, ironically, gradually began to regard him as the only internee with whom they could deal satisfactorily.

For the first two months of internment, until a Japanese camp superintendent arrived, it did not appear to be the policy of the Japanese to administer the camp directly. It was left in the charge of C. L. Chang, a puppet Chinese who had previously been employed by the National City Bank. Policing, which was very lax, was done by Indian and Chinese former police constables and by Chinese warders and wardresses from Stanley prison who did not seem to have been picked for any political connection with the Japanese. A foot patrol of three armed Japanese wandered round the camp several times each morning and there was an occasional small mounted patrol in the afternoon.

In March, Oda, a former Japanese consul in Hong Kong, was made the Commandant of the camp. He visited it very infrequently, leaving the daily administration to Nagasawa, a former clerk in a Japanese shipping firm in Hong Kong, and to Yamashita, a barber formerly employed in the Hong Kong Hotel.

Nagasawa would probably have liked to effect some improvements in the camp, but his weak personality and inferior social position rendered him powerless. Yamashita, however, was in close touch with the Japanese Military Police, who were to have a sinister influence over the camp in that they were responsible for inflicting appalling torture on some internees. Yamashita used his ability for his own ends, and Mr Gimson regarded Yamashita's appointment as a disgraceful exhibition of the callousness of the Japanese in fulfilling their responsibilities towards their captives.

The Military Police exercised a very wide general control which at times prevented lectures being given, entertainments being freely held, and gardens being cultivated.

The Japanese believed that the internees were in the camp for their own protection. Although this appeared at first sight to be ridiculous, in reality it proved to be true, for the Europeans would have found no employment in the Japanese-occupied Colony, and so they would have had no means of livelihood. Their activities would have been subject to intensive supervision by the Japanese, and torture and imprisonment would have been a constant threat, as it was for the Chinese in Hong Kong.

The Japanese scorned any reference to International

Law, and appeals to the Law of Humanity were largely ignored. The Japanese had signed but not ratified the Geneva Convention and only Japanese rules prevailed. Penalties, which included death, were announced for any infringement of the regulations. The Japanese issued instructions occasionally, with threats of collective punishment and reprisals if they were not obeyed. They adopted an extreme outlook whereby the very existence of the internees was dependent on the pleasure of their captors, and that the means of their livelihood had to be acknowledged item by item. This attitude required from the internees recognition of the granting of any request with the most effusive thanks, even when a refusal meant the infliction of considerable hardship resulting in serious danger to lives. The Japanese maintained that in Japan the total subordination of the individual to the state and the infliction of punishment was accepted without question, and so internees had to conform to these standards.

In these circumstances, it is hardly surprising that the internees' elected representatives were powerless to influence the Japanese, and replacements were frequently elected. 'To a perpetually starved, ill-housed and comfortless populace, all administrators appeared to be wrong, whatever they did,' recorded one internee. The harassed representatives were largely former businessmen, clergy and professional men, such as solicitors and doctors. They gradually succeeded in establishing order out of chaos and brought some hope for the future, but the internees began to feel that Mr Gimson might be better able to represent them in improving their lot with the Japanese.

A resolution asking him to accept the Chairmanship of a reconstituted Council was signed by 1300 British internees, and the existing Council resigned. It was tacitly agreed that Mr Gimson's assumption of the Chairmanship would not involve senior government officials being placed in executive positions in the camp.

Mr Gimson decided that his first priority was to try to improve the health of the internees. The problems included lack of suitable hospital facilities and medicines. The staff and patients of the Queen Mary Hospital had been installed in the old Indian single warders' quarters which had served as an emergency medical centre during the war. The Japanese had piled wounded patients into trucks without stretchers, causing them much agony, and on arrival at Stanley it was found that there were insufficient beds, no sheets, no arrangements for boiling water beyond one small stove that served also for cooking, no electric power and no facilities for dressings or operations. Permission to remove the operating and X-ray equipment from Stanley Prison hospital, which was not being used, was not given.

When subsequent batches of internees, staff and patients arrived, it was decided to turn the former Tweed Bay Hospital into an international centre for all communities. Doctor H. Gale of the American Red Cross and Doctor K. Utley ran the hospital committee.

The hospital had insufficient space, and initially all the patients had to be lumped together; typhoid cases had to be nursed in beds alongside patients with severe dysentery, while new babies were brought into the world alongside patients dying of tuberculosis. Admission to the hospital averaged 120 each month and so patients had to be put on the floor when dysentery became an epidemic.

Even so, due to the devotion and skill of the doctors and nurses, and the good climate and open air at Stanley, the sick suffered no worse than those in Singapore, where civilians were kept in a former prison living in the cells, workshops and dining-rooms. The patients with infectious diseases in Manila were housed in pre-war circus tents, and eighteen per cent of the internees had tuberculosis within two months of internment.

In Hong Kong many more internees would have died were it not for the relief work of Doctor Selwyn-Clarke whom the Japanese permitted to remain with his wife outside the camp. He had secured the confidence of the Japanese and was allowed to visit the camp at least once a week, providing he gave no news and discussed nothing but medical and relief matters. Everyone in the camp knew that all the improvements in diet, and the provision of medicines and clothing were the result of his untiring efforts. He also worked hard to relieve the distress among the prisoners of war and the Chinese population whose plight was immeasurably worse than anything the Stanley internees had to endure.

Within the first six months of internment at Stanley over 600 cases of vitamin B deficiency were recognised. The situation might well have been disastrous had the Japanese Foreign Office not allowed him to take additional food to the camp, including bread, milk and vitamin concentrates.

Quite unexpectedly in June 1942, the Japanese announced that the American civilians were to be repatriated in exchange for Japanese interned in America. The ship, *Asama Maru*, anchored off Stanley. She had huge Japanese flags with large white crosses printed on bow, stern and both sides. The *Asama Maru* already carried 432 repatriates from Japan, representing twelve nations. On a hot summer day the Americans lined up in alphabetical order and were hustled to small boats which ferried them to the ship. Some Americans gave all they had to their British and Dutch friends, while others kept everything.

It was soul destroying to see the Americans depart. 'We sat on the wall of the cemetery,' recalls one internee, 'and with deep emotion watched them go. We had dreams of good food, of fruit and ice-cream for the children. In their departure there was promise that our repatriation would follow. People were kissing each other goodbye and weeping. There was a shout, and a fresh burst of sobs and waves as the last boat pulled away.'

The Americans subsequently made known to the world the plight of the wretched internees left at Stanley.

It was fortunate that nobody then knew that the worst was yet to come. Malnutrition was to weaken the internees' resistance to infection to a pitiful extent. Some internees were to be executed on the beaches. The arrest of Doctor Selwyn-Clarke on a charge of treason was to be the culminating blow, for the life line of extra foodstuffs and medicines was to be severed. Not even the pessimists could imagine the horrors that lay ahead of them.

By January 1942, the Japanese had put the prisoners of war into three camps. 1500 Canadians and some of the Royal Navy were imprisoned at North Point on the island, while the Indians were segregated at Mau Tau Chung on the mainland, with the British at Shamshuipo nearby.

North Point Camp was alongside the harbour. The western end had been built on reclaimed land and ploughed up by shell fire, while the eastern end was littered with dead Chinese and animals whose bodies remained there for several weeks, badly decomposed. Shell fire had broken the water mains and so there was no running water.

Doctor A. J. N. Warrack had joined the Royal Army Medical Corps in 1937 and was posted to Hong Kong the following year to become the medical officer of the Royal Scots. He was sent to North Point with two medical orderlies when it was learnt after a week that the POWs had no medical staff.

He recalls on arrival seeing 'mounds of refuse covering several hundred square feet. We heard a low hum of flies and bluebottles which rose in an angry thick cloud at the noise of our approaching truck. The lavatories were out of order but not out of use. Around every choked, stinking pan was the tell-tale evidence that sanitary discipline had gone and dysentery had come. The type of dysentery was "Shiga" – the most virulent, which resulted in violent abdominal pains and high fever. Fortunately a severe attack of dysentery clarifies the mind of both officer and soldier as to the merits of sanitary discipline.'

Gradually latrines were dug, flies controlled and rubbish cleared. The Bowen Road British Military Hospital, near Victoria, sent what few medicines were available, and with the arrival of Royal Naval and Canadian doctors from Shamshuipo the number of serious dysentery cases was held in check.

The lack of lavatories was solved by visiting the edge of the sea where a stretch of wire had been nailed to large poles. There, the soldier dropped his trousers and undertook an uncomfortable balancing act. On the narrow ledge above the sea, he grasped the wire with one hand and held on to his trousers with the other. Such a process was rather difficult, particularly in a high wind, for those suffering from dysentery and chronic diarrhoea. One soldier revolutionised the lavatory arrangements by finding a cane chair, from which he removed the seat. The chair was placed on the end of a plank which projected out over the sea, the plank being secured at its landward end by a pile of stones. Unfortunately one night the soldier had to make a dash to his chair. He sank luxuriously into it. But someone had removed the stones that held the plank, and he fell headlong into the sea.

As there was neither sufficient food nor fuel in the North Point camp, and some men had no blankets or plates, the Japanese allowed small foraging parties to visit most parts of the island with a truck to gather what they could. Food was retrieved from buried stores and hundreds of books were salvaged from the Hong Kong Club. Building materials, tools and electric motors were found and used to rebuild the huts.

Although the Japanese soon stopped these foraging parties, a large sewer in the camp enabled small groups to go out at night to find food if they were prepared to squirm past several badly decomposed bodies lodged in the pipe.

On 1 February the crew of a Dutch submarine captured off Malaya arrived in the camp. The following night two Dutch, a Canadian and three officers of the Royal Naval Volunteer Reserve with a rating escaped through the sewer, stole a boat and eventually reached Chungking.

The senior Naval officer in the camp, Commodore A.C. Collinson, was harangued for half an hour by Colonel Tokunaga, the Japanese Commander of the POW camps, who spoke in French. 'As my French was little better than his, not much progress was made,' he recalls. 'I gather that he was threatening me with dire punishment. I later pointed out that it was our duty to try and escape and that in Europe this was recognised by all belligerents. He told me that I was to order the prisoners not to do so. I replied that I would not. Eventually after threats of sending me to a "dungeon", he said that I was to tell the prisoners that the Commandant did not wish them to escape. I said I would do this, and did so later, the message being received by the men with the first hearty laugh I had heard since capture.' The drain was blocked up and an electrified fence was erected around the camp.

After the escapes, rations became more scanty, and various curious foodstuffs came in occasionally. They included a small quantity of whale meat, some bird seed, and one fairly large consignment of old duck eggs which by this time had gone black. Such was the hunger that an egg had to be very bad before it was rejected. It was difficult to adapt to the inadequate and altered diet which usually amounted to one pound of low quality rice per day. Many Canadians whose home diet had included an especially high proportion of meat, bread and potatoes found the new diet particularly appalling. The staple vegetable was chrysanthemum tops which were not popular. The favourite pastimes were copying out recipes and discussing food.

The first of many to die in North Point Camp was Lieutenant-Colonel J. L. R. Sutcliffe, the Commanding Officer of the Winnipeg Grenadiers. He was suffering from beri-beri and dysentery. Repeated requests were made for him to be removed to hospital, but they were refused for two days and he died shortly after being admitted. Some felt he had died of a broken heart at the destruction of his fine Battalion. The Japanese provided floral wreaths for Canadian officers to take to the funeral as well as sending many themselves; the Canadians would have preferred food to flowers.

Rifleman D. L. W. Welsh kept a diary in which he daily recorded how little there was to eat. On 5 October he wrote that he had eaten nothing as he could not swallow.[1] He died that afternoon.

The future was at best uncertain: 'It was as if we had

54

known no other life,' wrote one Rifleman. 'The daily routine, the inadequate food, the shabby clothes and the daily humiliations seemed to be the real and only life we had known. All else seemed a dream and Canada just a name on some dimly-remembered map.'

Some Canadians knew that they should never have been sent to Hong Kong anyway. A year earlier, Winston Churchill had emphatically rejected the proposal that the Colony be reinforced: 'If the Japanese go to war with us, there is not the slightest chance of holding Hong Kong or relieving it. It is most unwise to increase the loss we shall suffer there. Instead of increasing the garrison it ought to be reduced to a symbolic scale. We must avoid frittering away our resources on an untenable position. Whether there are two or six battalions at Hong Kong will make no difference ... I wish we had fewer troops there, but any move would be noticeable and dangerous.'[2]

Why then were the Canadians sent at the eleventh hour? Major-General A. E. Grasett, commanding in Hong Kong until July 1941, had disagreed with this pessimistic view. On being posted to the UK, the General, who was Canadian-born, travelled to London via Ottawa and told the Canadian Chief of Staff, General H. D. S. Crerar, that 'an addition of two battalions at Hong Kong would render the garrison strong enough to withstand an extensive period of siege.' He did not specifically ask for Canadian battalions.

General Grasett's views were well received in London; the defences in Malaya were being strengthened and it was believed that reinforcements from Canada would deter the Japanese. Churchill therefore agreed unenthusiastically that Canada be approached for two battalions. In Ottawa, National Defence Headquarters had no map of Hong Kong, nor much knowledge of the defence plan, and the Minister of Defence was in America.

Nevertheless, the British request was agreed unanimously by W. L. Mackenzie King, the Prime Minister, and his Cabinet, because unallocated battalions could be spared. They felt that if Hong Kong was attacked by the Japanese, the United States would be in the war too. In addition the

Canadian Army had not yet had an opportunity of fighting. While Australians, New Zealanders and South Africans were heavily engaged in North Africa, the Canadian troops were bored, frustrated and angry. Some soldiers had loudly booed Mackenzie King on two or three occasions when he had visited training camps. To an Englishman this is a remarkable statement, true though it is. The superficial explanation is that high ranking politicians are not treated with as much respect in the Dominions as they would be in the UK. But, much more important, these incidents should be considered as symptomatic of the remarkable fighting spirit of the Canadians and their loyalty to the Mother Country, as is to be seen by the fact that their record at the end of the war was second to no other Dominion.

The choice of which battalions should be sent to Hong Kong was a matter of controversy and was made partly on political grounds. The Royal Rifles from Quebec was chosen to stir up enthusiasm and the fighting spirit in the province where the war was least popular, as the French-Canadians were reluctant at this stage to get too closely involved. The Battalion, although nominally English-speaking, was therefore drawn from a region where a high proportion of Canadians of French descent dwelt. The other Battalion, the Winnipeg Grenadiers, was picked because it represented one of the more western provinces.

These Battalions were therefore chosen to overcome the undercurrent of political disunity about the war in Canada. However, the choice of Battalions was made with inadequate consideration of military factors; neither Battalion was adequately equipped or trained. The Royal Rifles had previously been given one 2-inch mortar for training purposes, but no live hand-grenades or anti-tank guns, while some men from both Battalions had not completed their basic training. Nevertheless, as they embarked at Vancouver, 'We were the envy of Canada. When we left our families we thought we were going to some pleasant place for additional training and a good time,' recalls one officer. 'Little did anyone dream what our fate was to be and that we were not to see our families again for four long and tragic years.' The decision to reinforce the Colony was one of the blunders of the war.

Nine days before the Canadians sailed, General Tojo formed a new Japanese Government. He was notoriously sympathetic to Hitler and Mussolini and he represented the most extreme elements in Japan. Before the Canadians' departure a brief had reached Ottawa from London which did not gloss over the problems which would be faced in Hong Kong: '. . . The Japanese are established on the mainland, are carrying out operations in the vicinity of the frontier, and are in possession of a number of air bases within easy reach of the Colony. They also hold command of the sea and are therefore in a position to occupy the surrounding islands at will . . .'[3]

After the Hong Kong surrender, the Leader of the Opposition in Canada blamed Mackenzie King for not reconsidering the policy of reinforcing Hong Kong before the troops sailed, when the international situation suddenly became much more precarious.

A Royal Commission in Ottawa was established in early 1942 to examine whether any dereliction of duty or error of judgement had been made by those responsible for organising and despatching the battalions.'[4] The Commission, which concluded that nobody of importance was blameworthy, was labelled a 'whitewash' with good reason. Both the battalions which had been selected had been listed as 'not recommended for operational consideration' due to insufficient training. Moreover the Canadians arrived in Hong Kong without their 212 vehicles. They had been loaded on a separate ship which had sailed late, and only reached Manila by the time the war broke out.

Some Canadians understandably felt that they had been badly let down by those who had sent them to Hong Kong, for there was no way that the Colony could successfully be defended without an additional properly trained division and facilities for reinforcement.

'During the first few days at North Point,' noted Brigadier Wallis, 'a small number of Canadian soldiers started saying that, now they were POWs, everyone was equal; a camp committee should be formed by them, and that officers had nothing more to say. But fortunately some measure of discipline was gradually re-established.'[5] The Brigadier had been wounded during the fighting and he was admitted to hospital a month later. He remembers that before leaving North Point: 'One day among visiting senior Jap POW staff, there appeared a well-dressed and groomed officer in uniform, sporting the usual officer's sword. He had been my grocer in Nathan Road and had cashed me a cheque just before the attack. I told him that I recognised him and he denied being the grocer. This incident exemplified how the Colony had been full of spies and collaborators, and our difficulty in telling one Oriental from another.'

Captain H. L. White, the Canadian who had resisted the temptation to throw the grenades at the Japanese officers during the victory parade, kept a diary in North Point:

'Feb 15, 1942. There is quite a lot of criticism of so-called Democracy, the Imperial system, etc. There's a feeling among all ranks that we have been sold out.'[6] However most of the diary entries dealt with more immediate matters, and in particular with food:

'Feb 21, 1942,' he wrote. 'Still cold and wet. Everyone miserable. Ate some stinking cat fish today. The camp faces a main thoroughfare and Chinese going up and down all the time, clop-clopping on their wooden clogs. Anyone passing the Jap sentry-box who doesn't bow gets a bang over the head with a rifle. Today they had two Chinese women tied up to a telegraph pole all day without drink or food. Occasionally a Jap would beat them with a bamboo stick – don't know what they have done.

March 3, 1942. Had some very old eggs today. Oh! The stench! Quite a lot of us have lice. I'm longing to see my wife and family – haven't had a word since leaving Calgary – very home-sick. Always talking of when we will get out – two months to several years? Dare not think of it lasting more than one year.

Mar 14, 1942. We are always hungry, and the talk always seems to switch around to the dishes we'd like. Sometimes it nearly drives us crazy, then someone will yell:

"For Christ's sake, shut up," then the topic will change for a while. Oh Boy! Do I remember my wife's good cooking!'

In mid-March the Japanese announced that they would pay commissioned officers in military yen and a canteen was opened with a few articles, including cigarettes, on sale. As the other ranks had no pay and in order that everyone in camp should have if not equal at any rate some opportunity of making purchases, a fund was opened for their benefit on a voluntary basis. Officers were asked to contribute about sixty per cent of their pay to this fund. This led to a further improvement in relations between officers and men.

'On the whole I consider the morale of the camp by mid-April to be very good,' wrote Commodore Collinson 'in spite of the overcrowding, the lack of food and amenities, and the poor medical facilities.'[7]

Most suffered from the lack of cigarettes, and clothes were exchanged with the Japanese for tobacco. A few men would stoop to pick up the Japanese butts; a cigarette would be shared between half a dozen soldiers. One doctor claimed that cigarettes were as useful as medicines, such was the effect on morale of a good smoke.

Every effort was made to overcome boredom in North Point Camp, and an active sports programme was started but had to be abandoned when the men began to lose their strength and energy as a result of the starvation diet.

Concerts were held on most Saturday nights, for the Winnipeg Grenadiers had managed to keep their band instruments. The orchestra numbers were simple and somewhat crude, but they gradually became more sophisticated.

The Japanese Commandant of all the Prisoner of War Camps in Hong Kong, Colonel Tokunaga, occasionally visited the Canadians. He was gross, cruel and sadistic, and was hated and feared. He was aged fifty-four and had served in the Imperial Japanese Army for almost thirty years.

On 23 May he ordered everyone to sign an undertaking promising that he would not escape. The prisoners refused. As a result 'Colonel Tokunaga flew into a violent rage,' recalls Lieutenant-Colonel J. H. Price, who was now commanding the Royal Rifles. 'He told us that Japan was not a party to the Geneva Convention and we were subject only to the law of the Imperial Japanese Army – we would be treated like mutineers, and our refusal to sign would result in cutting down our meagre rations and inevitably many deaths. He produced a document signed by General Maltby and so we agreed to sign if Colonel Tokunaga personally ordered the men to do so. Accordingly the fat, pig-like creature addressed the soldiers and made it clear that the consequences of refusal would be unpleasant and treated as mutiny.'

The officers explained to their men that an undertaking under duress was worthless and not binding; if a chance to escape arose, it should be taken. 'One chap, Lance-Corporal J. Porter, Royal Rifles, refused to sign,' wrote Captain E. L. Hurd. 'At best he was always a little eccentric. The senior officers tried to talk him out of his stand, but they couldn't, and he was taken off to prison. We all admired his courage, but considered him foolhardy.'[8] Porter was returned to the camp almost a fortnight later in an emaciated condition, having signed.

Colonel Tokunaga's insistence that the undertaking be signed to prevent escapes had little effect. On 20 August, Sergeant J. Payne and Riflemen J. H. Adams, G. Berzenski, P. J. Ellis, all of the Winnipeg Grenadiers, climbed through the shell-damaged roof of the camp. Their escape was discovered at dawn when the barbed-wire fence was found to be broken.

The four Canadians found a small sampan to cross to the mainland. However it leaked badly and later sank in mid-channel. They drifted for four hours before being picked up by the Japanese Navy who took them to a prison in Kowloon. There they were interrogated for an hour by Colonel Tokunaga, who took a delight in watching their faces while Lieutenants Tanaka and Niimori beat them with a baseball bat when their answers were found to be unsatisfactory. A Chinese who was working for the Japanese, Mak Kee-shing, saw the Canadians dressed in shorts and shirts, their clothes stained with blood and mud.

Major-General Arisue, the Japanese Chief of Staff in Hong Kong, ordered that they be executed without trial forthwith. Colonel Tokunaga maintained later that he told General Arisue that the executions would not be considered legal in International Law. Arisue replied that prisoners of war would inevitably try to escape at night, and such escapes made not only the POW Camp staff but the Governor-General lose face. 'It is not the time to talk about International Law,' he said, 'escaping POWs are to be executed.' Ten Japanese soldiers shot the Canadians in King's Park, Kowloon. The bodies were buried there overnight and removed later to the POWs' cemetery.

It was reported to the Tokyo Bureau of Information that the Canadians had been shot during their attempt to escape. 'Our report to Tokyo did not state the true facts,' admitted Colonel Tokunaga later, 'as I did not wish to hurt the honour of the camp guards.' He added that he wanted to save General Arisue, 'from trouble, should a question arise of the ill-treatment of POWs.'

Tokyo was also continuously misled, in monthly reports compiled by the Japanese in Hong Kong, as to the desperate plight of the Prisoners of War and internees. As a result, when world opinion criticised the Japanese for their inhumanity, Tokyo dismissed the criticism as enemy propaganda which, they suggested, would harm the prisoners further. However a week before the Japanese surrender, one of their clerks amended the nominal rolls to show the truth. 'Executed' was then entered against over a dozen names.

A few nights after the four Canadians' escape, the prisoners were paraded at 11 p.m. while the Japanese searched the camp, convinced that another escape had been made. For five hours the POWs stood in the rain, with the sick on stretchers among them, until the Japanese satisfied themselves that everyone was present.

The senior Canadian medical officer in Hong Kong was Major J. N. Crawford, who retired after the war with the rank of Brigadier and later became Director-General of

Treatment Services, Department of Veteran Affairs, Ottawa. He was transferred to North Point Camp in late January and developed a relationship of sorts with the Japanese medical sergeant who, according to his limited ability, helped the Canadians as much as he could. 'I realised,' recalls Major Crawford, 'that we would have to use indirect methods with the Japanese. A direct request, however reasonable, was certain to be refused. On the other hand a Japanese could be placed in a position where the refusal of a personal request would result in loss of face. All my subsequent dealings with the Japanese were directed upon these lines. The little Jap sergeant spoke English and had studied Shakespeare in the Imperial University in Tokyo. He was very proud of his knowledge and I read Shakespeare aloud to him, and corrected his reading for hours at a time. A pathetic and resonant passage from *Romeo and Juliet* or *Hamlet* would produce assistance, when the urgent need of the moment would fail to do so. Shakespeare wrote better than he knew.'

Dysentery ravaged the camp continuously and in August diphtheria broke out. 'A large party had to be sent out of camp every day, for work on Kai Tak airport. There were not enough fit men to make up the required number, so we had to select the less sick, and send them out to do hard physical work. Our plight seemed hopeless for we could not increase our food supply or reduce the over-crowding, and so quarantine was impossible. We were unable to obtain anti-diphtheria serum and requests for throat swabs and isolation of the carriers were ignored.' Captain Hurd continued to keep up his diary:

'Mar 18, 1942,' he wrote. ' The Royal Navy party have a secret radio fixed up. The news is passed from one to another. The wet season has started and life is very monotonous. At night we walk up and down. The whole camp walks around and around, like a bunch of milling cattle. I'll never want to see caged animals again.' The entries in Hurd's diary continued to describe what the prisoners saw, did and felt:

'Apr 18. The Chinese are sure taking a beating – about

62

ten coffins go by each day. The Royal Navy party was moved out today leaving just the Canadians and a few Dutch.

'May 1. The senior Canadian officer refused to allow us to read the news bulletin made up from radio flashes which we pick up from time to time. This only antagonises us and makes life more miserable. He claims we pass on the news to our men and he's afraid the Japs will get wise.

'June 15. We sent a working party to Kai Tak airport today – the work was hard, cutting the sods from the airfield. Apparently the Japs intend to put in some runways, but it was fun and wonderful to get outside the camp. Later we had a most peculiar feeling – sort of unprotected, deserted and strange, and we were glad to get back inside the camp fence afterwards. From the camp we can see in the harbour half sunken boats, lots of funnels and masts sticking up from the water, very ghost-like at night.

'June 20. Had a long chat with someone who remembered my wife Maxine. Gave me a kind of weak feeling in the stomach. Last night I had a vivid dream of her – she was so clear I could almost touch her. Had to get out my snaps and old letters.

'July 14. It's rained every day this month so far. Typhoon threats all week. Some of the stews we made up for the men were pretty terrible; stuff you'd hardly feed the pigs back home. There was a lot of grumbling – had what nearly amounted to a mutiny in 'D' Coy; about a dozen soldiers charged with offences and some NCOs reduced to the ranks, and told they'd be turned over to the Japs if there was any more of it. I really don't blame the men, but what can we do?' Officers and men were not yet separated to different camps, and military discipline prevailed.

'Aug. 20. Another typhoon threat, hut roofs are leaking,' wrote Captain Hurd. 'The harbour is a wild sight, the sea smashing over our seawall, coming into the huts through the many cracks. Malnutrition starting to show up. Sores are starting on feet, mouths, throats.

'Sept. 17. Twenty-two Canadians have died of sickness so far at North Point Camp. Have got to wear masks across our mouths to prevent disease. It's a Japanese custom and damn good, although hard to get used to.

'Sept. 19. Was in charge of working party at airfield. The Japs are tearing down a section of the village; whole blocks of large concrete buildings, and two small hills, which the British couldn't have done, due to the hills being sacred. Our job is very hard – pulling down the hills with pick and shovel. We met some of the Royal Scots and Middlesex from Shamshuipo. Quite a lot of them are going to Japan, some think. They told us that conditions are much worse at Shamshuipo – lots of dead.

'Sept. 27. We were moved to Shamshuipo.'

Colonel L. T. Ride, the Senior Medical Officer at Shamshuipo Camp, on Hong Kong mainland, quickly came to the opinion that it would soon be impossible to stop the spread of dysentery with the primitive facilities at their disposal. The meagre diet of rice was such that the men would die of any epidemic, and in particular he feared cholera. He was convinced that he must escape, to force the Japanese to alter their policies by pressure of world opinion. He also hoped to smuggle vaccines and medicines into the camp. Colonel Ride told General Maltby on 9 January that he proposed to escape from the camp that night. General Maltby replied that Colonel Ride should leave his final decision until after an interview with a Japanese General who was about to inspect the camp.

'I witnessed that "interview",' wrote Colonel Ride shortly afterwards. 'Sentries were placed and our soldiers were forbidden to stand around. Twenty-five to thirty cars laden with officers drove on to the parade ground together with six lorries of armed soldiers, each lorry mounting a light machine-gun. When the Japanese General arrived, the POWs all assembled in a group which General Maltby and Commodore A. C. Collinson, RN, the Senior Naval officer, had to join. A photograph was taken, and then the cavalcade disappeared in the reverse order of their arrival. That constituted the camp inspection and promised interview. I called to see General Maltby again, but he was busy. I had the impression that he did not really believe that I would make the attempt or, if I did, I had very little chance of bringing off such a foolhardy scheme. This, I regret to say, was the opinion of most of the people with whom I entrusted my secret. They did not realise that their war was not over until peace was declared, and that the fighting spirit must be fostered by promoting the will to escape. One officer whom I asked to come with me declined because he "felt sure things would improve." Another, when I told him I was going, simply remarked, "Good Lord! Whatever for and wherever will you go?"' The Canadian doctor, Major J. N. Crawford, who was later moved to North Point Camp as already related, refused to escape with Colonel Ride because, he wrote later, 'First, it was obvious that medical officers were going to be urgently needed in the prison camps, and my duty seemed to be to remain with the men. Secondly, I felt that anyone of my unusual height would minimise the chances of anyone getting through; and third, I was damned scared and preferred to remain with the devil I knew. I deeply regretted my decision on many occasions subsequently.'

Colonel Ride persuaded D. W. Morley and D. F. Davies, both officers of the Hong Kong Royal Naval Volunteer Reserve, to accompany him.' They had been with him on the staff of the Hong Kong University before the war. They had to depend entirely on Private Lee Yiu-Piu, Colonel Ride's former clerk, who had escaped from a corner of the camp alongside the sea the day before. He returned with a sampan and crew of two at 8 p.m. on the following night. 'We all piled into the sampan,' wrote Davies later. 'There were searchlights playing across the water, otherwise it was quite dark and only the phosphorescence betrayed our movement. We disembarked about thirty minutes later and then scrambled up the hill-side. By dawn we were practically above Kai Tak aerodrome. We spent the rest of the day in rain, drizzle or fog.'

They passed many pill-boxes in which were sprawling hideous corpses; and they found ammunition but no food. 'By night we were completely lost in a mist on the top of a hill with a village below us. When the moon rose we stumbled down a ravine and we hid near the village while Lee sought information and food. He returned to report that we were in a place which it was our intention to avoid at all costs!'

Next day they marched inland. Lee returned, after a miserably cold night, with three pieces of bad news; no boat could be found for a reasonable price; Chinese who were pro-Japanese knew that three Europeans were in the area; and a band of robbers was operating in the neighbourhood.

'The last two pieces of news caused us to retreat still further into the wood, just in time,' wrote Davies in his diary, 'for there began a ten-hour search for us by the robbers, whose tramping and crashing around us did nothing to relieve our difficulties. Lee went back to the village to bargain for a cheaper boat and returned at 5 p.m. with the startling news that our "robbers" were guerrillas who were looking for us, shouting "where are our friends of the ABCD front?" [America, Britain, China, Dutch.] We left our hiding places and met the guerrillas who had been operating there for a week.' The guerrillas formed part of the Chinese forces fighting the Japanese, although mainly out for themselves.

Five days later, escorted by the guerrillas, they had reached a 'safe' village beyond which lay unknown territory, and 'free' Waichow about thirty miles away. 'Up to this very last day the actions of the guerillas in guarding and leading us had been worthy of the highest praise, but they failed lamentably at the last moment,' continues Davies. 'Contrary to all previous practice, the village was raided by Japanese troops and cavalry. The guerrillas had posted no sentries and the alarm was raised by small boys with whose help we scrambled up into the hills. Unfortunately Ride's and Lee's haversacks were left behind. Ride's contained some anti-Japanese lecture notes, while Lee's contained the names, in Chinese, of various guerrillas whom he had met. We parted from our one remaining guerrilla at the end of his "beat", and with a village boy as a guide, passed through Chinese territory into "Free China", arriving at a Seventh Day Adventist Mission, the Wai On American hospital, two weeks after we had escaped from Hong Kong.'

The two Naval officers reached Colombo by bus, train and plane almost two months later, leaving Colonel Ride and Private Lee with the momentous task of arranging an organisation, from scratch, to smuggle medicines and information into the Hong Kong prisoner of war camps – in particular to Shamshuipo where diphtheria was raging. Colonel Ride described the conditions in the camp to the British Ambassador in Chungking thereby enabling the British Government and eventually world opinion to receive first-hand reports of Japanese inhumanity.

Shamshuipo Camp contained 4400 men of the Royal Navy and British Army, and 800 Hong Kong Volunteer Defence Corps which included some Chinese and Portuguese.

'Discipline varied considerably. Some units had maintained it, while others had cracked somewhat,' wrote another escaper in April 1942. 'No man was handed over to the Japanese for punishment, but all the same it was difficult to maintain discipline because of the lack of effective punishment. It later became easier, as offenders were barred from using the canteen. There were four Courts Martial which awarded up to one hundred and twelve days detention.'[1] The sentences were served within the camp.

Before the Japanese landings on Hong Kong Island, and the surrender, evidence was being gathered against those few soldiers who had allegedly run away while in action. However the defeat put a stop to subsequent proceedings, just as the investigations into the pre-war corruption scandals had to be dropped.

For the first few weeks of imprisonment, General Maltby and his Fortress Headquarters staff were kept busy completing their war diaries which were based on the few records they had kept. These had been finished by the time Brigadier Wallis reached Shamshuipo from hospital. General Maltby expressed little interest in Brigadier Wallis' account, although he was the only Brigade Commander to survive the fighting, Brigadier Lawson having been killed in action.

Most of the diaries were wrapped in an old plastic gas cape, put into a tin and buried, and recovered after the war. Several, now in London, are not available for public inspection until the next century to protect those who are still alive from what can be nothing more than allegations since they were never put to proof.

The 1942 report of the Canadian Royal Commission cannot be read probably for the same reason. One Commanding Officer was never satisfied with his report and continued to redraft it for months in order to show his battalion in the best possible light. 'No amount of re-writing can alter the facts,' commented a more senior officer, 'but I appreciate the wishes of any commanding officer who tries to defend the good name of his battalion.'

The senior British officers were without privileges. They had to queue for their rice and were subject to the same humiliations as other prisoners from the arrogant guards. The rice was cooked in converted gasoline drums which added a taint to the taste. The average daily ration during the first months fell to less than nine hundred calories. 'We were constantly hungry, cold and bewildered,' remembers one POW, 'we were a pretty miserable lot.'

Sergeant A. J. Alsey was among those few who kept diaries in Shamshuipo. He had served with the Band of the Royal Scots at Aldershot and Quetta before moving to Hong Kong with the Battalion in 1937. Most of the diary entries inevitably referred 'to food or lack of it; real hunger was something none of us had ever experienced before,' he wrote. 'Men reacted in many different ways. Some assumed their stomachs would never accept an endless diet of rice – they died. Others accepted all that was offered – and existed. Others braved beatings and bullets and made sure they lived. The Grace of God was never more apparent.'

Medical care was urgently needed and a building was converted into a hospital. Sacking was draped over the gaping doorways and window frames; a billiard table, too heavy to have been stolen earlier, was turned into an operating table. Instruments were sterilised in a mess-tin over a small bonfire.

Surgery had to be done in daylight, as there were no means of illumination. Eventually an operating theatre was lit by a battery of twenty-four wicks burning in peanut-oil. The Japanese were particularly suspicious of documents of all sorts, including medical records which the camp doctors were most anxious to retain. 'After several sad experiences when some records were found and confiscated,' explained Major Crawford later, 'we resolved to adopt the principle that what is most obvious is best hidden. The Japanese controlled an orderly room which was quite swamped with their own "bumph", which was naturally beyond suspicion. We therefore surreptitiously placed our medical documents there. They were never disturbed and the records were subsequently used as evidence against the Japanese after the war.'[2]

In September 1942, Major Crawford with all the Canadians had been moved back to Shamshuipo from North Point Camp. The diphtheria and dysentery sick accompanied him.

'Now began the darkest period of our imprisonment,' he wrote later. 'The Indians had all been moved to a separate camp and many of the Chinese Volunteers had been released to go to their homes. A draft of British officers and men had left for Japan, but there was still no accommodation in the hospital for all the sick.'

By the end of October 230 new cases of diphtheria had been admitted to Shamshuipo's primitive hospital, the vast majority of them being Canadians. Forty-one Canadians died that month.

Lieutenant Saito Shunkichi, the Japanese medical officer in charge of the Hong Kong POW camps, had graduated from the Kyoto Medical College as recently as 1940. After two months on a post-graduate course for internal diseases, and service in Canton as a sergeant, he was made responsible for directing and supervising all the POW medical staff in Hong Kong. It is incredible that the Japanese gave someone of so few qualifications such responsibility.

Lieutenant Saito usually refused to permit the seriously ill to be moved to well-equipped Bowen Road Hospital, and appeared indifferent to the lack of serum in the camp. Although some medicines were still in Hong Kong most had been sent to Japan. When called to account after the war for his callous disregard of his responsibilities, he maintained that the Canadians 'did not like gargling because the liquid disinfectant had a fishlike smell; they freely walked in and out of the segregation wards and passed cigarettes from mouth to mouth because of the lack of tobacco at the time, thereby encouraging germs to enter throats; and they also refused to use face masks.'[3] His lies did not impress those trying him in Hong Kong in 1947 when he was brought to justice.

Beatings had become common occurrences and the Japanese turned their attention to the doctors. 'The Japanese had become very annoyed with me,' remembers Major Crawford. 'It was not the thing to do, to allow men who had received no serum to die of diphtheria, or men who had no food to die of starvation. Therefore they lined up my medical orderlies and myself, and gave us a bit of a belting. My dignity was hurt more than anything else, but I found it intensely annoying to be pushed around by a slant-eyed, bandy-legged Jap, whose neck I could quite easily have broken. But machine-guns trained on the camp are a great deterrent to riot, and I grinned and took it. What was equally upsetting was the fact that during the succeeding twenty-four hours there were no further deaths. Clear proof, the Japs believed, of the efficiency of their methods of treatment!'[4]

In early October small supplies of serum reached the camp hospital from the Japanese or through the black market which was run by the guards.

'One of the most difficult decisions we ever had to make now faced us,' wrote Major Crawford. 'Which of our numerous cases of diphtheria were to receive serum and which were not? We had only very little, and some must do without. We felt that such a power over life and death should be the prerogative of the Deity, but at the moment He seemed to have forgotten us. Our final decision was simple. Any man who had shown the symptoms of death forty-eight hours before the serum became available did not receive any. We gave serum only to fresh cases where a small quantity might do some good and save life.'

One of the very troublesome symptoms of lack of vitamins was an agonising pain in the feet and legs. The soldiers called this 'electric feet', which accurately described the pain. Such cases were grouped together in the hospital's 'agony ward'. 'Many a time have I made night rounds in this ward,' recalls a doctor, 'to find all the inmates with their feet resting on the cold cement floor or soaking their feet in cold water. I would find them rocking back and forth, and crying with pain; because the soaking treatment led to laceration of the skin and secondary infection it was strictly forbidden. But I could not find it in my heart to be too severe upon the offenders as I could offer them no other form of relief. Never have I felt so helpless. Death, starvation and maltreatment were all we had to look forward to, and many of us felt that those who had already died were the fortunate ones.'

The death-toll eventually forced the Japanese to action. What they called an anti-epidemic unit moved into Shamshuipo and carried out throat examinations on 500 POWs a day. The carriers were quickly discovered and segregated, and sufficient serum was provided from Tokyo to last five months. In November there were 137 new cases of diphtheria, but the worst was over. In December only nineteen new cases materialised, and by early February only one POW had diphtheria. Nevertheless by then an unknown but considerable number of British and 130 Canadians had died owing to the Japanese having initially been unwilling to take the necessary steps.

Strangely enough diphtheria saved some lives, for the patients were isolated for a long time instead of being sent on working parties; the rest undoubtedly saved some from death by exhaustion.

A quota of 800 POWs was required daily to extend Kai Tak aerodrome, which was used by Japanese fighters. POWs were also made to move bombs, fill fifty-gallon drums with gasolene and dig tunnels. G. A. V. Hall, previously an architect in the Public Works Department, told the Japanese of the dangers of constructing the tunnels in loose soil, but the work continued although collapses were frequent. On one occasion a tunnel entrance was sealed, and Hall was told that some Chinese labourers were left entombed.

Second Lieutenant E. H. Field, Royal Artillery, decided to complain to the Japanese that the work undertaken by the POWs was illegal. He discovered afterwards that Lieutenant M. Abbot, later to become Chief Justice of Bermuda, had also done so the same day. Field delivered the following letter to Colonel Tokunaga:

Sir,

I have the honour to refer to Article 6 of Chapter II of the Annex to the Convention Concerning the Laws and Customs of War on Land signed by Japan at the Hague on 18 October, 1907, which expressly states 'the work performed by prisoners of war shall have no connection with the operations of the war'.

The work commenced on 15 September, 1942, at Kai Tak by POWs is extending the airfield. This is, in my opinion, work which is directly connected with the operations of war.

I therefore protest against the employment of prisoners of war at Kai Tak in work which will help the Japanese operations.

I have the honour to be, Sir
Your obedient Servant,
E. H. Field. 2 Lt RA

Field was quickly summoned to Colonel Tokunaga's office where he was interrogated for half an hour by the Colonel's adjutant, Captain Yonai, who asked him if he was an expert in International Law.

'No,' replied Field, 'but I make the protest because I consider it my duty to do so.'

'Do you know that protests are not allowed?' asked Captain Yonai.

'No,' the Lieutenant retorted, 'I have always considered that a polite protest is the correct thing to do on such occasions.'

Captain Yonai was gradually getting angrier and angrier. 'Do you think that the Imperial Japanese Army would employ POWs in such work if it was against military law?' he shouted. 'Would you like to learn some International Law? I will teach you a little. Come here.'

Field was left in no doubt that something nasty was about to happen. 'I received the best hiding I have ever had,' he recalls. 'Yonai started with straight punching on the jaw and face, kicking when I fell, then nearly finishing me off by beating me with his sword, with the scabbard still on, I noticed with some relief. Finally, he gave me a heavy crack on the head with it.

'I was then helped to a chair where I was immediately attended to by a Jap medical orderly who had been waiting throughout the interview. My head was washed and dressed and after five minutes I was offered a cigarette and given a brilliant pep-talk by Yonai on my "bad thoughts", the impertinence of my protesting and, finally, that Kai Tak was purely a civil airfield, which convinced me that my protest was valid. Yonai then shook my hand, adding that we now understood one another and were friends. I left and saw Commander J. A. Page, our Medical Officer, who gave me a couple of aspirins and re-dressed my head.'

Working parties were woken at 4.30 a.m. and returned to Shamshuipo at 8 p.m. However they usually received a little extra food which some felt made the work worthwhile.

The working parties often saw women tied up against lamp posts and telegraph poles. Murder of Chinese was not uncommon. In March 1942, the POWs saw a Japanese sentry shoot a young woman who was digging for sea-shells. The sentry proceeded to walk over to her crumpled figure and then shoot her again at point-blank range. On another occasion a Chinese with his hands tied behind his back was brought into the camp by a sentry. He was taken out to the pier, stabbed with a bayonet in the kidneys, tossed into the water and then shots were fired at his head.

The Japanese policy was to discourage Chinese from approaching the camp in order to prevent them smuggling in food or information, or helping potential escapers. Nevertheless, some guards turned a blind eye to the POWs' relatives and Chinese girl-friends who brought food parcels one day a week. However, in mid-April, after an escape of four POWs, outside parcels were stopped for almost the remainder of the year, which resulted in many deaths from malnutrition.

Tinned tomatoes in food parcels had an unexpected bonus. The seeds managed to survive both the Chinese canning and passage through the bowels, and the POWs noticed little tomato plants growing wherever excreta had been left on the ground.

Doctor J. D. A. Gray was one of those who decided to cultivate the plants. The contents of the latrines were purchased at the standard price of one cigarette for each trough. One morning the latrine cart delivered Doctor Gray his order. 'To prevent flies swarming, I covered the mess lightly with loose soil,' he wrote later. 'This made me slightly late for the first roll-call. The sentry, known as "Cat and Dog" spotted me and rushed forward to club me with the butt end of his rifle. Unfortunately for him, the route he chose was directly over my hidden "minefield". He sank halfway up his calves and I went on parade with the utmost speed. The only tragedy was that there were no witnesses to enjoy the free show.'

Those who lived in Hong Kong had been subject to malaria before the war and the British had introduced control measures as a result of which there had been few cases. The Japanese did not initially take malaria seriously. In contrast to a lackadaisical attitude on this important matter, the Japanese offered rewards to POWs of cigarettes for every hundred flies brought to them, although this would have had only a marginal effect on the reduction of dysentery. Some soldiers left wet, cooked rice on the ground and, after the blue-bottles had laid their eggs, they were carefully covered by cloths until the flies matured. They were then gleefully exchanged for cigarettes.

Doctor Gray remembers that one of the Royal Army Medical Corps Corporals had qualified as a laboratory technician. He was particularly well-read, but also was a heavy drinker. After the fall of Hong Kong the Corporal drank ethyl alcohol and then finished off the highly toxic methyl alcohol and died as a result. 'The Japanese were most impressed,' Doctor Gray wrote later. '" Here at least," thought the Japanese, "was an honourable Englishman who is so ashamed at having been captured alive that he has committed hari-kari – although in a slightly unorthodox manner." So they gave him a slap-up funeral with huge wreaths, and there was much bowing over his grave.[5]

'Rats abounded and it seemed to me as a bacteriologist to be a specially refined tribulation to feel them running over me when I was trying to sleep, knowing that plague, carried by rats and their fleas, was by no means unknown to Hong Kong.' And so a 'camp rodent officer,' Second Lieutenant Evans, was appointed. He carefully primed rat cages with baits of rotting fish. Next morning there was great hilarity for Evans' catch was rats nil – kittens three. The monsoon rains proved more effective as they flushed enormous numbers of rats out of the cracks in the cement. Sally, a little black and white fox-terrier, had a marvellous time killing them. She belonged to the Royal Army Pay Corps, but when rations became really short towards the end of each month, she defected to the Japanese, always to return a few days later. It was a memorable sight to see men, stark naked except for their loin-cloths, standing in the bucketing rain encouraging Sally to still greater efforts. She was later electrocuted on the perimeter wire and gradually all the other animals died of starvation, including the regimental pets.

The padres were allotted a spare hut which was used as a chapel for Anglican, Greek Orthodox and Jewish services. 'In the first few months we all sang "God Save the King" at the end of each service,' recalls a POW. 'But someone tipped off the Japanese and the custom was thereafter strictly forbidden. So the padres arranged that immediately after the blessing we all came sharply to attention and remained so for the time it would have taken us to sing the National Anthem. The synchronising of our coming to attention and standing at ease was perfect, and the effect, at least on myself, was far superior to the usual singing of the Anthem.'

The Roman Catholic padre of the locally-enlisted troops held his services separately and rigged up a red electric light bulb, connected illegally to the mains, to indicate the Reservation of the Blessed Sacrament. Tokunaga found the lamp burning and had the padre severely beaten.

A Canadian padre heard that some of the POW working parties were being put on to shifting sacks of sugar and that there was a chance of pilfering some. The opportunity was too good to miss and he wangled a place on the next working party. In spite of the heat, he put on his battle dress trousers and sealed the bottom of each leg with a tight puttee. He succeeded in filling up both legs of his trousers with sugar so that he could still just walk. On return to camp, the working party was lined up unexpectedly for searching. 'What will I do with my sugar?' wailed the padre. The Middlesex Corporal standing next to him offered fatuous advice on where the sugar could be stuffed. However the Japanese lost interest in searching everyone and the working party was dismissed. The sugar had to be scraped off the padre's legs with a knife.

The Japanese gave Major Cecil Boon the unenviable job of being in charge of the Other Ranks at Shamshuipo. He was aged forty-five and was a regular officer in the Royal Army Service Corps. After he had served as a junior staff officer in the First World War, he had once been a professional ballroom dancing champion. 'I believe that Major Boon was at first horrified by his appointment,' noted Major A. R. Colquhoun, a former Battery Commander in the Hong Kong and Singapore Royal Artillery. 'Boon had never commanded troops in the whole of his career, having always held administrative jobs. The Japs probably spotted him as pliable material because of his subservient attitude and general obsequiousness.'[6]

Major Boon occasionally attended parties with the Japanese as he recorded, in Russian, in his diary: 'After roll-call had bananas, fruit and roll with Japanese officers . . . We went to dine with the Japanese Commander, plenty of beer.'

Brigadier T. MacLeod, the Commander Royal Artillery, and his Brigade Major, J. H. Munro, also dined with the Japanese, their host being the Commander-in-Chief,

77

Lieutenant-General Kitajima, himself an artilleryman. 'He was very pleasant to us,' wrote Major Munro later, 'and gave us a good but rather peculiar meal as he was trying to give us European food. He drank white port, his staff red port and us neat Johnny Walker. The General spoke no English and we conversed through Colonel Tokunaga who spoke quite good French. After dinner the General brought out his operational maps and for almost three hours we had a very interesting discussion about the battle, during which he said that his troops received many casualties and damage from our guns. During dinner I astonished everyone by consuming an entire loaf of bread. He gave us the only square meal I ate as a prisoner.

'Shortly after this I found two companions, Flying Officer Moore and Captain I. B. Trevor of the Volunteers, who were willing to escape with me. From a map published in a Jap newspaper it appeared that Waichow was still in Chinese hands. Friends gave us ten tins of bully from their treasured secret stocks. We also received a few logs of precious firewood with which to make a small raft to carry our food and kit. On 1 February 1942, we crossed through the wire and swam for forty minutes, pushing the raft in front of us. We eventually met Chinese who treated us with the greatest consideration and kindness, enabling us to reach Waichow eleven days later. From there we eventually went on to India.'[7]

Another officer who found himself being sociable with a Japanese was a Royal Army Medical Corps Doctor, R. L. Lancaster, who was a very keen bridge player. One day the bridge enthusiasts were asked to give their names to the camp office as it was hoped to organise a tournament. The Doctor jumped at the idea and was told to report at 7 a.m. the following morning. Only then did he discover that he had to teach bridge to the Camp Commandant, Colonel Tokunaga, in French. Doctor Lancaster had to play on and on, and he eventually staggered back at 6 p.m. complaining ruefully: 'It would not have been so bad if Tokunaga had not been so bloody stupid!'

One Japanese guard, Lieutenant Tanaka Hitoshi, had a

more sinister liaison with a POW. Tanaka received a message from a POW who reported that a certain hut should be watched as a particular officer was planning to escape. The message had been attached to a slate and hung in the guard's office. The Japanese watched the hut before accusing Lieutenant Hyland of being the potential escaper. Hyland admitted this had been the case and agreed not to do so.

The word spread rapidly among the POWs that there was a traitor in their midst. He was eventually singled out and tried by court martial after liberation.

The treatment of officers was somewhat different to that of the rank and file at Shamshuipo and also to that of the Canadians who were earlier at North Point Camp. In April 1942, the Japanese moved 500 officers from Shamshuipo to a separate camp, 'as the officers were too uppity, and to reduce the escapes', recalls Major Colquhoun. They were allowed to take with them 100 soldiers as batmen.

In most armies officers have personal servants chosen from the soldiers under their command, and in the British Army they are called 'batmen'. Their duties are to maintain the officer's equipment and, more important, to look after him in battle. Nowadays an officer's batman is expected also to be a wireless operator and driver.

In Shamshuipo there had been little for the batmen to do, but the officers accepted their presence with pleasure and they felt they might be able to save some lives by taking them to a new camp where better conditions were to be expected.

'We marched off in an easterly direction through the suburbs of Kowloon,' remembers Colquhoun, 'heading we knew not where, carrying our few remaining possessions. Finally we arrived at Argyle Street near Kai Tak, which had been built for the internment of Chinese soldiers who had fled from the Japanese in 1937. Ironically, just before the war, I had been a member of a Court of Inquiry which had recommended the extra wiring required around the camp to prevent Chinese escapes. It was surrounded by high, electrified fencing with six guard towers which mounted searchlights and machine-guns.

'We were met on arrival by one of the Japanese interpreters. He was Niimori Genichiro, nicknamed "Panama Pete", a smallish Japanese-American who had pointed ears and wore military boots and a khaki cloak.

Niimori was the senior interpreter, having spent most of his life in Chicago. He was dapper and diminutive and addressed everyone as "Youse guys". Another interpreter, Inouye Kanao, nicknamed "Slap Happy" or "Shat in Pants', was swarthy, usually unshaven and had eyes set closely together. He was a Japanese-Canadian whose uniform was so ill-fitting that the seat of his trousers hung in a pendulous kind of bag. He had a grudge against everyone and Canadians in particular.'

Kyoshi Watanabe, the third interpreter, had been a Lutheran minister, and he succeeded in combining Christian charity with his duties. He had a smooth, flat face that looked as though it had been dipped in flour. The other guards became aware of his many unobtrusive acts of kindness and he was therefore transferred elsewhere, as were other Japanese who appeared friendly to the POWs. Another helpful Japanese interpreter was 'Cardiff Joe'. He was stocky and bandy-legged, and was reputed to have money still in Cardiff to where he seemed anxious to return. Finally there was a lanky, short-sighted tubercular youth named Katayama who was such a negative character that he never received a nickname.

The Japanese interpreters were very important for all the requests to the authorities had to go through them. They wore military-type uniforms, and had little respect for the Japanese soldiers. The British in Argyle Street had two Japanese linguists – Wing Commander H. T. Bennett and Mr S. R. Kerr. They both had a wretched life, for they were required to translate at any hour, and upon their tact, charm and elaborate turn of phrase depended the success or failure of the trivial concessions being sought. The Wing Commander was a large man with a big moustache, and the Japanese loathed him if only because they never liked dealing with a larger man. Therefore the interpreting gradually fell almost entirely on Kerr, a former Secretary of the Hong Kong Club. If the Japanese felt that a point was being made by the British interpreter without the appropriate courtesy, they would suddenly lash out at the startled most senior officer nearby, for the interpreter was considered to be doing his best and so was immune from being hit.

The Argyle Street camp had been systematically looted and stripped of everything movable by the Chinese before the officers' arrival and so these POWs believed that they had been sent to the camp as a reprisal. No canteen facilities existed and the food was the worst of all the POW camps, consisting of a very small amount of rice per day, supplemented by carrot or turnip tops and chrysanthemum leaves.

The officers were given the equivalent pay in military yen of a Japanese officer of their rank. Most of the pay was passed to a central pool which was used to buy medical necessities and luxuries such as eggs for the hospital. Unfortunately the military yen depreciated so quickly that a Second Lieutenant had barely enough to purchase one box of matches per month – if there were any. A flourishing black market grew up through the guards who negotiated the sale of prisoners' watches, signet rings and trinkets.

Two officers of the Volunteers ran a black market involving the selling of food. They were owed hundreds of pounds and had a mountain of IOUs by the end of the war. Lieutenant-Colonel S. G. N. White, the Commanding Officer of the Royal Scots, asked to inspect the IOUs and had them all burnt, which was much to be commended.

The black market dealt mostly in food, which continued to be totally inadequate although the Japanese gave the officers 'ghi', a butter, presumably imported, made from Indian buffalo milk with a peculiar rancid smell which clung for days. 'Nevertheless,' noted Doctor Warrack, 'it was valuable in our state of malnutrition, and I was horrified to hear our Messing Officer, an infantry Major of rigid views, say to the Japanese supply Corporal: "Good God! We can't eat that. We are British Officers." Fortunately the day was saved by poor interpretation and we got the butter.

'Suddenly the camp was struck by illness, frighteningly similar to cholera. One of the victims was a member of the Volunteers who, through thick and thin, managed to conceal the fact that he was completely bald, having hung on to his toupé, his dearest possession. His sudden illness was too much for him and as he was carried, stretcher-borne, to the sick quarters, several horrified brother officers commented to me on the gravity of the symptoms which had apparently suddenly deprived him of his hair.'

The Japanese took immediate action. All carriers were isolated and white-gowned and masked Japanese had all officers paraded for rectal swabs. This may have been rather undignified for the senior officers, but the sick recovered and there were no fresh cases, while hundreds of Chinese in Hong Kong were dying of cholera.

The officers in Argyle Street came from a multitude of pre-war professions, and there were many odd characters. One officer in the Royal Army Service Corps had received a message from England a few days before the surrender, which told him that he had inherited a fortune of £89,000 from a relative. He was the biggest optimist in the camp: 'There will soon be another American Fleet in Pearl Harbor,' he joked. 'British aircraft from Malaya will rescue us.' But when he heard that Singapore had fallen, he turned his head to the wall, ate nothing and died of a broken heart and starvation, weighing less than five stone when he was buried, although tins of bully beef were found hidden beneath the floorboards under his bed.

Another POW, Major Lord Merthyr, a regular officer and former battery commander, later Chairman of Committees in the House of Lords, became a confirmed pessimist, and told his friends that the war would last ten years. He kept spare tins of food unopened. 'When asked why,' one POW recalls, 'he replied, though in more dignified phraseology, that when the crunch came, and we were starving, he would be laughing. I don't believe he ever ate the tinned food. However he was extraordinarily unselfish, often undertaking the most unpopular jobs in the camp.'

Another idiosyncratic character was J. Woodward, an Australian doctor. He had to report daily to a Japanese guard who spoke no English. The Doctor always bowed low and then, smiling courteously, poured forth a fearful flood of foul abuse at the guard who understood not a word, but gravely bowed back, well-satisfied with the apparent respect.

One of the most courageous individual acts occurred when, most unexpectedly, a Red Cross representative visited the camp, Rudolf Zindel, a successful Swiss business man who had lived in Hong Kong before the war. Zindel was permitted to visit Argyle Street only once every six months, and on each occasion he saw that the POWs looked more haggard and ill.

'I discussed my observations with a Japanese officer who accompanied me on my visits,' wrote Zindel later. 'He did not deny the deterioration in the appearance of the POWs, but put the blame on the POWs for not keeping fit, saying that they preferred to laze about doing nothing.' Each perfunctory visit lasted only a few minutes and Zindel was permitted to talk to no POWs whatsoever. The POWs, in turn, were ordered not to speak to him, and threatened with severe beatings if they tried to do so.

'During my inspection of one of the barracks, inside which the POWs were lined up on both sides of the passage, one of the prisoners stepped forward, just as I was about to pass him, and called out twice in French: "Nous mourons de faim." I was slightly taken aback. Some of the half-dozen or more Japanese who accompanied me rushed at the POW, who was Captain K. M. A. Barnett, and asked him what he was saying. "We are dying of hunger," he replied.'[1]

Captain Barnett was immediately knocked to the ground, dragged away, and severely beaten by Sergeant Harada Jotaro who afterwards explained that: 'When a person did not obey orders it was customary in the Japanese army to beat him.' Captain Barnett was carried to hospital where he remained for several weeks. Harada, nicknamed 'Napoleon', was often to be seen demonstrating his prowess with a sword by chopping off imaginary heads.

Zindel did not intervene when Captain Barnett was beaten because: 'I realised that I would render Captain Barnett's ultimate fate much worse, and it might result in active participation by the other POWs with disastrous consequences for all. After this inspection, I discussed with

Colonel Tokunaga my concern over the obviously inadequate diet which the POWs were receiving, upon which he became furious and shouted at me that if I dared to mention one word of my views to Geneva, he would immediately suspend the "parcel service" to all camps.' Parcels, delivered once more to the POWs by friends outside the camps when the escapes had stopped, were vital for their survival. The POWs felt that Zindel was doing nothing to help them, and that he was still in ignorance as to their appalling condition. The International Red Cross in Geneva failed to take a strong line with the Japanese, and their arrangements for discovering the prisoners' true circumstances were quite inadequate. Zindel appears incredibly naive not to have realised earlier that his visits to the POWs were simply being used by the Japanese for propaganda purposes. He was not helped by another Red Cross delegate, Monsieur Egli, who made a stupid statement that everything under Japanese control was wonderful. Egli later explained that he knew things were far from right but thought he could get more out of the Japanese by supporting them than by criticisms.[2]

Zindel remembered one other occasion when a POW contacted him during his visits: 'Outside the barrack block, Captain R. Egal, a Free French who had been fighting with the British, suddenly stepped up to me, and pretending to know me, heartily shook hands in the presence of the Japanese. While doing so, he slipped into my hand a small object which I succeeded in getting into my trouser pocket without arousing suspicion. Later, in my house, I inspected the object which turned out to be a small cutting of a bamboo branch. It had been hollowed out, but stoppered at both ends with a little straw. Inside the tube I found a note, written in ink, in exceptionally fine but clear writing, which gave valuable information concerning the Argyle Street and Shamshuipo POW camps.'

It was perfectly obvious to Zindel that malnutrition was rife and conditions were deplorable. Yet reassuring Red Cross reports ostensibly from him reached the International Red Cross at Geneva. On 3 July 1942, for example, he had visited all the POW camps, on which day several POWs had died. However, the report which reached Geneva read:

'North Point Camp . . . Men looked well . . . Large garden-plot available . . . Commanding Officer states that they are being well-treated and that they could not complain about the food.

'Shamshuipo Camp . . . Food said to be sometimes better, sometimes worse, with meat rare, but, generally speaking, no cause for complaint. The officers consulted, assured us that the treatment accorded to them and their men was good.

'Argyle Street . . . The camp is exceptionally well-drained, a bakery had started . . . A canteen was available.'[3]

These reports were cheerfully circulated by the International Red Cross in Geneva. The POWs in Hong Kong were apparently being well cared-for, but Zindel knew that the truth was quite different.

'Through a contact which I had in the censor's office in Hong Kong,' he wrote later, 'I learned that all my Delegation mail and cables were strictly censored. My first full reports to Geneva never arrived. At least one of them was given by a Japanese censor to his girl-friend, who in turn boastfully reported the matter to me. She was able to quote extracts from the report.' The censors altered Zindel's reports, or simply ensured that they never reached Geneva. One report, which eventually passed the Hong Kong censor after satisfactory explanations, was returned to Hong Kong by the censor in Tokyo three months later. The Japanese advertised an air-mail service from Canton which seemed preferable to the totally unreliable surface mail. Zindel, therefore, decided to send his reports to the Swiss Consul in Canton who could air-mail them. 'When no replies were received,' he records, 'I made enquiries by cable in Tokyo and Canton and learnt that the air-mail service had ceased to function many months previously, without the public being informed and, what was still more serious, that the Post Office, which was under Japanese supervision, had continued to receive the post, although they had no intention of forwarding such mail by air.'

Due to the misleading picture of the welfare of the prisoners and internees presented in good faith by the International Red Cross, it was difficult for the British, Americans and Dutch to prove that the Japanese treated their prisoners with callous brutality. Diplomatic pressure on Tokyo to improve their conditions was therefore relatively ineffective. 'International Red Cross delegates report that the general state of health of the prisoners in Hong Kong is good,' reported *The Times* on 27 October 1942, 'and that they are satisfied with administrative arrangements.' The Commander-in-Chief, India, cabled two days later stating that this report was in direct contradiction of the facts, for there were a minimum of three diptheria deaths daily in Shamshuipo. The Foreign Office and Colonial Office initially sat back and accepted the favourable reports from Geneva although there was every likelihood that the contrary reports from Chungking on Japanese brutalities were quite likely to be true.

Major Colquhoun recalls Zindel's first visit to Argyle Street: 'We thought something good would come of it, when we heard he was coming. The Japs selected the Volunteers' hut and brought in tables, chairs, table-cloths, light-bulbs – the lot. We were paraded, and in came Zindel wearing a neat grey suit and Panama hat, surrounded by high-sounding Nipponese who whisked him past at twice the speed of light, before removing the tables, light-bulbs and all.'

When spirits were lowest and the POWs had abandoned all hope that the International Red Cross or the Allies could help them, they suddenly received a splendid surprise: 'Got a Red Cross parcel today – 15 items in it. Oh brother,' wrote Captain White. 'We all went crazy – talk about kids at a Christmas tree, nothing to the way we danced around here.'

Another POW on 29 November 1942, wrote: 'We were amazed to receive the shipment of foodstuffs. Bully beef, cigarettes, jam, meat and vegetable ration, cocoa, dried fruit, sugar, and clothing. This changed the whole picture. We now had reason to hope that these shipments might be repeated and that we stood a good chance of surviving our internment. We did not allow our optimism to govern our judgement, and we doled out the foodstuffs very carefully, enough to bring the calorific value up to about 2800 calories, with a protein content from all sources of about 70 grammes. In this way we managed to spin out this supply of food for some fifteen months. It was just as well that we did, for never again did we get such a shipment.'

Colonel Tokunaga decided that he and some of his guards should have their share of the Red Cross parcels, although they had sufficient food already. In June 1943, Matsuda Kichi, a Japanese interpreter, and G. White, formerly employed by the municipal electricity company, visited Tokunaga's house to repair the fridge. They were shown over the house by the Colonel's mistress and saw stacks of Red Cross parcels in cupboards. After the war at his trial Tokunaga was asked for an explanation. 'They were given to me by POWs through Major Boon, their representative, as an act of affectionate gesture,' he replied. Tokunaga was also asked whether it occurred to him that he was taking food from the mouths of the POWs, and on what authority had Major Boon allegedly given him the food? 'I did not think an occasion for authority would arise,' the Colonel answered. 'It was a sort of affection of the POWs towards the people who looked after them. A large quantity of parcels arrived and some were given to me as an expression of mutual friendship, just as one gives presents to friends. It was a happy event and the POWs offered the goods to me as a sort of affectionate human feeling.' Colonel Tokunaga agreed that he had supplied food to Mary Wong, his Chinese housekeeper, who ran a local Chinese hospital, but he denied that he had passed on to her Red Cross parcels, medicines and drugs.

Nevertheless, these vital supplies frequently found their way into shops, as Major Harao Yoshio, the Japanese chief of the Military Police in Kowloon knew well. He discovered that the shops near the Peninsula Hotel were selling Red Cross tins quite openly, and confiscated two hundred tins. Two Japanese NCOs carried out a half-hearted investigation to find the culprits. Eventually Major Harao decided that the blame could be placed on coolies who had allegedly stolen the tins from broken packing cases when they were being unloaded and moved. The coolies in question were not found and no arrests were made. Red Cross supplies and medicines continued to be pilfered.

Fortunately the Japanese allowed POWs to receive food parcels from friends in Hong Kong, once the escapes had stopped. These parcels were pooled, and most POWs had something extra to eat on Christmas Day 1942, as two POWs in Shamshuipo noted in their diaries: 'For Christmas Day we really spread ourselves,' wrote Captain White of the Winnipeg Grenadiers. 'We had a special meal for the men with Red Cross tins. The orchestra played, and the officers gave each man a packet of fags. Afterwards we had a guitar player and singsong. A wonderful day – hope we are home next Christmas.'

Sergeant Alsey, the musician in the Royal Scots, had a rather different Christmas: 'Carol-singing lasts for an hour,' he noted in his diary. 'Three buns and a third of a tin of bully for Xmas dinner. Bed at 8.30 p.m., but got up at 2 a.m., and made a really good cup of tea at 4.30. My scabies are terrible and I scratch for hours, and my feet are aching like hell.'

Shortly after the officers' move to Argyle Street, those with musical experience were asked to put their names down for their particular instrument. 'I put mine down for the saxophone,' recalls Major Colquhoun, 'not because I had ever played one, but it was probably easy to carry and interesting to look at. Months later enough instruments for a complete orchestra were issued, and the camp lay back, anticipating the prospects of long summer evenings when jagged nerves would be soothed by the limpid strains of the violins. Unfortunately most players couldn't read a note and the Japanese wouldn't allow any form of band practice or rehearsal. We were ordered to play in the canteen before evening roll-call.

'The canteen was a wire cage about twenty-feet square, designed in happier days as a thief-proof store. Twenty of us assembled – army officers, naval ratings, legal and government officials, and former school masters – all united under the baton of Lieutenant-Commander Stanley Swetland, RN, who was elderly, caustic, sardonic, morose and completely imperturbable. With fingers like a bunch of sausages, he could coax real music out of anything from a tiny mandolin upwards. Earlier he had built the camp ovens and organised the bakers who made excellent bread until the flour ran out.

'The entire camp, including the Japanese guards, assembled in front of the cage. We sounded rather professional as we tuned up – so much so that the guards applauded under the impression that this was the first item in our repertoire. Stan Swetland tapped twice with his baton for silence, raised his arms and collected us with a baleful glare over the top of his steel-rimmed glasses. "Black Diamond Overture," he gravely announced. "Letter A. Count of three. Come in on the down beat . . ." We did. The resulting discord of sounds was excruciating. Stan Swetland blenched, and it was generally agreed that this was the only occasion he was ever seen to betray any sign of emotion. We cowered behind our music stands, thankful to be secure inside our cage and safe from reprisal from the audience who were convinced that they had been conned by a bunch of impostors. After this débâcle the orchestra disintegrated into "splinter" groups who could play by ear, quietly in the cool of the evening. They later benefited from two superb players – Len Corrigan and Noel Bardel, both Canadians. When the Japanese decided that we should do mass PT before breakfast, the "Worst Orchestra in the World" was resuscitated to lighten the burden, and Stan Swetland orchestrated some rousing marches and simple waltzes to which the POWs could jump and wave their arms. The only advantage of being a "musician" was that we didn't have to join in these capers, which were not popular.'

'I thought the physical training exercises were demoralising,' recalls Sergeant Alsey in Shamshuipo whence all the officers were later moved when Argyle Street camp was closed. 'I felt physically weak, had no adequate footwear and was in no frame of mind to put heart or soul into wasting my small supply of energy on PT.' Evidently he did not feel such points could be discussed with his officers because he added: 'Perhaps a lot more could have been done in the way of regular meetings between officers and NCOs to explain and discuss day-to-day events and grievances. But because hunger was a great divider or leveller, it became a battle for survival with everyone for himself; imposing rank at such times was rather meaningless.'

Apart from the very occasional Red Cross parcel – few received more than three in as many years – morale depended on mail from home, and whatever the POWs could do to amuse themselves.

Once a month the POWs were permitted to print one postcard not to exceed fifty words. This was later reduced to twenty-five words to make the Japanese censors' job easier. The POWs' letters had to follow a standard format which could convey no information on sickness or any adverse circumstances. The first batch of incoming mail was delivered on Christmas Day, 1942, and letters arrived infrequently thereafter; the lucky ones received them with rapturous excitement. During the last two years of the war large quantities of mail reached Hong Kong more frequently. The Japanese censors were unable to cope, and the mail accumulated until Colonel Tokunaga ordered that letters which contained more than fifty words be burnt. Six wooden trunks containing mail were also burnt two days before the Japanese surrender.

Some POWs received many letters while a few received none, although their wives and sweethearts were writing from home as frequently as the regulations permitted. One wife impregnated her letters with scent hoping that the censor might sympathetically let it through. An officer in the Royal Artillery received only one letter in three years; it was from his tailor in Sackville Street, demanding instant payment.

The Japanese used mail as a bargaining counter. Officers were asked to submit a two hundred word statement on general camp life, emphasising the amenities. It was obvious that the statements would be used as propaganda and so they refused. Niimori retaliated by telling Lieutenant-Colonel White that if the statements were not submitted, both inward and outward mail would be stopped which would have a serious effect on the morale of the POWs and their families. It was therefore decided to comply partially with the request, and innocuous statements were passed to the Japanese. They proved unsatisfactory for propaganda so the Japanese tried a different approach in October 1943. The POWs were told that a few of them could broadcast messages to their families. Captain White was one of the ten Canadians selected to broadcast because he had received no mail from home. The Canadian authorities had earlier intercepted a broadcast picked up in New York giving substantial details of Japanese interviews with Canadian POWs which indicated that they were in good spirits and gave no hint of disturbing conditions, but the broadcast came through a German-controlled agency called Trans-Ocean and was therefore suspect.

Throughout the war the Japanese attached considerable importance to these broadcasts, particularly from Japan to the United States. It was an excellent method of reaching the families of POWs and the Japanese realised that the faint chance of hearing a loved one created a large and willing listening audience. At first messages were broadcast at a regular time each day. Later the time was lengthened with the addition of news items and music. Occasionally personal messages were sprinkled among the news items at any time. The forlorn hope of hearing a personal message was therefore continually dangled before the mothers, wives and sweethearts. These broadcasts gave the Japanese a chance to insert false statements.

By 1943 about a third of the messages from the Tokyo area were recordings of prisoners' voices, and all messages from other areas were read by announcers. The themes included the impression that the American soldiers were receiving kind treatment from their captors, had now understood the 'holiness' of the Japanese cause and 'had come to hate the American Government.'[4] In April 1944, the Japanese developed a slander theme which sought to drive a wedge into Anglo-American unity, both in the Pacific Combat Zone and in the homelands. It stressed the higher pay of the American officer which was alleged to have resulted in moral looseness with the wives and sweethearts of the British allies. The 'amorous exploits' were elaborated upon at great length in the broadcasts in a smear campaign directed against allied friendship, and their friends and relatives at home.

The broadcasts from Hong Kong, however, were considerably less sophisticated, and there is no evidence that those to Canada were of any propaganda value since the POWs like Captain White had chosen their words with care.

The occasional concerts in Hong Kong's POW camps were an immense success for they enabled the POWs to forget for the moment the malnutrition and miserable surroundings. 'The improvising in the play last night was really amazing,' wrote Captain Hurd on 21 May 1943. 'Wigs were made from the string of rice sacks, evening dresses from mosquito nets and the chorus "girls'" wings from wooden frames.' A Portuguese, "Sonny" Castro, invariably played the leading lady with such success that some POWs to this day are unsure of his sex. The Japanese enjoyed the shows as much as anyone else, and they provided coloured chalk for makeup. They sat in the front row and roared with laughter, although they only had one interpreter among them and so could have understood very little. Their presence meant that the lyrics had to be re-written just before hand, otherwise they would have found them very offensive. Plays produced included *Journey's End, You're No Lady* and *The Merchant of Venice*.

Evening lectures were popular and in one month alone they included 'Scents and Perfumes', 'A Holiday in a Lunatic Asylum', 'Gamekeeping', 'Murder and Armed Robbery in Shanghai', 'Communism', 'Hollywood', 'A Cruise in Swedish Waters', 'Ten years in Destroyers', and 'Training of a Minister of the Church of Scotland'.

The camp magazines were professional and enabled the POWs to amuse themselves. For example the camp cobbler's shop was run by an Etonian, Harrovian and Wykehamist which prompted the following:

> Though your boots were made by Maxwell
> And your shoes designed by Lobb,
> Aren't you still a social climber
> Aren't you candidly a snob?
> Are you suited – we'll go further
> Are you booted by Lord Merthyr?
>
> With a coronet on every heel to mark the finished job?
> Need we prove our gentle breeding,
> Need we show our pedigrees?
> Eton, Winchester and Harrow – aren't they always
>   guarantees:
> One and all we pull together,
> Put the 'polish' into leather,
> Won't you let us be your 'sole'-mates, fit you with our
>   family trees?

Despite the camp magazines, few POWs could divert their attention from food for long, as is suggested by the following poem:

A Prisoner's Prayer

> You know, Lord, how one must strive
> At Shamshuipo to keep alive.
> And how there isn't much to eat –
> Just rice and greens at Argyle Street.
>
> It's not much, God, when dinner comes
> To find it's just chrysanthemums.
> Nor can I stick at any price
> Those soft white maggots in the rice.
> Nor yet those little, hard black weevils,
> The lumps of grit and other evils.
>
> I know, Lord, I shouldn't grumble
> And please don't think that I'm not humble

When I most thankfully recall
My luck to be alive at all.

But, Lord, I think that even You
Would soon get tired of ersatz stew.
So what I really want to say
Is: if we soon don't get away
From Shamshuipo and Argyle Street,
Then please, Lord, could we have some meat?

A luscious, fragrant, heaped-up plateful.
And also, Lord, we would be grateful
If you would send a living boon
And send some Red Cross parcels, soon.

The prisoner's prayer was answered in an unexpected and dramatic fashion.

At night on 24 October 1942, United States aircraft from 14th Air Force in China bombed Hong Kong. The morale of the POWs soared; the war was catching up with them. One of the aircraft carried B. A. Proulx, the Canadian who had escaped through the sewer from North Point Camp. He had made contact with General C. L. Chennault, commanding the Americans, and briefed the pilots on the location of the POW camps. He flew in the leading bomber to indicate the targets. Bombing raids took place on each of the following two days and incendiary bombs were dropped. The next raid occurred ten months later after which they averaged almost one a month. On each occasion the POWs were placed in some danger since they were not allowed to dig air-raid shelters, and some oil drums containing high-grade aviation gasolene were stored in pits within Shamshuipo camp. Due to the accuracy of the bombing no POWs were hit, although some internees at Stanley were killed in a tragic incident which will be related later.

At Shamshuipo, however, several prisoners were injured by a Japanese anti-aircraft battery close by which opened fire as the American aircraft came in low over the Kowloon hills; live shells from the battery fell within the camp. The

Japanese ordered Colonel White to sign letters of protest to General Chennault. The Colonel, who invariably showed his utter contempt for the enemy and always did his best to save his officers and men from Japanese outrages, refused to co-operate. Instead the Japanese were shown the shrapnel and shell cases with their own markings.

The American targets were ships, oil depots and dockyard installations. Occasionally Chinese districts were hit, making hundreds homeless. Each raid was an opportunity for much rejoicing among the POWs, as Captain Hurd recorded: 'We had our first bombing from our own planes. What a thrill – we don't worry about danger to ourselves. Complete blackout and at night there are all kinds of wild shooting for the sentries are very jittery.' His diary usually lay buried since they were forbidden and searches were frequent. Nevertheless he could not resist digging it up on 2 September 1943, to note: 'We sure had the fireworks today. Dive bombers came over the hills just behind the camp and bombed the former Texaco Oil dump a mile away. We had a perfect view of the twenty tanks which went up with a terrific explosion – flames 500 feet up. The windows in our hospital rattled, the ground shook – Wow! What a thrill! Sure bucks you up a thing like that. We'll beat these little yellow bastards yet.'

The most dramatic raid took place almost three months later on the cricket field adjoining the Hong Kong Club in the centre of Victoria. A large Japanese parade was being held, and the aircraft attacked without warning from low cloud at the exact moment the parade was called to attention to hear a proclamation from the Emperor. The prison guards later confided to several POWs that there were many casualties because the troops could not escape from the cricket ground as it was surrounded by six foot high vertical steel railings.

This incident, which was hushed up, suggested to the Japanese that there must be allied spies in Hong Kong since the bombers knew where and when to strike. The Japanese were right for Colonel Ride's British Army Aid Group had courageous Chinese agents working amidst the enemy.

In February 1942, Colonel Ride arrived in Chungking after escaping from Shamshuipo. He proposed to Major-General L. E. Dennys, the British Military Attaché in China, that an organisation be established to arrange the escape of POWs and internees from Hong Kong.

General Dennys was sympathetic, but no men, transport, arms or wireless sets could be spared, and Ride's plans were considered to be too pretentious, and a modified proposal was approved. Ride was told to remain in South China to 'do what he could'. He was authorised to retain the temporary services of any escapers, as it was impossible at that time to provide a formal establishment. For security the organisation was called 'The British Army Aid Group', with the cover role of helping Chinese refugees. General Chiang Kai-shek gave the scheme his personal blessing and issued orders that the Chinese should support it.

In March Ride returned to Kukong where he started to recruit anyone who had escaped, including the members of the Special Operations Executive who had evaded capture with the MTB party. Colonel Ride asked Captain R. D. Scriven, Indian Medical Service, who had escaped from Shamshuipo the previous month to return to Waichow, forty miles from Hong Kong. Scriven had been the Middlesex Battalion medical officer and spoke Cantonese fluently. 'He told me I should do anything I could to find out what was happening in Hong Kong, and to contact guerrillas who might be helpful in guiding further escapers,' recalls Scriven.[1] 'I was also told to ingratiate myself with General Cheung who was commanding the Chinese forces in Waichow. And so I set off with a good supply of medical stores and a Chinese, Henry Chan, who had been a tour guide in Hong Kong before the war. How long my mission would last I had no idea. We reached Waichow hidden under sacks after passing Japanese patrols.' Waichow was a small and unimportant town which had been occupied by the Japanese three times. It had a population of under 100,000, many of whom were connected in some way with smuggling between Hong Kong, Canton and the interior of China. The town was in a state of almost complete ruin with no cars or electric light.

'I set up my quarters in the Italian Medical Mission,' remembers Scriven. 'The Italian Catholic priests had been "removed to safety" by the Japanese on one of their occasional hit-and-run attacks, leaving a most admirable Chinese priest, Father Ma. Within minutes of my arrival, there was an air raid, and the Japanese anti-personnel bombs caused many casualties. I bustled about arranging their treatment and removal to the Mission, receiving an encouraging response from the Chinese civil and military.

'Next day I was invited to dine with General Cheung and the City officials, and I am convinced that the dinner was the beginning of the British Army Aid Group's eventual success. I was thanked profusely by General Cheung, the civilian mayor, the bank manager, the Communist party representative and the guerrilla leader, all of whom proceeded to try and drink me under the table. Tongues loosened, the passage to Hong Kong for Henry Chan, the former Hong Kong guide, was arranged and I was told of three other Hong Kong escapers, led by Major J. D. Clague, Royal Artillery, who were two days march away. I walked back to the Mission with General Cheung, and he came in for a nightcap and to meet Father Ma. The drinks finished, I bid a courteous goodnight to him, and fell senseless to the floor, smashing an oil-lamp and a table in my descent. Father Ma put me to bed, and assured me I had acquired much face.

'Henry Chan returned from Hong Kong a few months later having actually talked to some POWs through the wire at Shamshuipo, and gathered much information. I was able to send detailed reports to Colonel Ride, while acting as the medical officer in charge of Waichow, chief of air-raid casualties, morale raiser, and confidant of all. However in

June Major Clague arrived to replace me, for the Indian Medical Service in New Delhi had become restless that one of their officers should be employed on "other duties".' Scriven later commanded a medical unit in Burma, reaching the rank of colonel. He returned to Hong Kong after the war to start a flourishing practice.

Major Clague's advance post, which consisted of five British officers and ten Chinese, started to plan ways of contacting POWs in Hong Kong. By now Ride had received an operational directive from Brigadier G. E. Grimsdale, the next Military Attaché in Chungking: 'You are appointed M19 representative in China,' it read. 'Your objective is to effect the rescue from camps in Hong Kong of POWs, whether Army, Navy or RAF, regular or volunteer, British, Indian, Chinese, American or Dutch . . . It is of the utmost importance that everything you do should be done with the knowledge of the Chinese Military authorities. You must be prepared at all times to give all the credit for any success you may have to the Chinese. You should collect all kinds of intelligence about general conditions in and around Hong Kong . . . I have so far failed to get permission for you to use cyphers.' The Military Attaché failed to appreciate the vast distances between him and BAAG, and Ride seldom received the help from Chungking which he deserved.

The difficulties with which the British Army Aid Group was set up were nothing compared to the Chinese hostility, and danger, particularly for the agents, amidst which they were to work over the following three years.

China was not an Allied war theatre; there was no Combined Allied Staff to plan and control military operations. It was instead purely a Chinese theatre, under the nominal supreme command of the Generalissimo, Chiang Kai-shek, with an American Chief of Staff, General J. Stillwell, a notorious Anglophobe, whose personal character is best described by the fact that he became universally known as 'Vinegar Joe'. He had little regard for the British apart from a more than sneaking admiration for Admiral Mountbatten and General Slim.

The Special Operations Executive had been set up by

Churchill to 'set Europe ablaze'. But by mid-1942 the SOE's days in China were over, as General Headquarters in India was informed in a report from the British Embassy in Chungking: 'The SOE got into such bad odour with the Chinese, largely because its personnel were almost exclusively representative of British interests, and their tactless and misguided activities, so that Chiang Kai-shek himself ordered them out of China and refused permission for them to operate.'[2]

BAAG therefore found that it alone had become a potential source of the operational intelligence which the Americans needed.

General Stillwell's interest became centred on those Chinese units which were fighting the Japanese in Burma, but the US General Chennault had established forward bases at Kweilin, Lingling and Hengyang for air operations against the Japanese in South China, including Canton and Hong Kong. There then sprang up between Chennault's Americans and BAAG a very close, though unofficial, liaison of mutual benefit.

BAAG's relationship with the Chinese was usually strained. China was in the transitional stage between the old provincial war-lord system and central control through a Ministry of War. The changes had taken place on paper but not in practice, and in the provinces there was a multiplicity of formations with military or semi-military responsibilities. They consisted of Central Government troops, provincial troops, a Pacification Bureau, Military Police and Communist guerrillas. The importance of each formation varied from area to area, and depended on the political status and personality of the commander and the closeness of his association with Chiang Kai-shek. South China was divided into four war zones, but their commanders had control only over their regular Central Government troops who were mainly stationed at their Headquarters or in large cities. The troops and junior commanders were all locally recruited and would never serve under an outsider; the limit of their allegiance was their War Zone, and when driven from it the units tended to fade away and cease to exist.

Marshal Li Tsai Sum, the strong man of the South, distrusted Chiang Kai-shek and did not accept his leadership.

This military set-up, complicated by local politics, personalities and intrigue, made BAAG's work most difficult. They found the Chinese system to be largely incomprehensible, and a policy which worked in one area failed in another. Finally, BAAG never formed an integral part of any Chinese military body. Its existence was usually recognised by both the Americans and Chinese, its presence tolerated, and its help accepted, but officially it was ignored.

'We were never at any time taken into the confidence of our allies as we should have been,' wrote Ride. 'Any co-operation we had or any help we were able to give was purely the result of our personal contacts. All British officers were compelled to have passes issued by Chungking and strict orders were given by Brigadier Grimsdale that on no account was an officer to move without a valid pass. Unfortunately these passes were valid for a few months only and had to be sent each time to Chungking for renewal. Thus an officer was immobilised every few months for a period of four to six weeks. This order of Brigadier Grimsdale was all the more futile because Chungking passes were never recognised in the forward areas, and the owner of such a pass was looked upon with suspicion. The only pass of any value in the provinces was either an ordinary visiting card or a pass issued by the local commander who regarded any other pass as an affront.'[3]

BAAG wireless permits were also issued by Chungking, 'and these took months and months to obtain and in many cases permission was not granted,' reported Ride. 'Yet frequently the local general, fully understanding the operational necessity of having wireless communications between our posts, would instruct us to go ahead and set up our stations; of this we were never able to take advantage owing to the measure of our control from Chungking.'

Ride found the biggest stumbling block was that Britain's prestige in China had reached an all time low. 'Many leading Chinese had been misled by our propaganda about the impregnability of Hong Kong', he wrote later, 'and did not trouble to hide their resentment at having lost everything when the Colony fell, and in their view the British were wholly to blame. Our surrender, before the promised arrival of what would have been a poorly-equipped and half-trained Chinese relief force, gave the Chinese ample grounds for expressing their disgust for the decadent British. So anti-British feeling was rife and anti-British sentiments were constantly expressed both in conversation and in the press. From 1942 the Chinese became intensely world power conscious, not through any achievement of theirs in the battlefield but mainly because our failures proved to them the fallacy of our supremacy. If the defeated British were considered to be a world power, why not the undefeated Chinese?'

Moreover many Chinese resented the idea of a British escape and evasion organisation in China, the evasion side of this applying to American aircrews shot down when bombing Japanese objectives. The Chinese national pride and politeness made them look upon all escapers, evaders and refugees as the guests of their country and it was their duty and privilege to look after them. For BAAG to do this instead was a loss of face, though the Chinese help to escapers began and ended with official entertainment on their safe arrival in China. Meanwhile the thousands of wretched Chinese refugees received neither encouragement nor support.

BAAG's problem, therefore, was to learn to do the real escape, evasion and refugee work, while still allowing the Chinese to save face by receiving the publicity.

Many Chinese believed that the British had been driven from the Colony forever, and it was their aim to re-occupy it without British participation. BAAG was therefore not welcome in many official circles owing to the belief that the organisation was an expression of British imperial policy by which they could keep a foot in the Hong Kong doorway.

China's contribution to the total war effort has not been adequately recognised. When the Pacific War began in December 1941, China was engaging twenty-two Japanese divisions plus twenty brigades, compared with ten divisions and three brigades which Japan used in its offensives in the Dutch East Indies, Malaya, Hong Kong and Burma, and by the war's end well over a million Japanese troops were in China. During Japan's war against China, almost 400,000 Japanese troops were killed, which belies the later charges that China did not really fight.[4]

South China was divided into spheres of influence, due to the internal political web caused by the Communist anti-Chungking faction which hated Chiang Kai-shek. North of Hong Kong was the Japanese-occupied belt, beyond which lay the 'unofficial' guerrilla belt occupied by Chinese Communists. To their north, further inland, the 'official guerrillas' held sway. They were Chinese who ostensibly accepted Central Government direction, and were under the command of whichever general nominally controlled the area.

The Communists thus formed the buffer between the Japanese and the Chinese Government Forces, and they were occasionally attacked by both. Nevertheless the Communists were usually the most active, reliable, efficient and anti-Japanese of all the Chinese forces. There was no overland route into or out of Hong Kong other than through Communist territory, and no one, be he Chinese, American or European, could pass in or out without Communist permission and help.

Chiang Kai-shek's Government regarded anyone who had dealings with the Communists, including the escapers, as immediately suspect. Privates D. Hodges and J. Gallagher, two soldiers of the Royal Scots, escaped from Shamshuipo in 1942. Both were quickly found by the Communists who looked after them at their headquarters for six weeks, during which time the soldiers gave them instruction in small arms and machine-guns. The Government immediately accused Colonel Ride and the British Ambassador in Chungking of training the Communists to fight against them, and the two men had to be discreetly moved out of China as rapidly as possible. This was typical of the stupidity of Chiang Kai-shek, or his advisers, which caused so much trouble. Even three years later the accusation that the British had been engaged in training the Communists was resurrected by the Central Government authorities.

A more awkward incident occurred in February, 1942, when Superintendent A. Bathurst of the Hong Kong Police escaped from Stanley Internment camp. He returned without authority to the Communist area to arrange another escape from Stanley with the help of Communist guerrillas. However his plans failed, and so he went to Chungking where the Chinese protested so strongly about his behaviour that the British Ambassador agreed that Bathurst must leave China and not return. Unfortunately, on his arrival in India, a new secret organisation, officially known as the British Liaison Office to the Consul-General in Chungking, recruited him to work in China. He now returned with the rank of Lieutenant-Colonel and began to wear uniform. This confirmed to the satisfaction of the Chinese that their orders were being circumvented and BAAG, being the accredited military organisation in South China, had to bear the full brunt of accusations and suspicion.

Thus many difficulties, caused by Britain's loss of prestige, Chinese unhelpfulness and their enmity for the Communists, seriously prejudiced the escape and evasion organisation which BAAG hoped to set up.

Gradually Chinese were recruited, usually from the refugees fleeing from Hong Kong who could be returned to the Colony for extremely dangerous work. Some had previously served with the Volunteers or the Police, and so knew the Colony well. So, of course, did the principal British officers, Colonel Ride and Majors Monro and Clague who were commanding BAAG's posts having all themselves escaped from Hong Kong. None of them had received formal training in the intricacies of escape or evasion. In London a school, with the non-committal title of Intelligence School 9, was training officers from all three Services for such work, but there was insufficient time to send BAAG officers to London, and south China was too far away.

BAAG initially found that contact with the POWs could not be established since the Japanese guards shot at anyone approaching the camp's perimeter wire. In June 1942, a BAAG group of five, commanded by Captain D. R. Holmes MC, who had evaded capture when Hong Kong fell, was sent by Ride into the hills near Hong Kong on an escape reconnaissance. From there they saw in the distance the POW camps. They had maps stolen from the Japanese which showed the complete drainage system of Kowloon, including the sewers beneath Argyle Street POW camp which had been occupied before the war by Chinese who had been interned after fleeing from the Japanese in China. Many of these internees had escaped through an underground nullah which passed under the camp and opened into Kowloon Bay. BAAG now planned to help POW officers to escape through the sewers, but unfortunately the plan was not found to be feasible. In September Captain Holmes's team was withdrawn because the Nationalist Central Government would not allow BAAG to send money or supplies to them, for fear that such items would fall into Communist hands and be used eventually against Chiang Kai-shek.

The possibility of establishing a regular system of communication with the camps seemed remote. But in September 1942, POWs from Shamshuipo started to work at Kai Tak airport. The Chinese prisoners in the Hong Kong Volunteer Defence Corps found it possible to chat with the Chinese construction overseers, some of whom were friendly. The following month several of these prisoners were surreptitiously given messages written on small slips of paper. They passed them on to their Commanding Officer, Captain R. K. Valentine, one of the camp's medical officers.

One such message read: 'I am in touch with friends outside and I am anxious to make contact with the Senior British officer in your camp. Acknowledge receipt of message, giving your name. Signed No 13.' Another message was addressed to Major Boon, and said that assistance was available for parties planning to escape.

These messages caused consternation and the few British

officers left in Shamshuipo suspected a Japanese trap. Major Boon, it was felt, was the last officer who should receive them because he seemed too friendly with the enemy.

Captain Valentine confided in Captain D. Ford, now the senior Royal Scot at Shamshuipo after most officers had been transferrred to Argyle Street. Ford, aged twenty-four, came from Edinburgh and had joined the Battalion in Hong Kong three years earlier. The messages began to arrive daily and appeared to be originating from Major Clague.

Captain Ford gave Sergeant R. J. Hardy and Corporal Bond a guarded reply to hand to a Chinese contact identified only as Number 68. The two NCO's were working daily at Kai Tak. Corporal Bond spoke Cantonese and cross-examined Number 68 very thoroughly before handing over the message which read: 'Do you know where the messages originate? We are not interested in organising an escape party. Send a note signed by Major Clague whose signature we can identify.'

A few days later a reply was received by Captain Ford: 'Post established at Waichow. Agents organised to carry messages. Anxious for news of personnel and conditions in camp.' Clague's signature was recognised as genuine, and the excitement was intense. At last, after almost a year, a link had been established through contact 68 to China and the outside world. Captain Ford reported to Waichow that Major Boon was 'not acceptable to the small group dealing with the communications'.

The next message from Major Clague told Captain Ford that it was the duty of every officer taken prisoner to escape as soon as possible and rejoin his unit. Every help was promised including Chinese agents from Chungking who would guide the POWs to safety; escape plans and routes would be provided.

Knowledge of the link with BAAG was confined to only five in Shamshuipo: Captains Valentine, Ford and D. L. Prophet, and the two NCOs Hardy and Bond. They felt that General Maltby in Argyle Street must be told of the contact and be consulted on escape policy. Fortunately Lieutenant-Commander J. C. Boldero, RN, arrived in Shamshuipo from hospital, and as his transfer to Argyle Street seemed probable, he was shown all the messages and given a written note for General Maltby which was hidden in shaving soap. Before Boldero was moved to Argyle Street in early December, he appointed Captain Ford to command the Shamshuipo link with BAAG. It was agreed that if General Maltby confirmed this appointment, Ford would be sent 15 yen from Argyle Street; 10 Yen would be the sign of General Maltby's disapproval. A few days after Boldero's departure, Ford received 15 yen; from now on his voice could speak with absolute authority.

Meanwhile the messages from Waichow still urged the POWs to escape. BAAG had been established to arrange escapes and there was no apparent justification for the organisation if no POWs were rescued.

Colonel Ride told General Headquarters, Delhi, that: 'The main reason why there were no escapes was the complete lack of escape-mindedness among the prisoners'. It was of course known to Regular Officers, although there were not many in Hong Kong, that it was their duty to try to escape in order that more enemy manpower should be tied up in trying to prevent it. Although there had been no training in Hong Kong in the techniques of escaping this was common in England and routine for those most liable to be captured such as aircrews, parachute troops and commandos.

One Commanding Officer, commenting on the escape of a brother officer, stated that the escaper would be court-martialled on arrival at Chungking for deserting his troops. Colonel Ride was told through smuggled messages from a senior officer in Argyle Street that, 'such was the lack of enthusiasm for escaping, there would be none unless a senior staff officer was sent from Delhi to carry out the operations.' Ride reported that the POWs were deterred by lack of knowledge of conditions outside their camps, 'there was no information on where an escaper should make for or how far he should have to travel before reaching safety; it was commonly believed that all the Chinese had turned pro-Japanese; there was a peculiar psychological attitude almost universally prevalent in the early days of imprisonment whereby even the most fantastic rumours were believed and passed on as true. For example the Canadians all believed that they were to be repatriated, and it was universally believed that Mr Churchill had broadcast that Hong Kong would be re-taken within three months.'

These reports which criticised the POWs for failing to try to escape were factually correct but misleading, as Commander D. H. S. Craven, RN, imprisoned in Argyle Street, reported to the Admiralty in 1945: 'Incoming messages were at first concerned with blaming us for our apparent lethargy and unwillingness to escape. We pointed out that the question of escape had had to be shelved for the present, on account of the brutal Japanese method of wholesale retaliation on those remaining behind. Understandably this point was not appreciated outside. We informed one BAAG officer in plain words that his own escape, contrary to the instructions of General Maltby, had indirectly caused about 150 deaths in a few months from starvation and neglect.'[5]

Major Clague in 1942 in a further note ordered that all officers be informed of their duties to escape 'and to attach no sentimental value to those incapable of getting away'.[6] BAAG informed the POWs that '*all* previous escape parties had arrived in safety in Free China.' However this was not the case; four Canadians, and two Royal Engineer Other Ranks had already been executed by the Japanese after being recaptured before the Communist guerrillas or BAAG had had an opportunity of helping them. Although BAAG must have been unaware of this, they had reported to General Headquarters, Delhi, on 17 February 1943, that four internees from Stanley had been recaptured after escaping in early 1942.

By 1 May 1943, BAAG consisted of thirteen officers and four soldiers divided between their Headquarters at Kweilin and outposts at Chungking, Waichow, Macao and Dunming. A further thirty-five British and Chinese staff served at their Headquarters as clerks, accountants, medical staff and messengers.

Ride had begun a year earlier to plan an attack on Hong Kong to liberate hundreds of POWs, since they were unwilling to escape in small numbers.

The first plan involved a Chinese guerrilla attack on the Japanese in Hong Kong which could be extended to liberate the prisoners. In October 1942, Colonel McCooper, Chief of Staff of the American-China Task Force visited Ride to discuss his proposed operation. 'He immediately left for Washington and London,' noted Ride optimistically, 'to place our whole plan before President Roosevelt and Churchill.'

Until the Autumn of 1943 the overall strategic plan had been first to re-open the 'Burma road' linking India to China, and then with re-trained and re-equipped Chinese armies to attack Japanese formations in the Canton-Hong Kong area, synchronised with an allied amphibious attack from the Pacific. Next would be a move northward in China, to establish bases for heavy bombing of Japan. But the American success of 'island-hopping' in the Pacific and the development of long-range bombers resulted in a new plan – to defeat Japan without Chinese bases and without major operations in China. And so plans for the early liberation of the Canton-Hong Kong area became a low priority.

However, by May 1943, Colonel Ride had finalised an audacious plan to free the POWs. BAAG optimistically reported that: 'In Shamshuipo, on the whole, the prisoners are willing and eager for a mass escape. Morale is on the upgrade for some time due to efficient communications between us and the camps. But it must now be considered to be at its peak. Morale in Argyle Street is fair, and officers are only willing to participate in a complete evacuation escape. I foresee difficulties if the scheme of escape necessitates forwarding them even a brief outline of plans. I do not consider that the POWs there are fit to criticise advantage-ously any operation plans.'[7]

Ride calculated that in Shamshuipo over 250 Canadians were then in the camp hospital and a similar number of British were too weak to play an active part in an escape, while the majority of those in Argyle Street would need assistance in travelling more than a short distance. Nevertheless Ride urged that a coup-de-main airborne raid was required within three months. It would achieve surprise, he argued; 3000 prisoners would be liberated as opposed to dying of starvation. The formidable logistic difficulties were not glossed over. 165 aircraft were required to land the attacking force of 1500 men to evacuate the POWs; the operation would take at least three hours during which Kai Tak airport on the mainland must be held.

Wars are not won by defensive measures, but the plan was suicidal. Virtually all the towers around the POW camps were manned by ruthless guards who would not hesitate to machine-gun the defenceless POWs when a liberating force approached. This attacking force would have been outnumbered, lacking artillery or armoured support, and the Japanese still had air superiority. The officers in Argyle Street would not have agreed to such a plan if they had known the details, which is presumably why they were to be deliberately kept in the dark.

Ride somewhat foolishly concluded that plans to liberate the POWs, and an even bolder one of retaking Hong Kong permanently should be made on what he considered to be tactical grounds 'and therefore in line with the Prime Minister's policy when he said at Quebec: "You may be sure that our soldiers' lives are expended in accordance with sound military plans, and not squandered for political considerations of any kind".'

General Headquarters, India, examined BAAG's proposed operation and decided that air transport was insufficient at that stage, but the plans were to be kept on ice and brought up to date occasionally as the war developed.

BAAG decided to bring out of Hong Kong anyone, POWs, Europeans, Chinese or Indians who would be useful to the allies' war effort. All the Indians had been moved to a separate POW camp at Mau Tau Chung near Kai Tak, where they were subjected to intense propaganda to join the pro-Japanese Indian National Army (INA) which sought the expulsion of the British from India. Approximately 200 of the 1530 POWs of the 2/14 Punjab and 5/7 Rajput

Battalions eventually volunteered for the INA and they were sent to Singapore.[8] Some welcomed the opportunity to work against the British while others merely went through the motions of co-operating in order to get better food. Many of those who did not join the INA were employed on guard duties and fatigues in Hong Kong, Canton, Hainan and Swatow.

Hakim Khan, 2/14 Punjab, fully supported the INA cause and did his utmost to change the allegiance of the other Indians. The Japanese gave him the rank of Major and sent him to a conference in Bangkok from 15–22 June 1942, at which the representatives of the Indian communities in all Japanese occupied territories decided to raise a national army to 'liberate' India from the British.[9] On Hakim Khan's return he beat up some of those POWs who refused to join his activities. The majority of Indians rejected the overtures and were to continue to do so until the end of the war. They showed the same courage with which they had already fought alongside the allies.

BAAG's Chinese agents got in touch with them and arranged for parties to desert and come into Free China. On passing through Chinese territory they were disarmed by the Communists who wanted the weapons which the Japanese had given them when they acted as guards. This, of course, infuriated the Central Government.

On two occasions large scale desertions of Indians near the Chinese border were arranged while a Communist attack on another frontier post was used as a diversion. However BAAG's Chinese agents had little respect for, or trust in the Indians, and they were unwilling to try and effect their escape from inside their POW camp. It was too risky to send in Indian agents from outside as there were too many potential traitors.

The Chinese agents' work was extremely dangerous. Contact was made with an Indian whom BAAG considered they could trust, and agreement was reached upon the training, size of the parties and the men to be rescued. However the numbers and quality of the Indians brought out to China were often disappointing.

BAAG was severely criticised by General Headquarters, India, because some of the rescued Indians were blatantly anti-British. 'Being unable to go into Hong Kong and handpick bodies,' explained BAAG, 'we were completely at the mercy of those making up the parties. Jealousies and feuds were so common among the Indians that any other method would have resulted in a disgruntled Indian giving plans away to the Japanese. The rescue of any Indian working for the enemy, no matter how disloyal to the British he was, meant that the Japanese had to persuade another Indian to fill his job or else use their own people.'

Indian civilians were allowed to travel to the neutral Portuguese Colony of Macao which is on the coast about fifty miles to the west of Hong Kong. There they were contacted by BAAG agents who led them into China where BAAG had to feed, house and finance them and arrange their transport to India. At one time in 1943 over a hundred Indians were at BAAG's Headquarters in Kweilin.

Presumably for intelligence purposes BAAG preferred to bring out of Hong Kong the Europeans who had not been interned owing to their country's neutrality or because they were too useful to the Japanese being employed, for example, as bankers or mechanics. However BAAG reported in 1943 that: 'Contact with Free Europeans had resulted in little advantage to anybody least of all us. Much time, money and risk of life have been wasted in contacting them.'

The Japanese kept sixty British, American and Dutch bankers in the Sun Wah hotel and forced them to liquidate their banks. They were each made to sign five hundred bank notes a day, thereby making them legal, which took them less than half an hour each day. The Japanese supervisors treated them leniently.

BAAG felt that it was of great importance that some bankers were brought to China so that the Japanese economic plans for Hong Kong could be known. One of BAAG's most successful exploits took place in October 1942, when R. J. J. Fenwick, the Chief Accountant at the Hong Kong and Shanghai Banking Corporation, and J. A. D.

Morrison were contacted by a Chinese who introduced himself as Sergeant Lo. Before the war he had been a chemist and had served in Ride's Field Ambulance with the Volunteers. He told Fenwick and Morrison that Colonel Ride had sent him to help them escape. The following evening the two bankers walked out of the hotel, which was unguarded, and travelled with Lo by tram to a beach where they were rowed past Japanese MTBs to the mainland. 'We then started on our trek to Free China,' wrote Morrison later. 'We hadn't been walking for more than fifteen minutes when suddenly and with no warning there was a rush and we found ourselves surrounded by about fifteen armed men, looking down the barrels of rifles and revolvers. Fortunately the strangers turned out to be guerrillas, led by a former cook at the Peninsula Hotel. I cannot speak too highly of them, and their kindness will always be remembered with the deepest gratitude. On reaching Waichow we got a rousing welcome from BAAG. But when we eventually reached the British Consulate at Chungking, we were questioned by the Vice-Consul on the doorstep of the Consulate although it was dark, snowing and we were bitterly cold in our khaki shorts. He explained there was nothing he could do for us as a parliamentary mission was due to arrive and they had their hands full with that. We spent a cheerless night at a hostel, but the following morning the US Air Force were very good to us and gave us a lift to India. We reached London a few weeks later.'[10]

BAAG also contacted other bankers, including Sir Vandeleur Grayburn, head of the Hong Kong and Shanghai Banking Corporation, and D. C. Edmonston, both of whom refused to escape, probably because they feared Japanese reprisals on their families and friends. Some bankers were surreptitiously smuggling money out of the banks which was used to buy food, medicines and clothing for those interned in Stanley. Both Grayburn and Edmonston were arrested and accused of being involved and both died of ill-treatment. BAAG planned to kidnap all the bankers but the plan was frustrated when in May 1943, they were all interned in Stanley, their work for the Japanese having finished.

Another incident which occurred concerned three neutral Danes, named Herschend, Jacobson and Anderson, who went for a picnic in the hills near Kowloon one Sunday afternoon. They had just finished their lunch when they were pounced on by Communist guerrillas. The Danes violently protested that they had no wish to leave Hong Kong, but the Communists decided that the Danes knew too much, and so they were 'involuntarily escorted' to China where they arrived two days later in a high state of indignation.

BAAG contacted doctors in Hong Kong and pointed out to them that it was their duty to join the allied forces. A number of Chinese doctors responded and were led to safety through the Japanese lines, eventually joining the Royal Army Medical Corps to serve in India and Burma.

As explained earlier, the Japanese had not interned Doctor Selwyn-Clarke as they knew he was doing his best for the health of the Chinese community, in his capacity as head of Hong Kong's medical department. Selwyn-Clarke brushed off approaches from BAAG because, as he later explained: 'My activities were medical and humanitarian in character, and I believed that I could best – indeed could only – serve the prisoners, the internees and the people of Hong Kong by giving the Japanese no unnecessary pretext for eliminating me. Concealment and evasion were often needed for looking after my own network, and although BAAG was instrumental in bringing in certain medical supplies, the less I knew about other people's secrets the better it would be for all of us.'[11] Selwyn-Clarke refused to acknowledge the right of BAAG to deal with his doctors who, he felt, had a duty to remain in Hong Kong where they were needed most. When one named Stott escaped, Selwyn-Clarke sent out a message via Macao that the doctor should come back to Hong Kong and dedicate himself to helping the sick as the medical work was seriously prejudiced without him. These instructions were contemptuously ignored by BAAG.

BAAG had little difficulty in making contact with the

Chinese who had fought for the allies or who had served as civilian employees in such places as the Naval Dockyard or Kai Tak airport. Most of the Chinese servicemen had not been imprisoned as they had slipped away after the surrender and returned to their homes. When the Japanese military police became organised, these Chinese were in great danger of arrest through informers. Many of them had given long and faithful service to the Crown and some were highly skilled specialists. Without wasting time in getting a ruling from GHQ India, Ride had word sent to them that it was their duty to come to BAAG where they would be well looked after.

Some hundreds responded, bringing with them their wives and families which created problems in security, morale and discipline. However most of the agents and also BAAG's Chinese staff were recruited from them. While the War Office and Admiralty disputed who should pay them, over a hundred formed a unit, later known as the Hong Kong Volunteer Company, which fought with distinction with Major-General Orde Wingate's Chindits in Burma.

BAAG's attempts to set up a counter-espionage organis-ation in Kweilin were interrupted by the enemy offensive in South China in 1944. Logistic problems were almost insurmountable. For example in Kweilin it was impossible to obtain petrol and BAAG's only truck had to be converted to charcoal fuel. This proved a failure and alcohol was used instead; it was made locally from vegetable extracts and caused irrevocable damage to the engine. Another problem was that BAAG officers in the forward areas found themselves undertaking some of the work of other British organisations including the Ministry of Information, British Red Cross, Aid to China Relief and the Special Operations Executive. Much of these extra responsibilities duplicated work which the Americans were undertaking, so the relationship between Colonel Ride and the Americans was occasionally acrimonious.

'I believe that half our trouble with the Americans here is due to the complexity of our organisations which they find difficulty in grasping. So do I,' reported Major-General

E. C. Hayes, the new Military Attaché in Chungking, to Lieutenant-General Browning, the Chief of Staff to Admiral Mountbatten.

General Wedemeyer was suspicious of some British organisations in South China and he sometimes obstructed their operations. He considered that all resources should be used to stop the occasional Japanese offensive, whereas he believed some British were more concerned with their post war colonial aspirations. Despite the lack of British soldiers, they had in China a British Lieutenant-General, a Major-General and five full Colonels, 'a number which for reasons of face, I cannot reduce, much as I would like to,' reported General Hayes.

However BAAG's work with 14 USAAF in South China was appreciated by the Americans. BAAG's forward posts supplied weather reports from the Hong Kong–Canton area twice daily which enabled the Americans to plan their flying operations, and BAAG produced long and detailed weekly intelligence reports. Even so, the Americans set up their intelligence network, based on their own diverse organisations. They included the Office of Strategic Services and Air Ground Air Service which was responsible for rescuing shot down aircrews and for gathering intelligence.

'With the penetration of BAAG area by American agents, it became increasingly difficult to maintain the morale of our people who naturally felt that their own work was either not efficient or not appreciated,' reported Colonel Ride. 'Had some Americans achieved their aim to put us out of the business altogether, there is no doubt that the major portion of our escape and evasion system inside Hong Kong would have crumbled.' Colonel Ride faced many bitter frustrations. The Americans would not allow BAAG to see aerial photographs of Hong Kong on the grounds that the Chinese had issued orders not to show them to the British. To make matters worse the Chinese, whose troops invariably failed to salute British officers, imposed wireless restrictions on the British, but not on the Americans.

In September, 1943, an American Lieutenant named Schoyer showed Colonel Ride a signal from General G. C.

Marshall, the American Chief of Staff in Washington, which stated that the War Office and War Department in Washington had agreed that for the purposes of escape and evasion: 'To USA belongs primary responsibility for China, but agree to retention of Colonel Ride's organisation under the British.' BAAG's plans to make contact with British POWs in Shanghai and Formosa collapsed; BAAG no longer had the authority to operate outside Hong Kong and Canton. With the arrival of the American Military Intelligence Section for escape and evasion, known in Europe as MIS-X and in China as Air Ground Air Service, BAAG no longer had a part to play in helping shot down American air crews. BAAG was sceptical as to what the Americans could achieve: 'They had no one on their staff who knew the country, the local conditions or the language, or who had ever had dealings with guerrillas or Chinese provincial troops,' reported Colonel Ride, 'yet they were going to undertake the safe conduct of evaders through enemy territory at a distance compared to that separating England from Turkey.' BAAG proudly claimed that they and the Communist guerrillas had already rescued one American pilot shot down over Hong Kong within a few hundreds yards of an enemy post. BAAG justified their existence by being an escape and evasion organisation, but there were now no POWs who were escaping, and no Royal Air Force crews were in South China.

Nevertheless throughout the war BAAG and Communist guerrillas helped 33 British and allied servicemen who had already escaped from Hong Kong by their own efforts. Over 400 Indians, 100 Europeans and nearly 4000 Chinese who had been servicemen or civilian employees in Hong Kong were encouraged to leave and helped on arrival in China.

BAAG's most significant contribution to victory in the Far East lay in its intelligence service which will be described later. For some of the POWs and internees, however, gathering information within the camps for this intelligence service was to prove disastrous, for the Japanese had infiltrated spies in the tenuous lines which lay from Hong Kong through China to Delhi and London.

In September 1942, the Chinese agents of the British Army Aid Group in China had established contact with five British POWs in Shamshuipo Camp by passing messages through POW working parties at Kai Tak airfield. However, the work on the airfield stopped in December, and for several weeks the link seemed to have been broken until Lee Lam, a Chinese truck driver who delivered rations to the camp, handed a message to Driver T. Farrell.

Lee Lam, aged thirty-eight, and nicknamed 'Sunny Jim', had been employed before the war in the finance department of the Hong Kong Government. He was now working for the Kowloon Omnibus Company which provided the vehicles for the delivery of rations.

Driver Farrell passed Lee's message to Captain Ford to whom it was addressed. A regular system of passing secret messages to Shamshuipo was thus established. The first incoming messages, which initially were signed '68', enquired about the health in the camp and it became apparent that many were originating from Major Clague in Waichow.

Contact with the officers' POW camp at Argyle Street started three months later. The delivery system was very risky particularly when it began. Lieutenant J. R. Harris recalls: 'In March 1943, on a brilliant sunny day, I was a member of a truck unloading party. A group of Japanese fighters had just taken off from Kai Tak airport when the supply lorry arrived. It contained a load of wood for the cookhouse, and as it was being unloaded I strolled to the front where the Chinese driver sat in his cab. Standing by him was a Japanese guard, and eight others were twenty feet away. Just as the last log was removed the driver gave a warning cough and threw out an old cigarette packet. I picked it up with the sweepings of bark off the floor of the truck.

'My heart was thumping as I carried the packet into the latrines, but it had nothing in it, and I did not then know of BAAG. I took the packet with some disappointment to Colonel L. A. Newnham, aged fifty-four and a former Commanding Officer of the Middlesex Battalion, and one of General Maltby's principal Staff Officers. He fetched a piece of charcoal from the cookhouse and held the paper up to the heat. Immediately a message became visible; our excitement was intense. I was struck by the extreme bravery of the Chinese driver for he had no idea who I was and his trust had to be absolute.'[1] Lieutenant Harris was given a reply by Colonel Newnham which was hidden in a cigarette packet and left in the truck when the same driver was next on duty.

The other POWs did not understand why the same two officers, Lieutenant Harris and Captain G. V. Bird, both in the Royal Engineers and responsible for the messages, appeared on each occasion that the supply lorries had to be unloaded. Colonel Newnham therefore decided that each POW hut should have an officer to pass the messages, and so nine more officers were told about BAAG.

Gradually the concealment of messages became more sophisticated. A note was sent to the outside contacts telling them to fix three nails in a precise position in a dark corner under the floor of the truck, between which messages could be held by rubber bands.

Lieutenant R. B. Goodwin, RNZNVR, who thought up this system, made a small wooden model on which the officers practised despatching and receiving messages until everyone was confident. The rubber bands held a tightly rolled message firmly, and it took only seconds to remove it from between the nails.

Now that Newnham had a reliable system of communication with BAAG which could be used almost daily, he wondered how he could obtain important intelligence on Japanese shipping, gun positions and unit strengths. He hit on a remarkably successful and simple method. Captain J. L. Flynn, of the 2/14 Punjab Regiment, of course spoke Hindustani, and occasionally worked in the Argyle Street vegetable garden alongside the Indian Mau Tau Chung

POW Camp. The Indians established their own intelligence system through their friends who were employed by the Japanese on guard duties throughout Hong Kong and neighbouring towns which were under Japanese control. Several Indians close to the wire would speak loudly to each other, enabling Flynn to hear what they wished to convey. The Formosan and Japanese guards nearby, some of whom spoke a little English, never discovered what was happening.

Indians who were ostensibly pro-Japanese were made to guard the officers' Argyle Street camp. Some would descend from their watch-tower and patrol outside their perimeter wire within the Argyle Street garden. Altogether they left about twenty-five messages in cigarette packets for Flynn. Some were of about 200 words, and a typical message dealt with Japanese strengths and locations, results of American bombing raids and details on crews shot down, Japanese morale, shipping, aircraft at Kai Tak, Indian National Army activity, and traitors and informants.

Captain Flynn passed these messages on to Colonel Newnham in a lavatory, or during camp work such as when sawing wood. Newnham re-wrote the reports and arranged for them to be hidden on Lee Hung Hoi's truck. Often this information was of considerable value to BAAG, the United States Air Force in China and General Headquarters, India. Colonel Newnham very wisely confided the whole scheme only to General Maltby.

The truck was also used to smuggle in medicines, and each incoming truck had to be searched for messages. A small green towel on the perimeter wire among the washing outside the guards' latrine indicated to Lee Hung Hoi when there was an outgoing message for him to collect. It was arranged that a red towel was to announce that all messages were to stop immediately. Thus, by March 1943, BAAG had established a flourishing intelligence service in Hong Kong, and General Maltby's despatches had been passed by BAAG to Chungking.

In June 1942, Ts'o Tsun On, a former superintendent in the Hong Kong Police Reserve, had started to recruit

Chinese to work for the organisation. He persuaded Yeung Sau Tak, employed by the Japanese Navy in the dockyard, to steal secret documents from the planning room and copy them in invisible ink. In March 1943, Yeung began operating a short-wave transmitter from his room at 39, Lockhart Road, to report on the movement of Japanese warships.

Chan Ping Fun, a construction engineer at Kai Tak airport, obtained intelligence on Japanese aircraft and installations, while Cheung Yuet and Loie Fook Wing reported on the importation of foodstuffs and military supplies into Hong Kong.

Cheung Yung Sam, a mechanic in the shipbuilding yard, discovered which ships were undergoing repairs, and Lau Tak Kwang, a fireman, described progress being made on restoring various industries.

Europeans in Hong Kong, who had not been interned since they were believed to be doing essential work for the Japanese, were also recruited to gather information. Loie Fook Wing persuaded W. J. White to set up a wireless post in his home at 97 Wanchai Road. White was a chauffeur and mechanic in the Public Health Section of the Japanese Governor-General's Department. He received instructions from BAAG by wireless and passed them on to Loie. A. C. Shinton also worked for the Health Section, and he arranged for Leung Hung, who drove the ration truck to Stanley Internment Camp, to smuggle twenty secret messages to the internees at Stanley. The internees already had two wireless sets hidden in the camp and were regularly listening to news programmes. Two bankers, L. C. R. Souza and C. F. Hyde, who were helping to liquidate the banks' assets, were listening to a wireless set in Hong Kong and were also in touch with the underground.[2]

The mass of intelligence which was gathered was summarised in written reports which were carried by Lau Tak Oi and Ho Yau to Waichow, the messengers returning with funds to pay the agents.

Initially all the information was embodied into a weekly Waichow Intelligence Summary which went to the Military

Attaché at Chungking and the Director of Military Intelligence, India. This was an inefficient arrangement as the reports took three weeks to reach Delhi and permission had not been given by the Chinese Central Government for the use of wireless or cyphers. Urgent intelligence was sent from Waichow via the Chinese telegraph service, in a simple code which was most unsatisfactory, but even then it took up to seven days to reach India. However, by 1943 the Chinese allowed BAAG to use wireless and reports arrived within four days. Operational intelligence was passed to the United States Air Force's 68th Composite Wing Headquarters at Kweilin, and the Americans came to depend on BAAG's agents since they did not at this stage have sources of their own.

By March 1943, the agents in Hong Kong amounted to over thirty. They covered every significant branch of intelligence and their reports included the enemy's army, naval, air and economic activities with details also on Japanese security, censorship and deception. They managed to smuggle to India copies of special enemy publications, and a complete set of Japanese printing type and official Japanese note-paper which were useful for forging documents.

Meanwhile the intelligence organisation within Argyle Street was working well. 'But, as Colonel Newnham and I realised,' wrote Commander Craven later, 'it would only be a matter of time before the Japanese Military Police got wind of it. I am afraid we did not give as much consideration as we should have done to their obvious reactions. Warning of approaching trouble reached us in mid-June, when we had an SOS from Lee Hung Hoi telling us that Lee Lam had been arrested. Naturally we closed down the business at once.' But it was too late.

On 1 July the lorry drove into the camp as usual, but Lee Hung Hoi, now acting under Japanese orders, suddenly tossed a piece of paper towards Lieutenant J. R. Haddock, HKRNVR, who, by chance, happened to be nearby. Haddock picked up the paper when he felt it was safe to do so, and hid it on top of a lavatory cistern and then strolled to his hut. Ten minutes later he was sent for by the guards and arrested. Captain Bird retrieved the piece of paper from the cistern and applied iodine all over it, but without success; it was blank.

'This made me suspicious that it was a plant,' he wrote later, 'but I could not connect the plant with Haddock's arrest because I was told that no Japanese had seen him pick it up, yet it was not found on him. I put the piece of paper back on the cistern, and on checking later it had mysteriously been removed.'

On the same day that Haddock had been arrested at Argyle Street, the Japanese struck in Shamshuipo. A guard, Matsuda, removed Flight-Lieutenant H. B. Gray from the camp, but this aroused no suspicion as Gray had been taken before to buy sports equipment. However a few minutes later the ration lorry drove into the camp and the Chinese driver picked out his two contacts: Sergeant R. J. Ruttledge, Royal Canadian Corps of Signals, who was arrested, as was Sergeant R. J. Hardy shortly afterwards. The Japanese had therefore identified the truck drivers' contacts at Shamshuipo and one of the eleven contacts at Argyle Street, but the two key POW organisers, Colonel Newnham and Captain Ford in their respective camps had not yet been betrayed.

The few POWs in Shamshuipo who knew about BAAG already had their suspicions that the network had been penetrated two months earlier when an urgent message had been received from Lee Hung Hoi. It had asked Captain Ford to show himself at a particular time in a corner of the camp which was overlooked by the road beyond. He did not do so, as this was considered unwise. The Japanese, it was felt later, were probably watching the spot through binoculars in order to identify the contact. The last few messages sent to BAAG could not have been more incriminating if intercepted by the Japanese; they had dealt with the possibility of a guerrilla raid on the perimeter fence to free POWs, although fortunately messages via BAAG to the Canadian representative at Chungking had been passed successfully. The Shamshuipo POWs, unlike those in Argyle

Street, had refused to report on Japanese shipping as they thought this too dangerous.

For ten worrying days the POWs in the know waited for the mass arrests which they felt to be inevitable. On 10 July Colonel Newnham and Captain Ford were arrested at Argyle Street and Shamshuipo respectively.

'I saw the Colonel being taken away,' remembers Captain Bird, 'and I went to the underground hiding place outside his window in which a precis of all messages was kept. General Maltby decided to burn them together with the maps. I kept only six front collar studs, which concealed compasses sent to me by BAAG.'[3]

Thus by mid-July 1943, BAAG's organisation in Hong Kong had collapsed. The Japanese had infiltrated their spies into the agents' organisation both in China and in Hong Kong.

Lee Lam, who was the first to be arrested, was tortured and eventually named three other Chinese who in turn identified their principal POW contacts. Gradually the trail led to the discovery of each wireless set in turn, and every Chinese agent named in this chapter was arrested and brutally interrogated for several months.

The Japanese started to use *agents provocateurs*, one of whom persuaded a very brave Indian to plan a mass escape. He was Captain M. A. Ansari, 5/7 Rajputs, who was the only Indian officer left with the Indian POWs in Mau Tau Chung camp. He was in touch with BAAG and was the mainstay of the resistance among the Indians only to be betrayed by another Indian when sufficient compromising evidence had been gathered.

The Japanese decided to eliminate him for he had been arrested several times before, and despite inhuman and humiliating treatment they had failed to break his spirit.

The resistance groups among the bankers in Victoria and within the Internment Camp at Stanley collapsed, too, due to an unfortunate series of events. Doctor Talbot, a British internee at Stanley, had become seriously ill and was taken to St. Paul's hospital in Victoria for several days. Just before he returned to Stanley, he was given a number of messages for the internees and 4000 yen by the Hong Kong and Shanghai Bank. Doctor Selwyn-Clarke insisted that the messages be destroyed, but Talbot kept the money for the internees. On arrival at the Wong Nei Chong Gap police post, the truck was stopped for a routine search. Talbot objected and was rude to the Japanese who responded by a very detailed search. They found the money beneath the Doctor's bandages and he was promptly arrested. Sir Vandeleur Grayburn, the most influential of the bankers, bravely went to the Japanese Chief of the Foreign Affairs Department and told him that he had asked Doctor Talbot to take the money to Stanley as it was partly for the nursing staff of the camp's hospital. The Japanese responded favourably and released Talbot, but they were simply biding their time, and Sir Vandeleur's arrest followed two weeks later.

Security among the internees was poor. Some were indiscreet and knowledge of the radio sets was too widespread. One day the Japanese came into Stanley Camp and went straight to one room to search for a radio which was not found. Later a radio engineer was arrested and he was forced to dig in a bank where one set was found. The other was voluntarily surrendered, but too late to avoid the mass arrests of those who had been in touch with BAAG.

The Japanese were indifferent as to individual charges and trials, and everyone was accused of spying, or of inciting or assisting espionage. The penalty laid down for espionage was death, and nobody had illusions as to the extreme gravity of his position.

Nevertheless, most of the messages passed from Stanley Internment Camp had concerned trivial matters, such as the health of the prisoners. None of their wireless sets could transmit, and they were able to receive only normal broadcasts from the world's capitals. The Stanley internees in particular had committed no form of espionage, although some had been in touch with BAAG.

On 19 October 1943, twenty-seven British internees, Chinese and Captain M. A. Ansari, were tried by five Japanese officers presided over by Lieutenant-Colonel

Fujimoto, who was a tired, wizened old man. Lieutenant Yamagouchi, the Superintendent of Stanley Prison, asked each prisoner in the first group a few simple questions as to what they knew or had done. When an accused answered with a denial, Yamagouchi uttered, with a sneer, his stock phrase: 'We know the Military Police know better.'

The Japanese regarded J. A. Fraser, the former Hong Kong Government Defence Secretary, as the ringleader. He was questioned about the wireless news received in Stanley Internment Camp, and about the receipt of secret notes from 'spies' in Waichow. Yamagouchi tried to implicate Mr Gimson, the Colonial Secretary, against whom the Japanese could find no evidence and had not arrested, although Gimson was well aware of everyone's activities. Fraser replied, boldly and clearly, his voice ringing resonantly through the courtroom, that he alone was responsible, that he had acted solely on his own judgement, and that he had the right to act as he thought fit in the best interests of British nationals interned in Stanley.

After each of the accused had been briefly questioned, the prosecutor, Major Kogi, made a speech which lasted the greater part of the morning. The Chinese interpreter translated infrequently and so badly that the prisoners were scarcely aware of what was being said. Occasionally Kogi would pause, a silence and whispering followed, and then the interpreter would make an attempt to translate, but he failed miserably.

The President, Lieutenant-Colonel Fujimoto, at one stage put his arms on the table, rested his head on his arms and for half an hour seemed to be asleep. On awakening he went to the lavatory to smoke a cigarette, while the prosecutor continued. The interpreter briefly translated that the prisoners were preventing Japan's progress in bringing about a New Order in East Asia. At 2 p.m. Kogi mopped his brow, bowed and sat down amidst much applause from the Japanese. The interpreter asked a question in Japanese and there was a confusing discussion before he finally translated: 'In the eyes of the law, you are all guilty of High Treason, and the prosecution has demanded the death penalty.'

Lieutenant-Colonel Fujimoto then fumbled with the pages of a book on the table in front of him. Yamagouchi came to his rescue and found the appropriate pages. Fujimoto then called out each prisoner's name before being helped to find the place once more. Finally he announced that, 'All are sentenced to death. The Court is adjourned.'

Throughout the trial, which had lasted for almost four hours, the accused had been forced to stand rigidly to attention, and Katanawa had patrolled behind them beating anyone who had protested his innocence too volubly.

Finally the prisoners were removed and given their first meal of the day. 'I need hardly say that it was a very sad party that sat down to the food,' wrote W. J. Anderson, one of the condemned. 'Few touched their small bowl of rice. Some broke down due, no doubt, to the long strain of the morning. We had good warders and there was no restriction on talking. Fraser was quite unperturbed and chatted as we ate. Some prisoners felt that they still had some hope, for the President had ended by adjourning the trial which suggested that something was yet to follow.

For the following five hours the prisoners waited while a second group of eight was tried. When the Japanese adjourned for tea, the prisoners from both groups were able to meet in the lavatory, and learn that all but three of the second group had been condemned to death.

At 6 p.m. both parties assembled in Court. Fujimoto made a long speech with spasmodic pauses, as if labouring hard to find words. When he finished there was no interpretation, and no prisoner had understood what had been said. He then read, from the book in front of him, two lots of names and numbers, and announced the sentences. After at least two attempts by the interpreter, the prisoners were told that the first group to be named had been sentenced to death, and the names called last had received fifteen years' imprisonment. Another interpreter then asked each prisoner what his sentence was, 'while laughing and making a sign with his thumb, drawing it across his throat,' noted Anderson. 'I replied "fifteen years". While this wretched business of sorting out the condemned and reprieved continued, Katanawa beat Mrs Yung who was screaming and clinging to her husband who had been sentenced to death. I helped to carry her back to her cell. She had been reprieved.' Fraser was among the condemned. The Japanese permitted the victims to send a last message in writing; however this was a final trap to get more information, and none were delivered.

On 29 October, after ten days in solitary confinement, thirty-two men and one woman were led out to be executed. A group of children from the internment camp who were passing the prison saw a van drive out. As it went by English voices shouted out, 'Goodbye boys.'

'I was in the prison garden when I saw the prisoners leave on their last earthly journey,' wrote Anderson later. 'I was told that some had asked to be granted the services of a minister, but that this was refused. They were allowed to mix and talk to each other for five minutes before being tied up preparatory to their death march. Captain Ansari, I was told, gave them a "pep talk" which greatly cheered them. Warders who were present at the execution said that it was a cruel and bloody affair. All were decapitated, though the executions in their near final stage, were said to be so bad that some lives were ended by shooting.'[4] The dead were heaped together in a common grave making later identification impossible. After the war Colonel Fujimoto, the President of the Court, vanished into obscurity, and therefore escaped the fate which he so justly deserved.

On 1 December, six servicemen were taken to the Supreme Court in Hong Kong after four months of rigorous solitary confinement on starvation rations during which, with immense courage, they had refused to betray anyone. They were:

Colonel L. A. Newnham, MC, The Middlesex Regiment
Captain D. Ford, Royal Scots

Flight-Lieutenant H. B. Gray, AFM, Royal Air Force
Lieutenant J. R. Haddock, Hong Kong Royal Navy
   Volunteer Reserve
Sergeant R. J. Hardy, Royal Air Force
Sergeant F. J. Ruttledge, Royal Canadian Corps of
   Signals.

The Japanese had concentrated on breaking Captain Ford's will as they knew he was the first officer to take charge of BAAG's operations within Shamshuipo. Major C. R. Boxer, in a cell nearby, reported later that 'Ford gave nothing and nobody away, although subjected to severe physical torture to reveal the names and particulars of those involved. Ford took all the responsibility on himself, and maintained that no senior officers were involved, thereby saving General Maltby and Colonel Price of the Royal Rifles of Canada. Ford gave an outstanding example of cheerful and courageous fortitude which was an inspiration to all those who were imprisoned with him and which aroused the respect and admiration even of the Japanese.'[5]

The trial was presided over by Major-General Ashidate, and evidence was given that Ford, Gray, Ruttledge and Hardy had received over a period of three months, six messages from BAAG, after which they had compiled several reports on conditions in Shamshuipo. The Court was also told that Newnham and Haddock had received and sent out fifteen messages from Argyle Street.

The prosecutor did not attempt to prove that the information passed was of any military significance; he felt that it was sufficient simply to satisfy the Court that the POWs had been in touch with BAAG.

The Japanese were unaware that the POWs' activities were much greater than the evidence suggested. Colonel Newnham, in Argyle Street, had gathered important military intelligence through his links with the Indians, and so charges of spying were not unjustified. From Shamshuipo most of the POWs' messages had dealt with conditions in the camp and plans for the mass escape. Such information was most useful to the allies.

In the evening, after the trial was completed, Commander Craven saw the accused return 'We were mortified to see Newnham, Gray and Ford put in the condemned cell,' he wrote later. 'The remaining three were fortunate to receive fifteen years' imprisonment. Newnham and Gray were very sick, but behaved most gallantly during their seventeen days under sentence of death. Ford was fit, and his good spirits were an example we shall never forget.'

On the morning set for their execution, the condemned men were in one cell. Lieutenant H. C. Dixon, a young New Zealander in the RNZNVR, crept up the prison corridor while ostensibly washing the passage floor. When he was near their cell, Dixon asked if there were any messages he could take. Newnham requested that his love should be sent to his family, and Gray asked that his remains and his silver watch should be sent home. A warder then hustled Dixon away; Ford later said that he hoped his remains could be reburied one day in Edinburgh.

On 18 December the three officers were removed from their cells. Neither Newnham nor Gray could walk unaided, and Ford half carried them to a waiting truck. They were shot on the beach at Shek-o.

In 1946, King George VI approved the posthumous award of the George Cross to Colonel L. A. Newnham, MC, Captain D. Ford, Captain M. A. Ansari, and Flight-Lieutenant H. B. Gray, AFM, in recognition of most conspicuous gallantry while they were prisoners of war. The George Cross is the highest recognition for courage which can be awarded in such circumstances. The awards are a fitting tribute to the tenacity of these men who, well knowing the likelihood and fearful consequences of detection, nevertheless passed information to BAAG in China and subsequently refused under torture to betray their comrades.

Had the four officers survived, they would probably have said that the bravery of nearly all prisoners of war and internees in the Far East deserves full recognition. This, indeed, is the case.

Prior to the mass arrests and executions, Lieutenant Dixon in Argyle Street had found pieces of a wireless set in a bombed house while on a working detail. He was a radio technician, and when some valves were stolen from a Japanese set, in July 1943, the POWs were able to listen to broadcasts about four days a week from London, San Francisco, New Delhi, Sydney and Chungking. They also picked up a considerable amount of operational transmissions from American China-based aircraft, thereby becoming acquainted with their wave-lengths and methods of operation.

Lieutenant-Commander R. S. Young, RN, took over responsibility for the operation of the wireless set because before the war he had been in charge of communications. It was hidden in an old biscuit tin and buried when not in use. As Major Boxer was a Japanese interpreter he wrote out the news bulletins in such a manner that the guards believed the information was coming from Japanese newspapers which were allowed in the camps. Although the war news was not good, 'the tonic effect of genuine news to men living in our degrading existence on the borderline of starvation cannot be overstressed,' one POW remembers.

The wireless set was, potentially, of the utmost importance for Dixon had constructed it so that it could, at very short notice, be used as a transmitter to report to BAAG and the United States Air Force the movement of Japanese shipping, aircraft and troops – a situation which was almost unique. Very few in the camp knew of the set's existence and only three officers knew of its transmitting possibilities – Craven, Young and Dixon. 'I could never feel happy about the set,' wrote Commander Craven later, 'and I only hoped that we should not be betrayed and that the Japanese would not discover the set through their vigilance.'[1]

The arrests described earlier of Colonel Newnham, Captain Ford and the others who were involved in passing messages to BAAG increased the danger. General Maltby had protested most strongly at those arrests, but the Japanese had refused to tell him anything. Instead, General Maltby, Brigadier Wallis and thirteen other senior British officers were put in a special inner perimeter within Argyle Street, and on 4 August they were sent with seven batmen to Formosa.

Commander Craven, now the senior Naval officer in the camp, concluded that General Maltby and his principal officers had been moved because the Japanese knew they were involved in smuggling information, but there was no incriminating evidence 'and so with their complex Japanese mentality, they decided to remove them from their sphere of investigation. Despite the arrests, I did not think anything would be gained by suspending work on the wireless set, as the effect of reliable news within the camp would be as good as any quantity of medicines.

'The blow fell on 21 September 1943, when the wireless had been operating for a little under two months. During morning parade the camp was invaded by the Japanese Military Police, and while we were all kept on the parade ground the principal searching party went without hesitation to the spot where the set was hidden, and I was much embarrassed by seeing it brought out immediately; the false top of the box looked very stupid and inadequate.' The Japanese drove triumphantly out of the camp, having gone through the huts like a typhoon.

Commander Craven felt that they would be arrested immediately and that: 'it was really impossible to tell any watertight story. My instructions, therefore, to those involved were not to mention more names than possible. At 7 p.m. Young was arrested, which confirmed in my mind that we had been given away. I was arrested at 10 p.m. and Dixon half-an-hour later.' Craven faced the same Japanese interrogation techniques which were used on the other suspects, except that he was not tortured.

'My interrogation started immediately. I was told that I

prisoners had to squat all the time on their bedboard facing the wall, one hand on each knee and eyes directed immediately to their front. A spy-hole in the door enabled the Indian warders to watch the prisoners without themselves being seen.

The prison population was found to consist in the main of Chinese malefactors, but also some British POW Other Ranks, British civilians, and Portuguese and other nationalities who had offended against the Occupying Power. They were all dressed in khaki prison clothes with the broad arrow. They worked in the prison garden on a starvation diet of two meals a day, each of six ounces of rice, under the supervision of Japanese convicts. Most of the prisoners could hardly survive except by stealing vegetables from the garden. Severe punishment followed for those caught. Culprits were beaten before being hung by their hands which were tied behind their backs, and a large manure drum was suspended from their necks by a chain. However, as all the prisoners were ravenously hungry, punishment deterred nobody.

Two months later Craven, Young and Dixon were taken with other criminals for trial and sentence. The order of trial was Japanese, Indian, Chinese and finally the British. 'We waited eight hours before we were marched in to the Court Room,' wrote Commander Craven. 'The Prosecutor, Major Kogi, had a first-class reputation as a blood-thirsty criminal. Our statements were read and the wireless was produced for identification; we were then marched out. After waiting an hour and a half, we were recalled and the sentence was announced. "Prisoners are condemned," announced the interpreter, after which there was a deliberate pause, "to five years imprisonment".'

On Christmas Eve, dressed in white prison clothes and given cells in the old condemned cell block which also housed Japanese convicts, they were put to work in the prison garden.

The Japanese authorities apparently decided that in principle POWs should not be allowed to die, although by February 1944 they were all seriously ill from a near starvation regime. When deaths seemed likely the Japanese gave them six months' back pay with which they were allowed to buy a bottle of codliver oil from the former British prison stocks. Officers were also given a Japanese vitamin pill and they started to receive the same rations as the Japanese convicts.

They were later moved to Canton to join other convicted POWs from Hong Kong. Conditions were harsh, but all survived because of their courage and optimism that the allies would triumph ultimately.

Meanwhile the POWs still in Shamshuipo and Argyle Street had become very wary of any contact with outsiders in view of the arrest and possible torture of so many of their number. In November 1943, Major R. A. Atkinson, Hong Kong and Singapore Royal Artillery, was placed in a dilemma when an Indian sentry in a watch-tower said that he had a very important letter for the British which required an immediate answer. The Indian, whom Major Atkinson did not know, told him to come as close to the wire as possible where he would drop the message. Major Atkinson knew that the guard's beat was in full view of the Japanese officers and, if they were watching through binoculars, he would suffer the same fate as Haddock who had received fifteen years' imprisonment for picking up a message.

The guard climbed rapidly down from the watch tower and dropped a small folded paper as he marched smartly past Major Atkinson. 'In case this was a "plant", I did not stop to pick it up until I next drew buckets of water from the garden well,' he recalls. 'The sentry, who had returned to his tower, was very agitated until he saw me pick it up. This gave me some hope that it was genuine, but to be safe I buried it immediately a few paces away and did not collect it until the following day.'[2]

Atkinson took the note to Captain Bird, who had been responsible, with Colonel Newnham, for handling the earlier messages. Bird had served as one of the Colonel's staff officers in the fighting and had been badly wounded. He read the note and was startled to see that it was misspelt and was signed '68'; the writing was quite different from all previous messages from 68. Bird suspected a trap and ordered that no reply should be sent. This decision saved the life of both him and his friends. The original 68 had been arrested and the Japanese were now re-establishing links under their control in order to compromise others.

In December Lieutenant T. S. Simpson, Royal Engineers, and Major J. Smith of the Volunteers saw a message thrown in their direction by a Chinese. This note was also signed 68 and it expressed the wish that communications be re-opened. The message was passed to Captain Bird who consulted Lieutenant Colonel F. D. Field, DSO, MC, Royal Artillery, the senior officer now in Argyle Street. The message appeared to be genuine and they agreed to renew the contact, but not to send any written messages as there was no proof that BAAG was sending them.

Communications were maintained with the Chinese contact by Bird and Simpson walking to the wire talking to each other in a loud voice so that the Chinese contact, strolling beyond the wire on the road, could hear the camp news.

Five months later another note was dropped over the fence. It was in bad English, in unknown handwriting and was signed '54'. By now the officers were very suspicious and agreed to break off visual contact, and to pick up no more messages.

In early May 1944, the Japanese closed Argyle Street camp and moved the POWs to Shamshuipo. The following month Bird, Field and Simpson were arrested and removed to the Military Police Headquarters. Field was interrogated first and told the Japanese that the notes contained enquiries about the health of the POWs, and said that they had been signed 68 and 37. This last number was a deliberate lie to mislead the enemy. After each officer had been interrogated they were put in the same cell where they were relieved to discover that they had each told the same approximate story. Two Chinese, who were also in the cell, were suspected of being Japanese spies. Major Smith was also there, having been arrested the previous day. He had not been involved in any of the activities, apart from seeing the first note being delivered, and he sat in the corner with his head on his knees and refused to talk to anyone.

The Japanese believed that Captain Bird was the ringleader, and the big, tall interrogator, named Fujihara, singled him out for special treatment. Captain Bird was, indeed, the last remaining POW who knew the names of the officers in BAAG. He refused to tell Fujihara anything, whereupon Bird was told that he would be tortured until he talked.

He was taken downstairs to a back room where he saw in a corner a large concrete washing tub with a tap over it. The bath had been used in peacetime by amahs for washing clothes. Also in the room, apart from the guards, was the interpreter, Jerome Lan, a half-caste British subject who had taught typewriting before the war.

Fujihara told Captain Bird to take off his shirt and get into a coffin-shaped box. His feet and arms were tightly bound so that he could move only his head. 'I was then lifted in the coffin on to the washing tub and my head was placed under the tap,' he wrote later. 'A dirty cloth was put over my face, and the tap was slowly turned on to drip, drip, drip on to the cloth. I had no idea what was going to happen and I was very frightened.[3]

'Soon the cloth became saturated with water and my breathing became very difficult; I was gulping down vast quantities of water through my nose and mouth with every breath I tried to take. I got less and less air, and more and more water in my lungs. I stood it as long as I could, before telling Fujihara the numbers, 68 and 37, which Colonel Field had already given them. This satisfied him, but he then asked me for the names of the British officers at Waichow. I knew that if I refused to speak there was no one else who could tell him, and so I replied that I knew nothing about any of them.

'Back went the cloth over my face, on went the tap, and I was pushed under once more. Slowly my lungs filled with water and I was gasping, struggling and fighting for breath until I thought the end had come. I began to say a prayer which we Roman Catholics are taught to say on dying. It begins "Jesus, Mary, Joseph . . .". I had just managed to mutter "Jesus, Mary", when the cloth was whipped off and the tap stopped. Fujihara thought I was giving the names of the officers. Lan, the interpreter, was a Catholic too, and told Fujihara that I was merely praying. This made him very angry and I was pushed under the tap for the third time. I thought that it was all finished, but I automatically struggled and fought for breath. I just remember breaking the rope which bound my feet before passing out. Lan later told me that I was unconscious for forty minutes.

'I next remember being slapped hard on the face to revive me, and I was made to stand up, but my knees gave way and I collapsed on the stone floor. As I fell, Fujihara jumped forward and gently stopped my head crashing against the door. In the face of all that had happened, this seemed an odd thing for him to do, and it dawned on me that they were trying to avoid leaving any evidence of any maltreatment; I realised that they did not intend to kill me, and I immediately felt hopeful.'

Captain Bird was taken to the upstairs waiting-room from which Colonel Field and Captain Simpson had been listening to him being tortured below. Five hours later Fujihara came in and told them to stand up and remain standing to attention until he came back. He told the Indian guard who sat on a chair a few feet away to ensure that the order was obeyed. 'After about half an hour, the Indian guard winked at us and we sat down on a bench,' recalls Captain Bird. 'The Indian and Chinese guards were changed every hour, but they all allowed us to sit, and tipped us off when anyone approached. This little game lasted until 3 a.m. when Fujihara returned. He was very surprised to find me still on my feet after my session with him, and he hit each of us in the face and then, realising what had happened, hit the Indian guard, too.'

The interrogation was resumed the following morning. The Japanese knew that Captain Bird had been editing the news bulletins, and accused him of publishing allied news smuggled in from China. He replied that, if he was allowed back to the POW camp, he could show them an old news bulletin, which he had left tucked into a book, to prove that it was only a translation from a Japanese newspaper.

'They agreed to do this, and we drove into camp. All the POWs were paraded as I went to my bed space. The news bulletin had gone. Someone had wisely gone through my papers and removed everything they considered incriminating. Although news bulletins from Japanese papers were permitted, my friends had not risked leaving them. This made my story look pretty thin, and my hastily thought up excuse that there was a dreadful shortage of lavatory paper was not believed. They took all my papers away and I was locked in the cell for three days.

'On 14 June, Lan, the interpreter, warned me that the Japanese had found among my papers two copies of the International Morse Code which had made them deeply suspicious. The following day the interrogation was resumed. Lan now appeared to be discreetly helping me, and I felt that, when interpreting, he was putting my answers in the most favourable manner possible. I was later put in a cell with twenty Chinese. I had not eaten for sixteen hours, but the Chinese gave me little bits of fish which they had managed to smuggle in. The guards also slipped in little scraps at great risk to themselves; they were very kind and sympathetic when they dared.

'The interrogation on the next day took a different form. Fujihara accused me of listening to a radio in camp which I denied. As my answers did not satisfy him, he lit some Chinese firecrackers and threw them at me, trying to get them inside my shirt, but he missed and they exploded noisily on the floor. He then wound several layers of rag round my wrists and bound them with rubber-coated electric light flex, and I was made to stand on a stool in an open doorway. Fujihara jerked my arms up behind me and tied them to the fanlight over the door, so that only my toes were touching the stool. I noted the care he was taking to prevent leaving any marks on my wrists, and I saw a basin of water in the corner, so I knew that he had every intention of reviving me should I pass out under the forthcoming torture. This knowledge cheered me considerably.

'Fujihara drew up an armchair, and he and Lan made themselves comfortable. He continued questioning me, but I told him nothing; he then left the room. Lan started writing with his finger on the wall, but I could not make out what he was trying to say, so he whispered "This is a very painful torture; tell him about the Morse Code and he might stop." When Fujihara returned, I told him about it, explaining that it was an international code and that I was a keen yachtsman. It was not a convincing story and I was not surprised that he did not believe me. I now decided that it was useless to fight against being suspended in this fiendish position and the sooner I passed out, the sooner I would be relatively comfortable. And so I relaxed my taut body, taking my full weight on my arms. I hung like this for another half an hour and I was nearly unconscious when he started questioning me again as to where the radio was hidden. Since there was none, I could not answer him, and so he violently pulled the stool away, leaving me swinging by my arms, hitting my head against the side of the door before becoming unconscious.'

Captain Bird was imprisoned for a further six days and subjected to further interrogation, but the worst was over, and on 26 June Colonel Field, Captains Simpson and Bird were told that the investigation was finished, and they were returned to the POW camp, to the surprise of their friends who never expected to see them again. Lan told them that had they admitted any of the charges, they would have been shot. The three officers were freed from prison because they had never replied in writing to any of the Chinese messages. Most, if not all the contacts had been under Japanese control. Fortunately, Fujihara had not connected them with Colonel Newnham's activities. Ironically, Major Smith, who was innocent of all involvement, was convicted and imprisoned.

Captain Bird's courage in telling the Japanese nothing was recognised by the award of the George Medal.

Lieutenant-General Rensuke Isogai, a former Chief of Staff of the Japanese Kwantung Army, arrived in Hong Kong two months after the Colony's surrender, to become the Governor. He was greeted by many of the same Chinese élite who had welcomed Sir Mark Young five months before.

In his first address Isogai warned his audience that he would show no mercy 'to those who transgress the path of right'. Those Chinese who supported Japan's puppet leader in China, Wong Chang Wai, were surprised to learn that 'Hong Kong belongs to Japan' but, Isogai added, he would consider giving the Chinese some administrative responsibilities.

The following day he inspected Government House, which had been badly damaged before the war when air raid tunnels had been dug in the rock beneath its foundations. To his disgust he discovered that gaping cracks had appeared in the walls and balconies and the building had been shored up with masses of great timbers.

A British internee was removed from Stanley and questioned on the foundations. 'Your Governor,' he was told, 'must be a very brave man to have lived in a building in that condition.'

Government House was gradually rebuilt as a tiered and turreted east-west hybrid vaguely reminiscent of Japanese palaces and the Imperial Hotel in Tokyo. Its completion coincided with the Japanese surrender. During the rebuilding everything of value was looted. Sinn Chi Lam, a Chinese sub-contractor, remembers seeing a few broken safes and sofas. 'On the walls,' he recalls, 'there were three large oil paintings of royal personages which had been slashed across, and one which was intact. I persuaded a Japanese guard to let me have the one good painting on the plea that I wanted it as a mattress cover. I also recovered all prints from the rubbish and broken glass which littered the floor.'[1]

Before the Japanese attacked the Colony, a few of the best pieces of a priceless art collection were buried in a chest in the grounds of Government House, possibly in a chamber dug in the floor or wall of a disused air-raid ventilation shaft beneath the foundations. The collection formed the best part of the Chater bequest to the Hong Kong Government, and twenty-five pictures by George Chinnery, the well-known Scottish artist and one of the most distinguished to visit the Far East.

Sir Mark Young had directed that only three people should know of the collection's location – A. von Kobza-Nagy, a Hungarian picture-restorer, T. Harmon of the Public Works Department, and the ADC, Captain Batty-Smith. One by one the three died, each believing the secret to be safe with the other two.[2] The last survivor, von Kobza, on his deathbed, told his trusted assistant, Fung Ming, that he could only reveal the hiding place to the British Government. The secret died with him, and spasmodic searches for the treasure have been unsuccessful; the last one in 1979 was carried out by a team from London.

General Isogai had an undeserved reputation for good living and geisha parties, whereas he preferred to be studying calligraphy at his home in the abandoned house of a European which overlooked Repulse Bay. Isogai enjoyed walking in its garden in his slippers, to listen to the croaking of the bull frogs. When he did leave Government House, all streets and roadways were cordoned off and for three or four hours all movement, including Japanese transport, had to stop. However few had much respect for him; it was the Military Police which wielded the power.

Three neutral Swedes were killed by looters near the Governor's house, so Isogai moved to Chartered Bank House which was the only white building in the vicinity and so was sufficiently distinctive for him. Isogai saw himself as the protector of the Chinese in Hong Kong, yet was oblivious to the atrocities which were being committed in his name.

The first priority of the Japanese administration was to reduce the size of the Chinese population in Hong Kong to avoid the responsibility of feeding them. In the face of starvation, unemployment, reduced educational and other social services, over one million Chinese fled to China during the occupation, leaving only 650,000 in Hong Kong by 1945. Nothing was more damaging to Japanese propaganda than that so many were forced to leave with insufficient provisions to reach their villages in China, and many unfortunates never arrived at their destination.[3]

Ridding Hong Kong of the destitute and chronically sick was solved by more callous methods. Thousands of beggars and homeless were quietly rounded up and shipped to the mainland where they were each given a little rice and ten dollars. The stronger attacked and robbed the weaker before walking into China; the weaker were not seen again.[4]

Later, several hundred more of the destitute were collected in Stanley Prison where they were herded into large junks. They did not sail due to rough weather, and the Chinese could be seen by the internees crowded on the decks, all standing up, with no covering over their heads. They remained there for two days, probably with no food. Occasionally bodies were thrown overboard, which were washed up on the beach where they remained unburied.[5] The survivors were abandoned on Lantau Island.

An American internee was told by Father Jay, the Superior of the Jesuit Procurature, that inmates of the leper home at Pokfulham were loaded on to three Chinese junks which were taken out to sea and then sunk.

In view of the semi-starvation in Hong Kong, crime rose dramatically but draconian punishment kept it within bounds. Periodically there were mass executions of thieves who were first made to dig their own graves. A Catholic nun who was released from Stanley Internment Camp in July 1943, recalls that: 'A relative of one of our Sisters had a dozen buns snatched from her hand. Before she realised what had happened, the culprit had devoured all but one. Snatchers who were caught might receive any punishment from beheading to being savaged by a police dog. We saw a man tied up in a cage which was three foot high and three foot square. He was kneeling and begging for mercy from a Japanese soldier who was amusing himself by poking a stick through the bars. We were told that the man was going to have his head cut off.'[6]

The Japanese were apt to take the law into their own hands, but few went as far as Colonel Eguchi, the Director-General of Medical Services. Father Granelli, an Italian priest who fled to Macao, reported that Eguchi beheaded his cook at a dinner party: 'Eguchi was annoyed because the dinner was late and so bullied the cook before cutting off his head with his sword. A Portuguese lady who saw the whole performance had to go to bed for a week.'[7]

After the British surrender, nearly all allied military equipment, ammunition, fuel, medicines, food and other stores were shipped, methodically and efficiently, to Japan, together with any movable booty such as refrigerators, sewing-machines and electrical equipment. Cars and trucks were dismantled and the engines and tyres sent to Tokyo; the vehicle bodies were then broken up for scrap metal.

Chinese labour working in the dockyards and elsewhere were paid in rice which was afterwards disposed of on the black market. A close control was kept of food supplies, and prices soared. The price of a bag of flour before the war had been three dollars; by October 1943, it cost seventy dollars, but could only be purchased on the black market at a price of two hundred dollars. Every commodity was strictly rationed, and food queues were evident everywhere.

Electricity and gas for cooking were available at about five times the previous price, and there was a prohibitively high minimum charge for electric light, regardless of the amount consumed. Rents were fixed at a very low level but taxes were so high that property owners were very often unable to pay them, in which case their property was confiscated without compensation.

A Japanese sentry stood outside each public building and everyone had to bow ceremoniously to him. Failure to do so occasionally resulted in the victim being tied up and a small wooden plaque being hung from his neck which read: 'This is the punishment for not respecting a Japanese sentry.' One man was imprisoned and so starved that when his family smuggled to him a valuable cake of soap, he ate it.

The Japanese set great store on hygiene. On entering public buildings, hands had to be washed in a basin of antiseptic and feet wiped on a mat saturated with the same liquid. A cleansing regulation was introduced whereby any shopkeeper or householder whose premises were too dirty had the building barricaded with barbed wire for a week to prevent anyone from entering. These measures proved fairly effective.

Many public buildings were unrecognisable, due to the damage caused during the fighting and the use to which they were subsequently put. The University was intact while St Joseph's College became little better than a pigsty. The Colonial Secretary's records vanished, and hawkers wrapped up their parcels in official and confidential documents from government offices. Birth, death and marriage certificates were frequently found scattered in the streets.

The Japanese language was enforced in the few schools which continued to function. Large shops closed at 4 p.m. and restricted sales as much as possible to avoid running out of items; for example not more than one piece of cutlery could be sold at a time.

Despite all these difficulties, life in Hong Kong went on just as in cities in Europe under German occupation. It was not Japanese policy to antagonise Chinese or Indians, for there were vague plans for Hong Kong and India to have an eventual role in Japan's Greater East Asia Co-prosperity Sphere when the war ended, and this would need the co-operation of the conquered races.

An Indian Independence League was formed, and a delegation was sent to tour Japan but it returned unimpressed by wartime living conditions there. Some League members wore uniform with a green, white and orange flash on their caps, but they did not participate in military training, and membership did not imply that the man was a traitor, except, perhaps, to the Japanese. Indians who were unenthusiastic about joining or subscribing to the League

146

were threatened with their food ration being cut off, and passes were not issued to them. Some wealthy and prominent Indians were kept unobtrusively in custody. Their release coincided with an announcement in the local press that they had contributed large sums for the welfare of Japanese soldiers.

Several hundred Indian troops were quartered in Murray Barracks in Victoria. They were to be seen carrying out foot drill and bayonet practice with dummy rifles. On other occasions they marched to the former Hong Kong cricket ground where they charged across the pitch shouting wildly, led by Japanese instructors.[8] Local newspaper reports in December 1943, stated that Indian 'students' were about to undergo rigorous training before being sent to Singapore to join the Indian National Army. Those Indians who carried out guard duties in Hong Kong freed Japanese to fight elsewhere, which was also the case with those who served in the police. It was reported to China that the Japanese treated them on a basis of equality which the Indians had not enjoyed in the past.[9]

The Chinese had no alternative other than to co-operate with the Japanese if they were to survive, and the degree of collaboration would seem to have been no greater than in occupied territories in Europe. Occasionally distinguished Chinese, upon whom the British had bestowed honours, broadcast urging everyone to co-operate enthusiastically with the Japanese Government. On 27 December 1943, for example, Sir Robert Kotewall, KCMG, a former member of the Hong Kong Legislative Council, broadcast that: 'Great progress has been made . . . Hong Kong will become a model city in the co-prosperity sphere. War is often followed by plague. The Government has introduced such methods as compulsory inoculation, excrement examination and large scale house-cleansing, thereby reducing the death rate. Great strides have been made in education; the public library will be opened in the future. We have the duty to co-operate . . . although we may encounter certain difficulties.'

Sir Robert started to call himself Lo Kuk-wo as the Japanese frowned on British titles, and he became the chief spokesman for the Chinese under the Japanese occupation, for which he was vilified after the war, as was Sir Shousan Chow who also co-operated with the enemy.

It may be thought that they both should have been stripped of their knighthoods, just as Professor Anthony Blunt, the Russian spy, had his removed by the Sovereign in 1979. However both Sir Robert and Sir Shousan had been formally requested to work with the Japanese by the leading members of the former Hong Kong Government. Within a week of the British surrender, R. A. C. North, Secretary for Chinese Affairs, J. A. Fraser, Defence Secretary, and C. G. Alabaster, Attorney-General, had called on Sir Robert and Sir Shousan and specifically asked them to promote friendly relations between Chinese and Japanese, and to do their best to restore public order and preserve internal security since the British had become powerless.

'These gentlemen in carrying out their task, which should have been my duty, were abused and humiliated by the Japanese, and are now misrepresented and abused by some of their friends,' wrote Mr North immediately after the war. Sir Robert had his house placed under Japanese military jurisdiction for much of the occupation and was seldom free from Japanese pressures.

The Japanese tried to restore something like normality in Hong Kong. During most of the occupation public transport functioned, and light, power, water and telephones worked.

Racing at Happy Valley was restarted by a Chinese who had formerly been a Justice of the Peace and held the CBE. He told his friends that he had tried to get Chinese admitted to the Jockey Club for twenty years, and now he could ensure that no Briton was ever admitted to the race course. To his disappointment the horses frequently collapsed during the races, due to starvation and eventually the course was turned into a vegetable patch.

Conditions in Hong Kong deteriorated as an increasing amount of Japanese shipping was sunk, so less food arrived. The starving relied upon the generosity of the few who could obtain money from outside sources. Valtorta, the Italian

Roman Catholic Bishop of Hong Kong, was given $50,000 by the Pope to buy food and clothing for the internees. To win the co-operation of the Japanese, the Bishop gave $5000 to wounded soldiers, both allied and Japanese, but the local newspaper, for propaganda purposes, announced that the Pope had given $50,000 to the wounded. The Japanese spent the money allocated to the POWs on sports equipment for them, which seemed irrelevant to those suffering from malnutrition or dying of diphtheria.

Bishop Valtorta asked to buy food direct from the Food Control organisation rather than have to pay absurd black market prices, but this was refused. Nevertheless the money sent in monthly to Stanley enabled the sick to receive, for example, eggs, which were an unheard of luxury since at one stage they cost £4 each on the black market.

The Japanese treated the Bishop with little respect. It seemed that his only hope of obtaining information about casualties would be if requested by the Vatican, but the Japanese ignored him, and wives at Stanley could not discover if their husbands in the POW camps were still alive. However the Vatican had some influence for when some Irish priests were arrested in Hong Kong, Bishop Valtorta was refused permission to send them clothing until he threatened to report it to the Pope, whereupon permission was granted.

The Anglican St John's Cathedral was occupied by the Japanese Army immediately after the surrender, and used as a stable. Fortunately, Doctor Charles Harth, a German Jewish refugee, prevented the Japanese from taking over the Anglican Bishop's house where services continued. Before the war he was suspected by some British of being a German spy. Now his nationality and reputation enabled him to stay at liberty although he was accused by the Military Police of helping the enemy when he sent prayer books into Stanley Internment Camp which contained prayers for the King. Doctor Harth noted that: 'The Chinese Christians behaved marvellously during the occupation, and there was a fine spirit of co-operation with the Roman Catholics. Bishop Valtorta wrote a strong letter of protest when Japanese

Buddhists tried to take over the Cathedral; the French Fathers kept the vestments and Cathedral plate, and the Irish Superior of the Jesuits brought personally to me the Holy Vessels of our burned-out Peak Church.'[10]

G. S. Zimmern, the British Warden of St John's Hall, was a lay reader and, in the absence of English speaking clergy, he took the services until he was arrested with Doctor Selwyn-Clarke and Sir Vandeleur Grayburn for alleged spying. 'How I came out alive can only be attributed to divine grace,' he recalls. 'On my release, I was avoided like a leper and so services stopped. Indeed by the autumn of 1943 many worshippers, including Chinese clergy, had left Hong Kong for Macao and Sunday attendance had dropped to six.'[11]

Macao remained a colony of neutral Portugal throughout the Second World War, and so became a natural refuge for the homeless from Hong Kong. The Americans bombed Macao towards the end of the war apparently under the impression that the Japanese were occupying it. The Colony was full of Chinese, European and Japanese agents. The Japanese Consul, Fukui, was murdered there by, it is believed, a North Korean who was later liquidated in China.

A BAAG source in Hong Kong smuggled a message to Colonel Ride that two British Consulate officials in Macao were in danger of being kidnapped.[12] This report may have been accurate. The officials one night heard prolonged rifle and machine-gun fire and discovered that the Japanese had hijacked *Sai On*, a ship in Macao's harbour, in which they may have believed the officials were living. The Japanese had boarded *Sai On* after which tugs towed the ship to Hong Kong, but they later returned her when they found that only miserable refugees who originally came from Hong Kong were on board. Two Chinese in the ship were reported to have been placed in Hong Kong's Stanley Prison where they were executed. Among others executed in the prison at the same time were three women, all aged about sixty, for allegedly eating human flesh, and two prisoners for attempting to pick their cell locks with chopsticks.

In June 1943, Sir Vandeleur Grayburn, head of the Hong Kong and Shanghai Bank, who had been forced to liquidate its assets, was seen to arrive in Stanley Prison in handcuffs looking emaciated and 'as grey as a timber wolf'. He was looked after in prison by an Indian sanitary Corporal who fruitlessly sought help from the Japanese on three occasions. On the third the Corporal was soundly beaten, but he managed to get word to Doctor Talbot in Stanley Internment Camp who feigned sickness and was admitted to the prison hospital. He saw Sir Vandeleur Grayburn but by that time he was in a coma and it was too late to do anything for him. In August, Sir Vandeleur's body was given to his widow without any warning. It had to be hurriedly buried as it was in a bad state of decomposition, since he had died several days earlier. An unopened bottle of vitamin pills was returned with the remains. Lady Grayburn had sent it to her husband many weeks previously, and the pills would have helped his beri-beri had he been allowed to have them.

Doctor Selwyn-Clarke, as explained earlier, was the Director of Medical Services in Hong Kong. 'He is a strange character,' wrote an internee who was later repatriated. 'His enemies fear and hate him, while his friends consider him a saint and martyr. The Japanese make him swallow humiliation after humiliation, yet he gets milk for the hospitals still open, and every second day he has two people brought in from Stanley ostensibly for an X-ray, and gives them a happy two days. Their gratitude and appreciation is pitiful.'

Many POWs and internees are alive today only because of Selwyn-Clarke's success in sending medicines, money and food to their camps for eighteen months. 'He is surrounded by puppets and traitors,' reported a doctor who fled from Hong Kong. 'He is not allowed to speak to anyone on the telephone and he is continuously watched, for the Japanese suspect him of being the head of the British Secret Service.'

Selwyn-Clarke knew that his days were numbered because his protectors Colonel Eguchi and Mr Oda, the helpful head of the Japanese Foreign Office staff, were posted away from Hong Kong in the spring of 1943. 'From then onwards,' he recalled, 'I anticipated that the Japanese

Military Police, which corresponded to the German Gestapo, would soon come for me.'[13] Eight months earlier, Selwyn-Clarke had sent a message via Macao and Lisbon to the Foreign Office 'stating that he would be able to do more with the Japanese if the knighthood he has heard he will receive can be advanced.'[14] The Foreign Office knew nothing about a knighthood and one official noted: 'It's a novel idea that this could help; the Japanese have little interest in decorations other than their own.' Neither Sir Mark Young nor Sir Vandeleur Grayburn had been helped by their rank.

'On 2 May, I heard hammering on my door soon after dawn,' Selwyn-Clarke remembered. 'I was accused of being the head of British espionage and of sending messages. The Military Police appeared to have made a close study of a pamphlet issued in the reign of Marie-Thérèse of Austria, in about 1768, as a guide to village magistrates on the value of the thumb screw, burning of the skin, and the like. Modern improvements included starvation and ballooning-out of the stomach and bowel with gallons of water introduced by rubber tube.' The Doctor was placed in solitary confinement which in some cases was totally destroying to morale. 'One man whom I knew went mad after a relatively short spell,' Selwyn-Clarke wrote later. 'I could hear through the wall his imaginary telephoning of instructions to his wife to send the car for him.' Although the Doctor had been agnostic, the Bible comforted him.

Sometimes a group of internees in Stanley Camp nearby would sing songs like 'There'll always be an England', and their voices would hearten the wretched prisoners, as did the drone of American aircraft and the crump of explosives.

Selwyn-Clarke had been meticulously careful not to get involved in BAAG's activities, but he had very occasionally sent messages to Mr John Reeves, the British Consul in Macao. Most of the messages urged Reeves to stir up the International Red Cross in Geneva to some positive action. More important, the Doctor had been collecting the donations, which amounted to over one million dollars, from the Hong Kong and Shanghai Banking Corporation,

Major-General C. M. Maltby after surrendering Hong Kong on Christmas Day, 1941

Allied prisoners of war watched by Japanese march to Shamuipo POW camp, 30 December 1941

陳申秦英將軍率領香港陸海空軍官兵由港抵達惠州留影 29TH DEC. 1941

ADMIRAL CHEN CHAK WITH BRITISH OFFICERS
AND MEN WHOM HIS EXCELLENCY LED THROUGH
THE JAPANESE LINES AFTER THE FALL OF
HONG KONG AND ARRIVED SAFELY AT WAICHOW

The one-legged, wounded Admiral Chan Chak sits with
British servicemen who escaped from Hong Kong

Rear Admiral C. H. J. Harcourt, liberator of Hong Kong, meets F. C. Gimson the
Colonial Secretary, on his release from internment

A Japanese fighter turns to attack American
bombers above Hong Kong

Major-General Umetichi Odada signs the surrender document in
Government House, 16 September 1945

Above right: Allied prisoners kept records on the prison walls, prior to their
execution, which the Japanese unsuccessfully tried to efface

Sister S. M. Augustus attends a severe case of malnutrition
after liberation

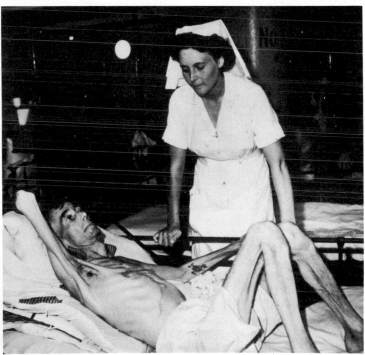

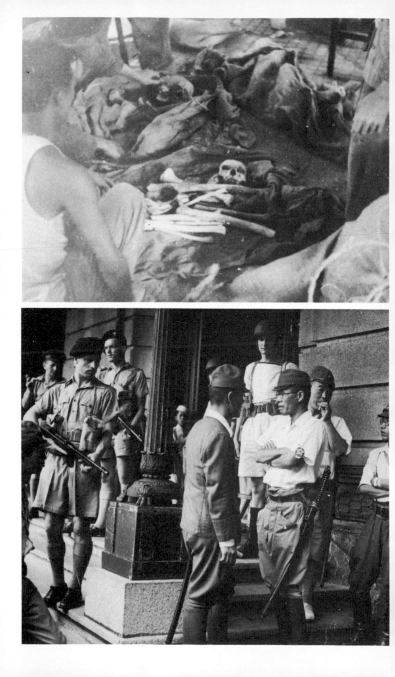

Liberated POW's cheering their US Navy rescuers at Aomori, Japan

Above left: Identifying remains of Canadian war dead
at Hong Kong, April 1947

British servicemen guard Japanese soldiers
after their surrender

Wendy Rossini, an internee shows a bowl
of rice, which together with a bowl of stew was
the daily ration for her 'room' of five people

and Indian and Chinese individuals. This money had enabled him to purchase food, medicines and clothing for the needy.

Sixteen months after the Doctor's arrest, he was formally tried, if one can so describe a process in which there are no opportunities for making a defence. The Japanese had no evidence against him and he was given the light sentence of three years' imprisonment. However, after only three months he was unexpectedly released to join his wife and daughter at the Mau Tau-Wai Internment Camp. After the war Selwyn-Clarke was knighted and in 1947 he became Governor of the Seychelles, a much deserved and unique appointment for a man of his profession.

Selwyn-Clarke's very urgent appeal for funds to buy food and medicines had reached the War Office in London through Macao in May 1942. The Treasury was willing to make a special payment of £10,000, and the Swiss Minister in Tokyo agreed to help transfer this sum to the Doctor, but it was later decided to pass it to Zindel, the International Red Cross delegate. Pressure from the Colonial Office and what was known as the 'Prisoner of War Department' induced the Treasury to transfer £10,000 monthly for the relief of internees and dependents of those POWs who were enlisted in the Volunteers. This money was put up by the Hong Kong Government from their own funds in London and reached Zindel in November 1942. He sensibly used these resources also for the POWs, to the dismay of the War Office which believed that 'proper care and maintenance of the POWs is the duty of the capturing power'.

The responsibility for British POWs fell upon the POW Department which held a meeting in the Colonial Office in London on 26 January 1943, at which a representative of the Colonial Office said that he did not agree to any part of the £10,000 being spent on the prisoners of war if civilians might be deprived thereby. The Colonial Office had earlier concluded, quite erroneously, that Zindel already had more money than he needed.

Mr G. Ignatioff, the Canadian representative, had long been greatly disturbed at the continued failure of the

International Red Cross to obtain specific information on the POWs in Hong Kong. At this meeting it was announced that the Canadian Government had already authorised the Argentine Government, then the Protecting Power, to make a minimum payment of five Canadian dollars monthly for each Canadian POW in Hong Kong. Representatives of the Treasury and of Australia tended to agree with the Chairman who said that it was unfortunate that the Canadian Government had made payments for their prisoners of war without consulting other Governments first. However Mr G. A. Wallinger, representing the Foreign Office, announced that the United States had been consulted five weeks earlier and in the absence of a reply, he suggested that such payments for POWs should be made. This was agreed, and the monthly allocation to the International Red Cross was later increased to £60,000.

Two weeks earlier, the Canadian authorities had complained to the International Red Cross about their lack of activity. The complaint was fully justified, and it is astonishing that Zindel, the delegate in Hong Kong, did not realise earlier that his telegrams to Geneva were being altered by the Japanese. A man of greater resource and energy would surely have ensured that the truth was reaching the allied Governments. However a British official felt that: 'We should express our disapproval of the largely unfounded complaints of the Canadian authorities . . . This complaint strikes me as a typical piece of selfishness on the part of Canada. Their POWs amount to 2% of the total of the British alone and for that reason, if for no other, Canada should, I think, have consulted other Governments before complaining to the International Red Cross in this fashion.'[15] (The 2% presumably applied to the proportion of all British POWs throughout the Far East including those in Singapore and Siam.)

Yet BAAG was sending accurate reports on the POWs' plight: '. . . 250 Canadians in hospital, while only 40% of the rest are fit. In Argyle Street one-third are in poor health. Medical facilities are utterly inadequate while drugs are quite insufficient . . . mortality from any epidemic is likely to be very high. Japanese have pilfered Red Cross supplies . . .'[16]

Such opinions were widely circulated in Whitehall, and the Foreign Office was passing the information on to the Swiss Minister in Tokyo for his comments because until the end of the war the only communication link with the Japanese was through him. The Canadian Government were entirely justified both in taking a strong line with the International Red Cross and in providing money for the Canadian POWs.

The International Red Cross has been criticised for the negative part they played in helping the Hong Kong POWs and internees. Nevertheless they were under a considerable handicap because the Japanese authorities refused to recognise their status, and they did not agree that the Swiss Minister could represent Britain's interests in Japan. The Colonial Office expected the International Red Cross to achieve more in time, 'reaping the benefits of their cautiousness.' Yet the opposite occurred. By August 1944, 'Zindel is working under a great mental and nervous strain,' wrote the Red Cross delegate in Chungking to Geneva. 'Zindel's office and flat have been searched by the Jap police who call weekly and look into everything. It is doubtful whether Zindel is allowed or would dare to send you reports stating the true facts.'[17]

The internees' circumstances had deteriorated rapidly after Doctor Selwyn-Clarke's arrest, and it was obvious to them that Zindel could achieve little. 'Zindel's last appearance in Stanley was a humiliating one,' noted Gimson, 'all internees had been confined to their quarters as he toured the camp, isolated between Japanese officers who walked in front and behind him.' Zindel knew that Red Cross parcels were being sold in Hong Kong, but his protests were of no avail. The food supplies in Stanley were hopelessly inadequate, but D. L. Newbigging did his best to supervise a fair distribution. 'He showed patience, imagination and understanding,' wrote Gimson later. 'The internees owe him and his assistants a great debt. All displayed an outstanding record of devoted sevice.'[18]

By 1943, Gimson had become exasperated by the British Government's inability to achieve anything for them. 'If it is the British Government's wish that we stay here and perish, we accept that fate, provided that we know a full and true report is in the hands of Mr Churchill and Mr Eden,' wrote Gimson in a long report to the Foreign Office, which was to be secretly carried by one of the Canadian civilians about to be repatriated.

The repatriation of 1500 people in the Far East, including 600 British from Stanley, was prevented by General MacArthur, commanding the south-west Pacific Area, and by the Australian Government. The Japanese had 330 merchant seamen interned in Australia, and some were believed to have been spying before the war. General MacArthur, whose area of responsibility included Australia, objected to the proposed exchange as the seamen were thought to know too much about the Australian coast line and harbours. On military grounds it is impossible to criticise the General's decision.

'We do not feel disposed to lay waste to the lives of the wretched citizens caught here,' wrote Gimson to the Foreign Office, 'but in view of the imminent repatriation of Canadians, and that of the Americans last year, we logically assume that Great Britain wishes to safeguard their people as the United States and Canada are caring for theirs. It is surprising to see reasonably fit (camp standard) men and women ready for immediate repatriation, ahead of the sick and dying, both young and old; we cannot but feel that, were it not for erroneous and rosy reports known to have reached Whitehall and Geneva, our sick and dying would have been exchanged first.'[19]

Ironically enough, a few months before the war in the Far East, wives who had been compulsorily evacuated to Australia were clamouring to rejoin their husbands in Hong Kong. In July 1941, an appeal had been made to Duff Cooper on behalf of 3000 of these wives. He had been sent by the War Cabinet for a short time to Singapore to investigate proposals to co-ordinate civil activities there. 'We are bitterly resentful at the unjust treatment meted out to us by the Hong Kong Government. We obeyed evacuation orders because we thought we were doing our duty. Actually we were duped by the Government,' ran the wives' protest. Some exaggerated claims were also made about the mental, moral and financial strain of the separation.

The wives' indignation had been inflamed by the very evident injustices of the Government's evacuation scheme. Exemptions to evacuation had been so obviously unjust. For example the wife of the Commissioner of Police, Mr King, had been exempted, together with both his daughters and his mother-in-law on the grounds, presumably, that 'their presence was necessary for defence purposes,' it was reported to the Colonial Office. 'Yet the evacuation policy was rigorously enforced for those of lower rank.'[20] Many soldiers were deeply resentful at the back-door exemptions and favouritism in certain quarters. But the evacuation was, with hindsight, the best thing that could have happened.

After Hong Kong was captured many of the wives in Australia joined the East Asian Residents' Association and news bulletins spread what news trickled in from those imprisoned. These bulletins occasionally contained compromising information which endangered those still in Hong Kong. For example two months before the bankers' arrest, Bulletin No. 5 published in Sydney reported that: 'A British banker in the Sun Wah hotel had managed to smuggle out a letter.' Important information then followed on the bank's liquidation, an individual was named and it was stated that the letter ended with the initial 'F'. This bulletin could have been sent by Japanese sympathisers through a neutral country to Tokyo, and it may be more than a coincidence that all the bankers were interned a few months later and some executed.

A Hong Kong Fellowship was formed in London for the wives, widows and relations of POWs and those interned. At the first meeting in February, 1943, 600 members were expected, but 900 turned up, such was the desperate anxiety for authentic news. Meetings were addressed by the President, Lieutenant-General A. E. Grasett, CB, DSO, MC, who had commanded the Hong Kong Garrison until

June 1941, and later became Governor of Jersey in 1945. The band of the Middlesex Regiment usually played at subsequent meetings, one of which was attended by several of the 1941 escapees. Eight lengthy and informative news letters published by the Fellowship were of great comfort, particularly as they reproduced extracts from dozens of POWs' letters though they contained only reassuring news for otherwise the Japanese censor would not have let them through. Zindel's favourable but inaccurate reports were given prominence, and one news letter contained Japanese propaganda photographs which suggested that Stanley was a delightful holiday camp.

The British and allied Governments faced difficult decisions on how much they should tell the POWs' families and the general public about Japanese atrocities, not least because publicity could only cause alarm.

In February 1942, Lord Moyne, then a member of the Government, drew Churchill's attention to the Chiefs of Staff's wish that atrocities committed by Japanese against prisoners in Hong Kong should be published. For example, that during the fighting at Stanley wounded in one hospital had been bayoneted to death in their beds, some prisoners had been executed on capture, and three nurses murdered. However, Lord Moyne added that: 'Although publication might stimulate the morale of British troops, there is a danger of the contrary effect with oriental peoples in Burma, India and Ceylon. Indian labour is already very uneasy; terror and defeatism might be aroused. It is possible that some Orientals may even admire the Japanese for their attacks on our prestige. The telegram from the Military Attaché at Chungking announcing the atrocities states: "This studied barbarism is undoubtedly employed with the object of breaking morale". If this is the case, it would be playing the Japanese game to broadcast the news. Publication might also queer the pitch for negotiations with Japan for better treatment.'[21]

Churchill decided that publicity should not be given to the atrocities for the time being, but Lord Halifax, Britain's Ambassador to the United States was asked for his opinion.

He replied that the State Department wanted no such publicity in America, 'since it would only exacerbate feelings on the West Coast of America, where anti-Japanese sentiment was already running high and there was real danger of disorders.'[22] The Americans had received bad reports about the treatment of their prisoners in the Philippines and were already holding up news of the atrocities there. The US Army's department responsible for psychological warfare also opposed publication because the Army wanted to fight the war 'according to the civilised rules', and publication might encourage the Japanese to further brutalities. There was a hint, too, that racial questions should be played down lest they might induce negroes to side against the white peoples.

However, later the same month the Americans told the British Government that publicity in London would cause insufficient attention in America to cause a dangerous situation on the West coast, and so the British should do whatever they thought best.

On 4 March 1942, a meeting was held in the Foreign Office to decide the policy. The Foreign Office and the Ministry of Information strongly favoured publicity, arguing that it would have a good effect on British public opinion by showing what we were up against, and useful propaganda would be obtained abroad. The Canadian representative and the War Office were, on the whole, also in favour, whereas the Colonial Office had not studied the question sufficiently to make a worthwhile judgement. The Australian representative said that publicity was undesirable, while the India Office drew attention to the Viceroy's apprehension that it would cause inter-racial animosity. Nevertheless, overall, the meeting favoured publicity.

Churchill subsequently agreed, so the following week the Foreign Secretary, Anthony Eden, shocked the civilised world by recounting in the House of Commons the first news of Japanese atrocities, based on the reports from Colonel Ride. It is known that the allied broadcast which announced the details reached Imperial Circles in Tokyo, for an entry was made by Kido, Lord Keeper of the Privy Seal, in his diary for 19 March 1942, '. . . the Imperial Household Minister came to the office and told me about Eden's address in Parliament concerning our soldiers' atrocities at Hong Kong, and we exchanged opinions.'[23] Seven months later Lord Simon, the Lord Chancellor, announced in the House of Lords that a United Nations Commission for the Investigation of War Crimes would collect evidence against those committing atrocities, but it was not until 1944 that the Commission came into being. Meanwhile the announcements of Eden and Simon failed in any way to undermine Japanese morale, nor did they curb the excesses of the militarists.

However, when Zindel's inaccurate reports that conditions in the POW camps had improved were published in Geneva, it was erroneously believed this improvement was the direct result of Eden's statement and the publicity given to the atrocities. General William Donovan, head of the American Office of Strategic Services, cited the House of Commons' statement as evidence that America should also publicise atrocities committed against their own people. The US Government therefore made a statement on atrocities committed against Americans and British in the Far East.

By September 1942, deaths in Shamshuipo Camp were running at the rate of five or six a day, 'and became so commonplace that, unless it was a personal friend who had died, it generated no more interest than a junk sailing down the harbour,' remembers Lance-Corporal A. J. Taylor of the Hong Kong Signal Company. 'Such was the state of affairs that a few extra grains of rice or a puff at somebody's cigarette was a subject of conversation. One day Japanese soldiers arrived in the camp, leant their rifles against a wall, donned white coats, and medically examined us to ensure that no disease should be carried to the graceful land of the Rising Sun. Each POW was inoculated and his anus was probed with a glass tube. It was rumoured that the inoculations were to sterilise one, and so some avoided the draft, leaving others who were less fit to make up the numbers.'[1]

The first draft of 700 POWs left at the beginning of September, and the second draft embarked in a 7000 ton freighter, the *Lisbon Maru*, on 27 September. They were not told their destination, but they were promised a place where the climate was better. However, it was common knowledge that they were off to Japan.

This draft of 1816 British POWs was commanded by Lieutenant-Colonel H. W. M. Stewart, OBE, MC, the Commanding Officer of 1st Battalion, the Middlesex Regiment. He was sick with pellagra and malnutrition, and his batman carried a wooden box-like stool for him to sit on. Rumour later had it that a wireless set was in the box which was the only object never searched by the Japanese.

The ship was commanded by Captain Kyoda Shigeru, and the POWs were squeezed into three holds: the Royal Navy nearest the bows, the Middlesex and Royal Scots in No. 2 hold just forward of the bridge, and the Royal

Artillery in No. 3 hold in the stern. The *Lisbon Maru* also carried almost 800 Japanese troops.

The ship steamed slowly, hugging the Chinese coast for safety, and some POWs began to enjoy themselves. Food was good by Shamshuipo standards; the sun shone, and the nights were warm. Prisoners were occasionally allowed on deck for fresh air and exercise, and those who resembled prematurely old men began to get a touch of colour in their cheeks.

The ship's carpenters had built wooden latrines which hung over the sides of the ship, but these were too far away for those with dysentery and diarrhoea who were too weak to climb the ladders from the deepest holds. 'With little air percolating there, the temperature built up, and the stench too,' recalls Taylor. 'Some men could only lie where they were, and being unable to clean or wash themselves, the filth and slime was terrible.'

It probably did not occur to the POWs that they were in danger from allied submarines, but this possibility had struck Doctor Selwyn-Clarke before his arrest. He had sent a message to the British Consul at Macao warning him that POWs were aboard the ship which was armed with two guns and carried no markings to indicate that POWs were aboard. Unfortunately Selwyn-Clarke's message never reached its destination.

At 4 a.m. on 1 October, USS *Grouper* of the Pacific Fleet Submarine Force, on patrol to the south of Shanghai, saw the *Lisbon Maru*.[2] Her Commanding Officer decided that the night was too bright for a surface attack, so took up position ahead of the ship to await daylight but, when dawn broke, the *Lisbon Maru* altered course, leaving the submarine in a poor position from which to attack. At 7.04 a.m. *Grouper* dived and began her approach. She fired three torpedoes at the maximum range of 3200 yards, but all missed. The *Lisbon Maru* remained on course, and so a fourth torpedo was fired. Two minutes and ten seconds later, the excited submarine crew heard a loud explosion. There were no casualties in the *Lisbon Maru* and the POWs did not know whether there had been an internal explosion in the engine-room.

Grouper's Captain raised his periscope and saw that the ship had altered course and stopped, but since no damage was visible *Grouper* moved to a new position for another shot. The Captain saw that his target had 'hoisted a flag and was firing at the submarine with what sounded like a small-calibre gun. Sharp explosions all around us.'

Grouper reached a fresh firing position at a range of 1000 yards and a fifth torpedo was fired, but missed. The submarine then fired its last torpedo and immediately dived to 100 feet where, forty seconds later, a loud explosion was heard 'definitely torpedoish'. Just before firing, the Captain had seen a Japanese light bomber over the target, and about two minutes later three depth charges exploded nearby. *Grouper* later came up to periscope depth; the plane was visible, but the ship had disappeared. It was assumed that the *Lisbon Maru* had been sunk. Mercifully, this was wrong; the sixth torpedo had missed, or the Japanese had destroyed it, according to the Japanese account published later in the *Japan Times Weekly*, although almost certainly untrue: 'Corporal Maji gave us the order to fire at the torpedo. Surprised beyond words, but faithful to the order, we charged our canon with a shell, aimed at the torpedo and fired. We then discovered that we had scored a direct hit.'

The POWs listened to the explosion of depth charges and the gun firing on the upper deck. For several minutes pandemonium reigned; it was the beginning of a long and increasingly anxious day. The ship was slowly listing, but the extent of the damage was unknown. The Japanese pulled heavy tarpaulins over the hatches, thereby sealing the POWs down and preventing fresh air reaching them.

Colonel Stewart shouted to everyone in No. 2 hold to be quiet. He told them what he thought had happened and asked for silence so that he could try to appeal to the Japanese.

'By this time many men were bursting to visit the lavatories, but as this was impossible, those in the bottom deck lifted a plank to let nature's wastes wash down the hull plates,' wrote Taylor later. 'Above them, on the second deck, men filled their water bottles from a fifty gallon drum which was then used as a lavatory. Nevertheless, the stench was asphyxiating.'[3]

Gradually, Colonel Stewart made contact with the other two holds. POWs in No. 1 hold reported, by tapping on the bulkhead, that two diphtheria patients had died and there was no way of escaping. Just before the tarpaulins had been pulled over the hatches, one tin of bad milk for the sick and a bucket were placed in No. 1 hold. The bucket was for sanitary purposes for 400 men. It was immediately filled and accidentally knocked over.

A prisoner in No. 3 hold shouted down a vent that the sea was entering their hold where soldiers of the Royal Artillery, working on the pumps, rapidly lost consciousness owing to the heat and lack of air.

At 5 p.m., the Japanese destroyer *Kure* took off all the Japanese troops, leaving only the crew and twenty-five guards under Lieutenant Wada. Arrangements were made to tow the *Lisbon Maru* to shallow water, and Captain Kyoda Shigeru discussed what should be done with the POWs. Lieutenant Wada said that there were insufficient guards to look after the prisoners, therefore the wooden hatches had to be closed. The Captain objected, knowing that the ventilation would be appalling, and if the ship sank all the POWs would drown. Wada replied that the Master of the ship had no authority to interfere. At 9 p.m. the heavy hatches were closed over the holds.

The POWs still confined to the holds had listened to the Japanese being transferred to another ship, and then the attempts to tow the *Lisbon Maru* towards Shanghai. Shortly afterwards the tow line was heard to snap.

The heat in all the holds was terrific. The night was made more hideous by the curses and moans of the sick, some of whom were calling for the padre. Everyone was told to lie quietly, stop talking and try to sleep to conserve air and strength.

By 9 a.m. on 2 October, over twenty-four hours after the torpedoing, the air in the holds was dangerously foul and it was evident that the men could not survive much longer, although by now everyone was calm. Colonel Stewart had earlier told Lieutenant W. M. Howell, Royal Army Service Corps, to make a hole in the hatch covers. He had already survived two previous shipwrecks. Howell was given a long butcher's knife which a POW had smuggled into the ship. He climbed up an iron ladder in the pitch darkness, but he had to abandon the attempt due to the lack of air and the difficulty of holding on to the ladder.

Captain Kyoda Shigeru knew that the ship was in imminent danger of sinking, and all the remaining Japanese, less five guards, were taken off, leaving the POWs to drown.

Colonel Stewart ordered Howell to try again.[4] This time he found the rickety wooden staircase which led to the hatch. He forced his knife between the baulks of timber above him, slit the tarpaulin and then with a great effort forced up one of the timbers. Howell eventually managed to climb through the gap, followed by Lieutenant Potter of St John's Ambulance Brigade who spoke Japanese. They saw some POWs from No. 3 hold struggling to get out through portholes on to the well-deck, and Howell opened the bulkhead door to release them, before making a second opening in the hatch at the point where the iron-rung ladder led up from the hold.

The Japanese guards, who had been watching their activity from the bridge, suddenly opened fire at the hole in the hatch, killing one man who was just emerging. They then switched their fire to the few who were on deck. Lieutenant Potter was hit, and Howell carried him back into the hold, where Potter died.

Colonel Stewart asked Howell about the state of the ship. There was a long pause, and everyone strained to hear the reply – that the position was desperate and the ship would sink at any moment. Just then, the *Lisbon Maru* gave a fearful lurch; possessions slid across the hold and water gushed in through the first opening in the hatch.

'Wild panic ensued,' remembers Lance-Corporal Taylor. 'Within seconds the ladders to the second deck were a mass of writhing, struggling bodies. Those first up discovered there was no room for them there, but others on the ladders below climbed over their backs before falling back into the bottom hold, crashing on to the men beneath them.'

Colonel Stewart ordered everyone to abandon ship, and another frantic rush for the ladders followed. Howell led the first group on to the deck. By this time the firing had stopped, for there were no longer any Japanese on board. Where or how they had gone remains a mystery, but it seems probable that some POWs, released by Howell into the well deck, had managed to make their way to the bridge, and had effectively silenced them.

Water continued to pour into No. 2 hold and there seemed little hope of getting out in time. However, order was quickly restored and the men formed up into long queues at the stairway and ladders. In the dim light which filtered into the hold, Captain N. H. Cuthbertson, Adjutant of the Royal Scots, carefully put on his Glengarry. Cuthbertson stated that he preferred to meet his God properly dressed.

The ship went down by the stern, but by good fortune the water was shallow and the stern rested on a sandbank while the bows remained clear of the water. The ship stayed in this position for about an hour while successive waves poured into the hold. Many of those in No. 3 hold, nearest the stern, drowned before they could get out.[5]

On reaching the deck, some immediately plunged overboard, while others lowered ropes down into the hold to increase the number of exits. Colonel Stewart was helped up one of the ropes and appeared on deck, immaculate as usual, complete with cap and swagger cane. Staff-Sergeant Ross, RAMC, collected a number of sick and injured on deck and gave them first-aid, displaying great devotion to duty and fine courage.

Lance-Corporal Taylor vividly remembers the scene on emerging from the hold: 'The deck was pitched at a very steep angle. We were desperately in need of water, but could find only a sack of white sugar which had been slashed open. We ate a little and found that in our dehydrated state we could not swallow it. The sunshine was brilliant, and the sun sparkled across the calm sea like a carpet of dazzling diamonds. The air was like wine after the foetid stench in the hold. Hundreds of men had taken to the water and a swift current was running westwards towards some islands about four miles away, which looked rocky and dangerous. Four Japanese auxiliary transport boats were slowly circling the *Lisbon Maru*. As the swimmers approached them, I heard rifle shots and small arms fire. The Japanese were picking off our men, one by one, using them for target practice.'

Signalman W. Parkinson saw several of those alongside him being shot. 'We swam back. Able Seaman Chilcroft and I found a small piece of wood,' he remembers. 'Nearby was a raft on which was sitting a Royal Scots private who was singing lustily to ten others hanging on to the sides. Two Able Seamen, both members of the Royal Navy water polo team were throwing a water-bottle to each other as if warming up before a match; neither survived.'

Taylor was still on deck, surrounded by friends who could not swim and most had no life jackets. He had been a Rover Scout in England and a member of the St Andrew's Rover Crew in Kowloon, and so he had little difficulty in making two rafts from ammunition boxes and planks. When they were completed, he wondered how he could launch them; the non-swimmers would have to drop into the sea and they would probably be quickly lost in the current. Just then, at 9.45 a.m., there was a muffled explosion from within the ship, and she sank instantly, sucking many down with her, including some of the forty injured and sick who were being cared for by orderlies in the Royal Army Medical Corps.

'It was a question of survival,' Taylor remembers. 'The longest swim I had ever had was some lengths of a swimming pool to qualify for a bronze life saver's badge. Having had no food or water for the last forty hours, and a starvation diet for nine months, I hardly felt qualified to swim over the horizon. With so many men in the water I was surprised that I could only see a few heads.'

The Japanese at last started to pick up those survivors who had not drifted past them, possibly because a number of

POWs were seen to have reached the islands, and some would live to tell the tale.

Signalman Parkinson swam up to a boat and saw a Japanese sailor leaning over the guard rail: 'So I offered my hand for him to pull me out of the water, but all I received from him was a slap in the face and I fell back in the water. By this time I was exhausted and really thought that I was going to die. Chilcroft had already drowned alongside me. Just then another POW, already aboard, grabbed my wrist and hauled me in. What a tragedy! Not one British POW should have lost his life; the Japanese had over twenty-four hours to save everyone.'

Lieutenant Howell was one of the first to reach the Sing Pang Islands which are in the Chusan Archipelago off the coast of Chekiang province. The islands were rocky and the sea dashed against the cliff faces.

Howell spoke Shanghai dialect and explained to the villagers that the numerous heads bobbing about in the water were British prisoners and not Japanese, whose fate the Chinese villagers had been cheerfully contemplating. The villagers immediately set off in junks and sampans to rescue about 200. Many other POWs were unable to obtain a footing and were swept past the islands before eventually drowning.

Company Sergeant-Major E. J. Soden of the Middlesex Regiment had been drifting towards the islands. 'We were feeling very weak and hungry, when a marrow came floating past which I grabbed and ate,' he remembers. 'At around dusk we were picked up by two Chinese in a lone rowing boat. One of them took my shirt and CSM's badge off my wrist, leaving me with only my 'fandoushi', the small piece of cloth covering my privates. It was then that I was violently sick, and thanks to the marrow I had something to be sick about. We were led to a warm shed full of fishing nets where women fed us hot vegetable soup and rice with bits of fish. The following morning a Chinese woman gave me an old overcoat for which I was most grateful.'[7]

Lance-Corporal Taylor had also been drifting towards the islands. He was supporting a Royal Scots non-swimmer named Ferris who had broken his back and was paralysed from the waist down. A Chinese fisherman in a small sampan saw them. Ferris was unconscious but they were both pulled aboard with a boat hook, and dumped ashore. Taylor crawled up to a small village nestling in the hill tops.

He knew a little Cantonese but only a small boy eventually understood that Ferris was still on the sea shore with his broken back. Four Chinese eventually unhinged a door and collected him. They were both then given a delicious meal before being left in a temple to sleep.

The following morning the villagers fed everyone again until they ran out of supplies. The Chinese had given clothing to those without any, and done their best for the many injured and sick.

At about mid-day three Japanese vessels approached the islands. All the Chinese males immediately collected their weapons and put on the militia uniforms of the Chinese Wong Chang Wai, Japan's puppet leader in conquered China. Two of them went down to meet the Japanese. The Chinese continued to be friendly and sympathetic until the arrival of Japanese marines who stormed the village and rounded up the prisoners 'while making a great fuss of proficiency, prodding the bales of straw with their bayonets.' The POWs were led down to the beach where they were made to return most of the clothing given to them by the villagers. 'A more bedraggled lot of skeletons you never saw,' recalls Taylor. 'Once on board we were squeezed on to the deck. During the afternoon we received a few tins of hot water but no food. The ship sailed in a convoy after dusk and the wind became cutting and chilling although we huddled together for warmth. At about midnight the first man died. We made such a fuss that the whole ship's company was mobilised, thinking that they had to quell a mutiny. When the Japanese eventually discovered that only a POW had died, they quite heartlessly tossed the body overboard without a hint of humanity. I later found that individual Japanese could be quite charming and natural, but witnessing this incident filled me with dreadful forebodings of the future. During the night three more men died. Rather than stir up any more animosity, we left them where they were; they were no colder than we were, just less animated.'

Some POWs in other ships received different treatment, as CSM Soden remembers. 'We were welcomed aboard by that most loved Commanding Officer of my Regiment – Colonel Stewart. The Jap officers on board treated us very well, stating that they had been trained by our Navy. They gave full military honours to those who died, and fed us well. On leaving the ship we noticed how quickly the mood changed when the Army took over. My coat was ripped off me, leaving me naked once more except for the 18″ x 6″ piece of loin cloth.'

By 5 October 1942, all the survivors of the *Lisbon Maru* had reached Shanghai, where it was established that, out of 1816 POWs who had sailed from Hong Kong, 843 had been shot in the water or drowned.

The Japanese decided to publicise the sinking of the *Lisbon Maru*, confident that the allies would not discover the truth. On 20 October 1942, the *Japan Times Weekly* announced that the Americans had sunk the ship, and gave the Japanese version: '"We must rescue the British prisoners of war" was the foremost thought which leaped to our minds when the ship met the disaster, said Sub-Lieutenant Hideo Wada. It was just the hour for the roll call of prisoners; somewhat taken aback, they were about to stampede. "Don't worry, Japanese planes and warships will come to your rescue," we told them. The commotion died down. It was encouraging to note that they had come to have such trust in the Imperial Forces during a brief war prisoners' camp life. All the Japanese, of course, were prepared to share a common fate with the British prisoners. That is why we all put on our lifebuoys at the same time. We remained on the bridge until the last of the prisoners was transferred to the lifeboats.'

When the POWs eventually reached Japan, the Japanese press stated that: 'With one voice and in the highest terms these surviving British prisoners referred to the strength and warm-heartedness of the Imperial Forces, and lauded the gallantry of the Japanese mariners.'

The dependents in Britain and Australia of those who died received a lower scale of allowance as their husbands were missing. The internees in Stanley were horrified to read in the *Nippon Times*: 'Atrocities by Americans – many British lives lost.' They knew neither who had sailed nor who had died. Mrs C. M. M. Man paraded with the other wives to receive the small allotment sent by their husbands in Shamshuipo. No money and no husband's signature authorising the payment meant that her husband was on the *Lisbon Maru*. 'I had been told there was money for me,' she remembers, 'and it was with tremendous relief that I joined the queue of wives and saw their joy and relief when they recognised the precious signature. It came to my turn and I was given a great deal more money than usual, but all I wanted was to see that signature. It wasn't there. I knew then that he was on the ill-fated ship.' Mrs Man feared the worst for eighteen months until a Japanese Brigadier named Otajima from Tokyo personally gave her a letter from her husband who had reached Japan safely.

The Japanese attempt to make propaganda out of the *Lisbon Maru* incident eventually failed because three POWs had escaped to Chungking to tell the true story. They had been helped by Woo Tung-Ling, the village representative on the Sing Pang Islands, who had hidden them for six days, thereby indicating the true allegiance of the villagers. Two guerrillas from neighbouring islands had later taken them to Free China.

The escapers were A. J. W. Evans, a civilian who had done air-raid precaution work during the fighting, Warrant Officers J. C. Fallace and W. C. Johnstone both of the HKRNVR.[8]

Their statements reached the Foreign Office in January 1943, and two months later the Swiss Government was asked to communicate to the Japanese Government the true facts, based on the first-hand evidence of the three escapees.

'His Majesty's Government appreciate that the Geneva Convention has never been ratified by the Japanese Government,' read the Foreign Office communication.

'Nevertheless, they expect the Japanese naval and military authorities to respect the principles embodied in the Convention and to treat prisoners of war in a manner befitting a civilised power . . . The treatment of the prisoners amounts to flagrant violation of the customs and usages of war . . .' The Japanese Government was asked to carry out a full investigation, and to report on the trial and due punishment of the responsible Japanese officers and men.

In November 1943, the Japanese Ministry of Foreign Affairs replied that: 'The British Government should be grateful for the measures taken by the Japanese authorities which resulted in the rescue of 900 prisoners. The Japanese Minister refuses to recognise the need for a Court of Enquiry.'

The responsible officers were brought to trial in Hong Kong in 1947, when the whole story emerged. However, for many POWs who survived the *Lisbon Maru*, the events of 1947 were irrelevant, for they had been so weakened by their experiences that they were dead. Lieutenant-Colonel Stewart died soon after his arrival in Japan, as did Ferris and 242 others during their first year there due to starvation. Thus of the original 1816 POWs, only 724 survived.

In December 1942, Japanese Secret Order No. 1504 stated that: 'Recently, during the transportation of POWs to Japan many have died and been incapacitated for further work due to their treatment on the journey, which at times was inadequate.' Instructions followed that prisoners should arrive at their destination in a condition to work.

This order had little effect, and in March 1944, Tominaga, the Vice-Minister of War, foreseeing the wrath to come, drew attention to the high death-rate among the prisoners. He added: 'If the present conditions continue to exist, it will be impossible for us to expect world opinion to be what we would wish it.'

He was right.

Eleven months after the *Lisbon Maru* disaster, the Japanese gathered in Formosa, now Taiwan, their most important prisoners captured throughout the Far East.

The voyage in August 1943, of the senior British officers from Hong Kong was unpleasant; they passed through several storms during which the sea swept over the decks, drenching the officers in their dark hold below, and their small ship barely reached the port of Kaohsiung in Formosa.

They were put in a camp at Shirakawa which was surrounded by a moat and a high bamboo stockade. Like the other four POW camps in Formosa, Shirakawa contained long bamboo huts built on stilts to avoid flood-water, rats and snakes. The POWs were issued with clogs, and ordered not to escape. Although they had been frequently searched, Brigadier Wallis still had his war diaries, hidden in the false bottom of a wooden box.

Also in Formosa were four Lieutenant-Generals, J. M. Wainwright who had taken over command of the United States Army in the Philippines from General MacArthur, Lieutenant-General A. E. Percival, the former GOC Malaya, Lieutenant-General Sir Lewis Heath, the former commander of the III Corps in Malaya, and General Hein ter Porrten, Commander-in-Chief of the Netherlands Indies forces. There were also four Governors imprisoned in Formosa – Sir Mark Young, Sir Shenton Thomas of Malaya and two Dutch: Tjarda van Stachouwer, the Governor-General of the Netherlands East Indies, and A. I. Spits, the Governor of Sumatra. Two British Chief Justices, Sir Percy McElwaine of the Straits Settlements, and Sir Harry Trusted of the Federated Malay States were also there with other British, American and Dutch senior officers and batmen, numbering 400 in all. The Americans had been captured at Bataan and Corregidor.

Fifteen months earlier, on Christmas Day 1941, Sir Mark Young had been separated from the other prisoners captured in Hong Kong. When General Maltby had ordered his Commanding Officers to surrender their units, Sir Mark was taken to the Peninsula Hotel in Kowloon to meet Lieutenant-General Takashi Sakai. The Japanese hoped to achieve the usual propaganda value out of the surrender, but Sir Mark protested at the presence of the photographer who was removed. After the Governor had signed the surrender, General Sakai told him that he could retain his sword, a symbol in Japanese eyes of his authority. Sir Mark expected to return to Government House, but instead was taken straight upstairs to a two-bedroomed flat in which he was locked for seven weeks. Subsequently he was treated with humiliation despite, or perhaps because, he was the King's Representative and the former Commander-in-Chief.

A suitcase containing clothes and books was sent to him from Government House, but he was allowed no visitors or newspapers. Although Sir Mark repeatedly asked to see Mr Gimson and other members of the Government, this request was refused.

A week after the surrender, he asked for an interview with the Japanese Commander. At last this was granted, but Sakai had left and his successor, General Isogai, treated him with no respect. The interview was a fiasco; all Sir Mark's requests were greeted with shouts from the interpreter: 'You are defeated. You have surrendered. You will obey.'[1] When he asked for news of his soldiers and of allied casualties, he was curtly told that it had nothing to do with him.

Sir Mark's period of solitary confinement was painful. He felt very keenly that he was the first Colonial Governor to surrender his command, was worried as to whether he had done the right thing, and denied the comfort of discussing this with anyone.

In early February 1942, he was asked whether he knew any private soldiers. On replying in the negative, the question was put to him again and again. He could not understand why the Japanese attached such importance to

174

this point, and he had the impression that he was not believed.

Meanwhile, Private J. Waller of the Middlesex Regiment was a POW in Shamshuipo. Before the war he had been studying to be a vet and on the surrender an officer asked him to be his batman as it was felt that officers might be better treated, in which case they could at least help their batmen. On 15 February, the day Singapore surrendered, Private Waller was told that he had been selected 'to go with an important British personage. I had no idea who he was or where I might be going,' he remembers. 'To look smart, I was given someone's Middlesex Regiment peaked hat and cap badge, and brass numbers to wear on my shoulders. The following morning I was taken to Sir Mark in the Peninsula Hotel. Privates don't meet Governors, and I did not know him before. He called me John and started by asking me how many press-ups I could do. I replied: "How many can you do, Sir?" He said "about fifteen."'[2] Waller felt himself to be very fit and they competed together. To Waller's mortification, he could only do five press-ups, whereas Sir Mark did fifteen for he had been keeping himself trim by pulling himself up to a ledge on the door.

The following day, the Governor and Private Waller were flown to Formosa. 'I had never flown before,' recalls Waller, 'and Sir Mark seemed mildly surprised when I asked him where the parachutes were. We sat between a Japanese Lieutenant and Sergeant who vomited continuously into their hats as the weather was bad. I felt almost as ill, but Sir Mark was quite imperturbable.'

After lunch in Formosa, they flew on to Shanghai where they were imprisoned at Woosung nearby. 400 United States Marines and 600 civilians were already there. The civilians had been captured at Wake Island which had surrendered after two weeks of severe air attacks and naval bombardment. Also in the camp were the British crew of a gunboat, HMS *Petrel*, which had been sunk near Shanghai, and the staff of the British Embassy in Peking.

On Sir Mark's arrival, the Japanese offered to build him a separate hut, but he refused saying that: 'Any money that was to be spent on housing should be spent for the benefit of the camp in general.' He lived instead in a room at the end of one of the barracks.

Private Waller, who was in an adjoining room, succeeded in smuggling in meat through the perimeter wire, with the help of British in Shanghai who had not yet been interned. However Sir Mark refused to eat this meat as it was not available to the other prisoners. He did not join the officers' mess which provided somewhat better and more varied food, as he was receiving no pay and so could not contribute. The Japanese refused to pay him on the grounds that they did not know what military rank a Governor was equivalent to. However he could order clothes and books from a British shop in Shanghai, the owner of which did not wish to be paid until after the war as the local currency was suspect.

Ten days after his arrival, Colonel W. A. Ashurst, the senior American in the camp, was given a certificate by the Camp Commandant which everyone had to sign. It read: 'I promise not to attempt to escape from control by the Imperial Japanese Army.' Colonel Ashurst had been the commander of the American Embassy Guard at Peking and also of the Marines in North China. On the outbreak of war he had complied with the Japanese orders to surrender for there was no possibility of fighting on virtually alone.

Colonel Ashurst took the certificate to Sir Mark, as the Governor was the highest-ranking person in the camp. They both agreed that nobody should sign it, and nothing more was heard about it for the time being.

The Governor told everyone in Woosung that no prisoner would be held guiltless who signed a promise not to escape unless he had been actually tortured; the threat alone was not sufficient justification for signing.

Sir Mark Young's views on escaping differed from those of most former senior officers in Hong Kong, presumably because he was unaware of the repercussions when the prisoners were treated much more harshly in Hong Kong after some POWs had escaped.

Lieutenant-Commander Wooley, Royal Navy, who had been captured in Shanghai on the outbreak of war, was invited by Sir Mark to eat with him. Wooley refused as he was planning to escape from Woosung and did not wish to compromise the Governor. Sir Mark was immensely enthusiastic at this news and typed out a brief report which he gave to Wooley on 10 March.

That night Wooley escaped with three Americans and Lieu, the personal servant of one of them. They planned to contact friendly Chinese farmers, but became hopelessly lost as soon as they had crawled under the outer wire. The farmers' sympathies lay with the Japanese, and they were all caught the following day only a few miles from the camp. Wooley destroyed the Governor's reports as the Japanese closed in on them. Two days later the escapers were paraded through the camp roped together, before being sentenced to ten years' imprisonment on a charge of desertion from the Japanese Army.

Colonel Yuse, the Japanese Camp Commandant, renewed his orders that everyone must sign a certificate stating that they would not escape. Colonel Ashurst eventually agreed that the Americans would do so after the following words had been added: 'Signed in accordance with a direct Japanese order, under duress and with the threat of terminal punishment.'

The Governor disagreed with Colonel Ashurst on a number of matters, and on this decision in particular. 'I don't think you should advise your Marines to sign,' he told the Colonel and the senior American officers. 'It renounces your rights. It is your duty to escape. You know what emphasis the Japanese place on "face". You are yielding, with no resistance whatsoever, to a blatant illegal order. They will not respect us in any way.'[3]

'Sir Mark,' replied Colonel Ashurst, 'we are miserable here in this cold and wet weather. Our rice ration nears the starvation level and we are completely at the Japanese mercy; I have the responsibility for the ultimate return to freedom of Americans in this camp. I have therefore advised each man to sign.'

After the Americans had done so, the Japanese were furious that none of the British would sign. 'The result was that we were confined to our quarters and the men were very badly treated and suffered from extreme cold and beatings,' wrote Sir Mark later. 'After some days I agreed to the men signing. Four days later I tried to end the impasse without conceding anything, and incidentally to give the Japanese an opportunity of getting out of their difficulty without losing too much face. So I drew up a different undertaking which said that I was not at that time contemplating or planning to escape. Colonel Yuse accepted my proposal with relief.'[4]

Meanwhile there was an extraordinary proposal to repatriate the Governor to Britain. It was made on 24 February 1942, by the Roman Catholic Bishop Ammann, a Swiss of the Benedictine Order in Nganda in Tanganyika, to C. B. Freeston, the acting Governor there, on the grounds that Sir Mark in his previous appointment as Governor of Tanganyika (now Tanzania) had allowed the enemy nationals, 600 in number, to remain at their Mission stations instead of being removed for internment or deportation. The Vatican cannot make war or peace, but it can and does influence, and there were at least 100,000 Roman Catholics in Japan.[5]

Bishop Ammann wrote to Cardinal Hinsley, the Archbishop of Westminster: 'Kindly ask the Holy Father to exercise his influence with the Japanese Government to set free Sir Mark Young, as he acted so generously towards the German and Italian missionaries, disregarding all opposition of some people.'

However the Colonial Office felt that: 'Much as we would like to see Sir Mark safely back, we feel that to make an exception in the case of the Governor of Hong Kong, especially in view of the deplorable treatment of our prisoners there, would arouse a storm of indignation in Britain, nor should we be justified in asking for special consideration for him . . . We would deprecate special treatment being afforded to any individual, however distinguished.'[6] It had already caused some indignation that the Governor of Singapore had been permitted to send a telegram to his daughter after the fall of that Colony, and the Colonial Office did not want to be accused of 'only concerning ourselves with people in high official places. The present state of tension and anxiety in this country would quickly express itself in criticism of this kind.'

Bishop Ammann's proposal was eventually forwarded from London to the Vatican with an accompanying note which said that the British Government would deprecate affording special treatment to anyone. The proposal was then dropped and no doubt Sir Mark would have agreed with the Colonial Office, for at no time was he prepared to accept the smallest of privileges which were denied to the humblest in the prisoners' camps.

A few exchanges continued to occur of British and Japanese who had been captured at the outbreak of war. Under these arrangements in August 1942, a Naval officer, Lieutenant-Commander C. S. Sheppard, was repatriated from Woosung. His report, which was forwarded to Churchill, stated that Sir Mark was robust and cheerful, although he had received no mail. 'He keeps his end up rigidly with the Japanese, refusing to accept benefits or favours, and he has as few dealings with them as possible.'[7] Lieutenant-Commander Sheppard also reported that the *Japan Times* article, which said that the Governor was 'dumbfounded' at Eden's allegations of atrocities in Hong Kong, was completely untrue; the Governor had never commented on Eden's statement.

Private Waller continued to serve Sir Mark. The Governor frequently strolled alone round Woosung Camp for exercise and all the prisoners treated him with great respect. In the evening he and Waller occasionally played chess, and they became great friends for life. They never discussed the battle for Hong Kong. Later, in different camps when Sir Mark occasionally became too weak and sick to walk, Waller looked after him as a brother.

The Americans worked outside the camp in fields where marijuana grew. Some Marines started to smoke it and so their officers persuaded the Japanese to have the plants destroyed.

In September, Sir Mark and Private Waller were flown to

Formosa. On arrival they set off at night for Karenko POW camp to join the other POWs. 'We had to walk through the streets which were lit by flares, while the locals jeered at us,' Waller remembers. 'Sir Mark's suitcase was too heavy to carry, and when I dropped it a corporal screamed and screamed unintelligibly at me, before pausing, and then saying inquisitively in perfect English: "Do you speak Nippon?"'

Sir Mark Young, General Maltby and the other prisoners from Hong Kong found it very interesting to listen to accounts of the fall of Singapore from the officers who had fought there. They were shocked to hear of what they were told of the sudden collapse of morale in Singapore, widely attributed to the lack of confidence in local leadership, and of sullen, armed deserters who had been seen forcing their way on to ships which were evacuating women and children. By contrast there had been no collapse of morale in Hong Kong.

The resistance in Singapore lasted no longer than in Hong Kong, although Singapore had a higher proportion of defenders to Japanese. Some units had fought well while at least two others had melted away. The commanding officers of these two claimed that during the battle they could scarcely lay their hands on a hundred men and yet they assembled almost 800 in captivity, having received few casualties.

It is not, however, fair to place all the blame for this remarkable collapse in morale upon the service and civilian leaders for having failed to inspire confidence. If blame has to be apportioned some must be placed upon the poor quality of some regimental officers. In the easy-going pre-war days most units, both regular and territorial, had some who were not truly battle-worthy. This was not apparent in the fighting which led to the retreat to Dunkirk because the orders were that no infantry company should go into battle with more than three officers, instead of the normal five, which allowed battalion commanders to be selective. It was not until the last two years of the war that almost all the misfits had been weeded-out. There is a well-known military maxim: 'There are no bad regiments, but only bad officers,' with which every experienced soldier can only be in total agreement.

The prisoners of war in Singapore were gathered on the Changi peninsula to the east of the island. Shortly after their arrival, a Japanese Lieutenant on a bicycle delivered a message which said that the POWs were to construct barbed wire around each unit and around the outer perimeter. The Japanese were quick to use disaffected Indians to guard the POWs. The Indians were much more aggressive than those in Hong Kong, and insisted on being saluted. Some British officers were so disgusted by these turncoats that they never left their compounds except to visit the wounded who were suffering terribly. An officer on a bicycle was almost the only Japanese individual that most POWs saw.

Vegetables such as sweet potatoes grew quickly in the warm climate in Singapore's POW camp at Changi. Huts were built and roofed with branches of palm trees. More important, a concealed wireless enabled the POWs to receive world news.

An increasing number of POWs were sent from Singapore through Malaya to an unknown destination. They cheered and waved as they departed and were envied by those left in Changi. It was not known they were to be used as slave labour and live in appalling conditions, building the notorious railway in Siam (now Thailand). Beautiful cemeteries of the Commonwealth War Graves Commission today indicate the large numbers who died. Nearby, close to the River Kwai, and the railway which leads to nowhere, the Japanese have recently put up a memorial in memory of those they killed so brutally. This is in a small, dusty, ill-kept enclosure, but it testifies to the friendly contacts between Japan and the western world today.

The POWs in Changi were left entirely on their own, and each senior officer remained fully in command of his men. Military discipline was enforced by each formation. Some courts-martial took place and miscreants were locked in unit guardrooms. The irony of being in a prison within a prison was brought home to some officers in unusual circumstances.

Eton College had been founded by Henry VI on 4 June 1440, and his birthday is traditionally celebrated by Old Etonian reunions all over the world on the Fourth of June. Major-General M. B. Beckwith-Smith, formerly of the Welsh Guards, discovered that he had thirty Old Etonians in the camp and decided to organise a party on 4 June 1942, in Changi. A deserted patch of scrub and palm was chosen; cooks produced a large variety of rice dishes and a doctor made a very intoxicating rice fermentation. The Old Etonians gathered as dusk was falling and a roll was called, but only twenty-nine answered their names. Where was number thirty? Consternation reigned. At last somebody remembered that he was a private soldier who had committed some minor misdemeanour and was locked in the guardroom!

For the following three months little occurred to break the unmitigating boredom. More POWs were packed into trains to be sent to Siam, and they continued to be seen off with envious cheers.

In September 1942, six months after the surrender, the senior officers and Government officials were assembled to be moved to Formosa. Generals Percival and Beckwith-Smith were driven from Changi and their men lined the road cheering and waving.

After medical inspections they were squeezed like sardines into a small ship's hold where they lay in three tier bunks. The ship was particularly crowded because a battalion of the Loyal Regiment had been included to make up the numbers. Ventilation was inadequate and because of the extreme heat few wore clothes. The prisoners on the top bunks lay three feet from the ship's bulkhead which dropped scorching hot moisture on to them. They were allowed on deck for twenty minutes each day where they were given a mug of tepid water to drink, wash, shave, or clean their teeth, which raised an interesting problem of priorities. The voyage lasted two weeks, during which time dysentery broke out and thirteen prisoners died.

Those from Singapore were disembarked in Formosa where they were sent to five different POW camps – the most senior going to Karenko. There they were joined by Americans, Dutch, and British. Formosa has an ideal climate which is never extreme. Apart from heavy showers, the sun shone daily and there were exquisite sunrises and sunsets.

The Japanese imposed extremely harsh discipline at Karenko. It was enforced by brutal beatings for the most trivial offences, and often for no reason at all. General Percival was severely beaten on the allegation that he had a speck of dirt under one of his fingernails,[8] and Sir Lewis Heath was so badly beaten that a blood vessel in one eye was ruptured.

Compliments had to be paid to all Japanese private soldiers and a favourite Japanese sport was to hide at night in the bushes on the route from the sleeping quarters to the latrines. If a prisoner passed any of the hidden sentries without saluting and bowing he was at once beaten.

Everything was done in Karenko to humiliate the officers and senior officials. Sir Mark Young and eleven of the oldest or most senior prisoners were employed as goat herds. If the goats strayed, and it was almost impossible to prevent them doing so, the goatherds were beaten.

Such was the craving for food that, after it had rained, many prisoners searched the ground for the large snails which were tough muscle and tasted horrible, but those who found the snails considered themselves lucky and wolfed them down. Most prisoners became increasingly weaker, and it was a pathetic sight to see them crawl up the steps to their huts. However the rice diet was said to have cured one Brigadier's duodenal ulcer which he had ascribed to a prolonged period of duty in the War Office!

On 9 November 1942, General Beckwith-Smith fell ill and the following evening he had great difficulty in breathing. A Japanese surgeon operated on him promptly, but the strain following diphtheria had been too great and he died of heart failure. It was a short illness and he was well looked-after by Colonel Bennett, RAMC. Brigadier E. H. W.

Backhouse wrote to the General's widow telling her that all the prisoners had assembled while the dignified and simple burial service was read. 'Throughout, the Japanese authorities have been most helpful,' he informed her, 'their officers have personally expressed to me their appreciation of "Becky's" character and personality.'[9] This report, which may have been intended to comfort the widow, conflicts with others to the effect that he was seriously ill for five days before the Japanese would treat him.

Beckwith-Smith's body was partly cremated near the sea. Afterwards his batman, using chopsticks, put the General's bones and ashes in an urn, a task which he found so gruesome that he fainted. For a time the much-loved General's death outweighed all other troubles. His Divisional Headquarters staff was transferred from Singapore to Siam where over half met their deaths through Japanese neglect.

At Shirakawa Camp in Formosa, where most of the senior officers from Hong Kong were imprisoned, at least one senior officer had grudging admiration for the remarkable discipline of their guards. 'The sentries were on duty for three hours at a time and were never once visited by an officer or NCO, yet they were always completely alert,' he recalls. 'When relieved they lay down on the floor of their hut and slept. They always ate sitting stiffly erect, after which they sat without speech or book. Their recreation consisted largely of dummy bayonet fighting. For half an hour they would thrust, lunge and make fearsome noises. As the Japanese guards had no canteens, music or wireless, their one and only relaxation appeared to be the weekly parade to the local brothel. Their wrong-doers received the same form of punishment as ourselves, for we were classed as third-class Japanese private soldiers. The Japanese sergeant at the gate would knock to the ground any of his men who returned from town drunk, and when the soldier got up, he would receive a second good punch. After the third the punishment was complete and the incident was closed. Just three biffs and all was over. Once this was understood one can see that our similar treatment was fully in accordance with the rules from Tokyo.'[10]

The Japanese continued to be totally unpredictable. '"Fall in anyone who has teeth trouble" we were told one day at Karenko,' remembers Brigadier T. Massy-Beresford, DSO, MC, who had commanded a brigade at Singapore. 'Having lost my false teeth on board ship, I fell in. We were marched to a dentist's surgery in a nice, clean little village. While waiting my turn for treatment, I was ushered through a paper door to find the pretty, smiling dentist's wife sitting on the floor preparing tea for me. I was invited to sit down and she served me. When the lady's back was turned, I filled my pockets with delicious biscuits which I shared with my friends in camp. Alas! this memorable outing was never repeated; inadequate, clumsy tools were given instead to our own dentist.'

One day the officers were ordered to work in the fields. Some generals protested. 'If you don't work, you don't eat,' they were told. 'I personally thoroughly enjoyed the new scenery and opportunity to sally forth from the camp for two or three hours a day,' noted Brigadier Wallis. 'We filed out of the camp accompanied by one or two sentries with fixed bayonets. We were a motley sight in our tattered shorts and shirts, and most of us wore conical-shaped bamboo hats against the sun. On our first day we were supposed to thin out long rows of green seedlings, leaving the strongest plants standing at nine inch intervals. We deliberately hoed up the lot and the sentries went almost mad. We claimed we didn't know a young turnip from a weed. After prodding with bayonets, face slapping and a Japanese demonstration, we did it properly.'

In March 1943, a vast amount of Red Cross supplies from South Africa reached the VIPs at Karenko Camp. 'It was a sheer miracle, and we knew that we were about to be saved from death by an avalanche of canned beef and other blessings,' wrote General Wainwright in 1945. 'It was too good to be true, and that was just about the case. The Japs told us that they would distribute this golden harvest "later" which was more numbing than any beating we had ever taken.'[11] However some tins were eventually given to the POWs.

One day without any warning all officers at Karenko down to the rank of Brigadier were ordered to pack immediately. For the British, captured in Hong Kong and Singapore, this took only a few minutes for they had virtually no possessions, but some Americans who had earlier been living in houses in the Philippines had trunks, suitcases and even hat boxes. The Japanese carted all this baggage around the Island issuing receipts for each item at every camp, but all this luggage was later lost at sea when the Japanese ship upon which it was being carried was torpedoed. The seventy most senior officers left in open trucks on a tiny light railway which meandered through beautiful scenery to another small picturesque camp called Tamasata in Formosa. The living quarters were an improvement on Karenko, but the food was much worse.

One day the Camp Commandant and his staff hastily erected a canteen and put on display what looked like the contents of Red Cross parcels. A special meal of fish, potatoes and fruit was served. The prisoners were contemplating these strange events when a Swiss Colonel named Paravicini arrived in camp, representing the International Red Cross. After his departure the Japanese hastily dismantled the canteen. However it achieved its purpose for Paravicini reported to Geneva that he had 'on the whole a favourable impression'.

The following day those prisoners who were below the rank of Major-General were separated from the VIPs and joined other POWs in Shirakawa. The only 'news' in their camp came from a Japanese propaganda newspaper which revealed nothing of significance on how the Pacific war was progressing. However it was possible to learn that the Germans were moving victoriously westwards in North Africa, which could only mean that Montgomery had broken through at El Alamein and was advancing upon Tripoli. The newspaper reported one remarkable feat of arms; a Japanese pilot, after sinking American warships, was not satisfied as one ship was still afloat and he had no bombs left. The pilot therefore drew his sword, the newspaper reported, and while flying low over the ship's bridge, he leant out and cut off the Captain's head, for which action he received a high decoration.

The most important news reached the prisoners in Shirakawa by accident. An interpreter announced that the POWs could write a short letter to their families. One American asked if his could be sent to his wife in Paris. 'No you can't,' the interpreter angrily replied, 'anyway she is in bed with an American soldier there.' Within minutes the entire camp knew that the long-awaited invasion of France had been successful and the allies were in Paris.

Even so, some prisoners believed the enemy's propaganda that the Japanese people would fight for a hundred years, and those few who took this news seriously lost interest in the progress of the war. The Japanese gave their version of events by parading everyone frequently, and then displaying three large boards, the first of which was headed 'Enemy ships SUNK'. Beneath this heading was a long list of aircraft carriers, battleships and cruisers. The second board was headed 'Enemy ships SUNK DOWN' with a similar list almost as long. The third board was headed 'Enemy ships THUNDER SUNK' which accounted for the remainder of the fleets. The prisoners found these parades fairly hilarious.

At Shirakawa senior Japanese officers occasionally came to stare at the prisoners who felt like monkeys in a zoo. 'They did not offer us buns or nuts,' recalls one POW, 'but an Admiral sometimes brought us a fat pig although it did not go far particularly as our guards liked pork, too. Each of us ended up with a piece the size of a fingernail which floated on the greasy surface of the water and leaves in our bowls.'

Some prisoners were moved around to other camps in Formosa. One explanation for these changes is that the Japanese expected an American attack, and they believed that General MacArthur's remark: 'I shall return,' referred to Formosa rather than to the Philippines.

By early October 1944, the Japanese decided to move to Japan the more senior officers and all the Governors,

Generals and Chief Justices, for by now the Americans had landed in the Philippines. Everyone was bundled into lorries, and as darkness fell the prisoners were taken to an airfield where they slept beneath the aircraft. So they left Formosa where they had been better treated than the thousands who were suffering in Japan, Siam, Singapore and Hong Kong. They had not been subjected to the same brutality, and their chief complaints were starvation and humiliation.

When the aircraft landed in Japan, the first to get off was a seventy-year-old retired Dutch General, H. D. de Fremery, who had lived in a Tokyo hotel before the war. The General immediately came face to face with a former friend, a Japanese interpreter who had been a waiter at the hotel. 'How are you, Sir? I am so glad to see you,' said the interpreter with lots of smiles, before suddenly remembering that Japan was at war and that he was now dealing with a disgraced prisoner. The smile was rapidly replaced by a wooden, bullying expression, and the General received only gruff grunts thereafter.

The prisoners were marched to an airport canteen where neat little waitresses in smart uniforms served a delicious meal, after which they were moved in a comfortable train to the pleasant seaside resort, Bappu. They saw three aircraft carriers at anchor in the bay. The prisoners spent several delightful days in small tourist hotels where the servants were friendly and often served second helpings. 'Another boon,' recalls Brigadier Massy-Beresford, 'was that we were able to indulge in hot sulphur baths which were about twenty feet wide and five feet deep. We were startled when the hotel girls jumped in and rubbed us down. The Americans started a rumour that we were destined for a luxurious villa where we could live comfortably under parole, walking around freely. However we were soon on a train speeding north once more. The rumours faded when we were crowded into a small overcrowded steamer which was in danger of capsizing. I won't try to define our despondency, as we lay in our denims on the decks splashed by spray. Thoughts of a luxurious villa were replaced by visions of some remote frozen camp where we would be neglected and forgotten.'

Visions turned into reality. After disembarking at Pusan in South Korea, they travelled north by train for three days and nights, arriving at a bleak western Manchurian village named Sheng Tai Tun, close to the Gobi desert. It was freezing cold and the prisoners' teeth clattered like castanets. In November 400 more officers joined them from Formosa.

Morale was raised by an issue of Red Cross parcels. A Japanese sentry was bribed by an American Colonel with such gifts as a wristwatch or fountain pen to borrow three newspapers from the camp commander's office for half an hour each day. The prisoners thus learnt that the allies had advanced to the Rhine and that Japan was being bombed by B-29s. Nobody knew what a B-29 looked like, but the fact that Japan was at last suffering gave the greatest joy to the prisoners.

On 20 May 1945, they were moved to a new prison camp near Mukden in Manchuria which the Japanese had apparently built on the presumption that the prisoners would remain working there for many years. 'If you obey all the camp rules for the next ten or twenty years, your relatives in America will be permitted to visit you,' the prisoners were told on arrival.

Some POWs already in Mukden had arrived there in 1942 to work in a brand-new factory which only needed the concrete floor laying. The Japanese collected about a thousand mainly American well-qualified electricians, mechanics and machinists from the POW camps throughout the Far East. On arrival they were told that they were to build aircraft after they had laid the concrete floor. The POWs were determined to sabotage the work, and so they started by deciding which small parts of the machinery were vital and could not be replaced by local stocks or manufactured nearby. Most of the machines had been made in America before the war and some parts were irreplaceable. When the concrete was ready for pouring these vital parts were thrown on the ground and covered over. Large holes in the uneven ground were filled with complete lathes and presses. By the time the floor was completed, the Japanese discovered that no machine in the entire factory could be operated.

A Japanese officer, a graduate of the University of California, arrived from Tokyo to investigate the sabotage, but he could not discover if Manchurians, Koreans or Americans were responsible for the damage, the Manchurians having moved the machinery to the new factory and North Koreans had assembled it.

The factory was useless for aircraft production and replacement machinery was not available, so it was gradually converted to manufacture presses for stamping out sections of the fuselage of aircraft. This conversion was completed by the summer of 1943 so then the POWs faced the problem of how to sabotage everything anew. They were given blueprints for the manufacture and assembly of the presses. Each set of blueprints already had at least one pencilled correction. The POWs started by tracing the corrections made on each set of blueprints. Carefully selected POWs then practised imitating the writing in which the corrections had been written. Others determined the crucial changes necessary to the blueprints which would prevent not only the press from operating but would also cause sufficient shorts, stresses and strains to ruin the entire machine. When the men were sufficiently expert at forgery, each set of blueprints was altered. When the machines failed to operate, the Japanese ranted and raved but they could spot no discrepancies between their blueprints and the completed work. Eventually they resigned themselves to complete failure. During the following two-and-a-half years, this factory which employed 1000 American, British, Dutch and Australian POWs, 1000 Manchurians, 1000 Koreans and 200 Japanese had turned out only one press.

Life was hard at Mukden and about 200 Americans died there during the first winter. By the time the senior officers had joined the survivors of that first winter, more news of the war was being received because again a guard had been bribed to provide small newspaper cuttings which were smuggled into the camp in the hollow heel of a POW's boot. The prisoners thus learnt that the invasion of Japan was imminent.

In early August 1945, all the POWs were seriously alarmed to hear that orders had been given to the cooks to prepare haversack rations. 'This meant an imminent move to some remote encampment,' recalls one POW. 'None of us could have marched more than a mile, and we knew that thousands of Americans had perished on Japanese forced marches in the Philippines. Intense uncertainty descended upon us.'[12]

The Governors, Chief Justices and the ten senior Generals had already been moved with sixteen batmen on 1 December 1944, to a camp near the small Manchurian village of Sian, about 150 miles north-east of Mukden. The allies were never to discover the location of this camp until the last days of the war.

Meanwhile, both the Russians in Siberia and General Chennault in Chungking were finalising their plans to rescue the prisoners in Mukden before they were slaughtered by the Japanese.

We will return later to these POWs in Manchuria.

The first draft of 616 POWs left Hong Kong for Japan on 3 September 1942, and the second sailed on the ill-fated *Lisbon Maru* three weeks later. A further 2000 POWs, including 1184 Canadians, were sent from Hong Kong in 1943.

The Japanese split up the British, American, Australian, Dutch and Canadian prisoners in Japan among about 120 camps. These were placed close to shipyards, docks, mines, quarries and factories in which the POWs worked. There were 250 more POW camps in Burma, Malaya, Borneo, the Dutch East Indies, Singapore, Thailand, Indo-China, the Philippines and Hong Kong. The numbers in the camps in Japan varied from a hundred to several thousand POWs who were often in requisitioned factories, converted warehouses, or sheds. All were surrounded by a wall or fence which was usually electrified.

Conditions in the camps differed considerably. Some POWs were treated as slave labour, working in semi-darkness in mines where there was a constant danger of being entombed by landslides. Others who worked at the docks suffered less partly due to their ingenuity in stealing food. The prisoners became increasingly vulnerable to American bombing raids, and some prisoners were near both Hiroshima and Nagasaki where the atom bombs were to be dropped. The prisoners left in Hong Kong were relatively fortunate, and a higher proportion of them survived.

Captain A. J. N. Warrack, the former Medical Officer of the Royal Scots, vividly remembers his arrival at Nagasaki in May 1944: 'Two hundred dirty and thin POWs disembarked from the ship's overcrowded and insanitary hold in which we had been sealed like sardines for all but ten minutes each evening. We were greeted by a posse of white gowned and masked figures wearing hygienic pads over their faces. Some carried cylinders on their backs or stirrup pumps containing disinfectant. As we walked down the gangway, this reception committee solemnly and literally soaked us with a grey antiseptic fluid. We were then directed to a long counter where we laid our meagre possessions. A Japanese gentleman in blue uniform, sailor's hat and sword, then told us that it was illegal to bring cameras, silk stockings or alcohol into Japan, none of which of course was in our possession, and that failure to declare such articles might lead to a heavy fine and even confiscation. We were next herded into an ordinary passenger train and told that we would arrive in Tokyo at 4.35 p.m. on the following day. We arrived dead on time despite being in the middle of a war.

'We were sent to a POW hospital at Shinagawa on the outskirts of Tokyo, which had been built on swampy land for Korean labourers. The huts were divided into small rooms each of which had a raised platform of thick straw mats or "tatami". On these mats we ate, slept, talked, wept, and some died until the end of the war. Roll call, known as "Tenko", was held at 5.30 a.m. I was woken the morning after our arrival by cursing, and the sentry shouting "switch on light". I was horrified to see on my chest what looked like half a cupful of strawberry jam which at once disintegrated into thousands of fleas. On our first morning we paraded outside an administrative office and waited for the appearance of a Japanese Infantry Major who was a stickler for military etiquette. Suddenly Hari, the interpreter, shouted "Kyotsky, Karaya" ("Attention, Salute") as the bleary-eyed Major emerged wearing the most beautifully shiny field boots, although his breeches were almost down to his knees. Above his waist he was wearing only a singlet. The Major, who was clearly suffering from one of his more Imperial hangovers, winced, snarled at Hari and lurched back into his quarters. "The Major is very cross," announced Hari, "he had only come out go to the benjo [latrine], and wasn't ready to be saluted." Hari often stood on a heap of rubbish like a cock on a farmyard dung heap, lecturing us on the great benefits which would accrue to both our nations when we traded together after the war.'[1]

In Hong Kong the prisoners had done their own cooking, prescribed their own medicines, such as they were, and exercised their own discipline, whereas in Japan they were under the direct control of their 'hosts' – their overall guardian being, as they were frequently reminded, the Emperor.

Although there was a reasonable supply of Red Cross medicines at Shinagawa, there were many cases of deficiency diseases. The sick arrived by train, truck, a motor bicycle's side-car and, on one occasion only, by ambulance. They were a sad sight – weary, disillusioned men, usually so weak that they were unable to stand. Some had cirrhosis of the liver, tuberculosis or chronic beri-beri. Three hundred cases of amoebic dysentery were treated, but there was confusion over the precise number of patients, for there was a flourishing 'trade' in the camp. Those with the illness gave their positive stool in exchange for two cigarettes to others who wanted to postpone their return to a camp where they would have to work. As in Hong Kong there were many cases of paralysis or 'electric feet'. The unfortunate men in some camps spent hours with their feet in cold water which later sometimes necessitated amputation, and the description of their symptoms was heartrending. More than one man committed suicide.

Sanitation in the camp was the responsibility of the Italian Naval Attaché, Captain Pirelli, who arranged for the emptying of the latrines weekly. He was a cultivated and amusing officer whose sympathies lay with the allies at least after Italy's collapse, whereas his secretary, a Pay-Master Lieutenant-Commander, still supported Mussolini. The half-dozen Italian seamen did not know which side to back. The Italians shared a small hut and accepted philosophically the menial tasks allotted to them by the British. Many were very likeable, and generously shared with the prisoners what they had brought into the camp.

The Japanese at Shinagawa took Christmas seriously. They arranged a compulsory church service under Roman Catholic auspices, and a small sum was deducted from the minute prisoners' pay to defray the cost. Colonel Sugi, the

Commandant of all POW camps in North Japan, attended the service. He was an elderly, rather distinguished man, and he arrived in a large, imposing car amidst a flurry of salutes from the Japanese. After the service, the Colonel addressed the prisoners at length. 'Both His Imperial Majesty and the Colonel hope you are well, and they think of you all the time,' translated the interpreter. One POW remembers that: 'We were then instructed to march up to Colonel Sugi individually to receive our Imperial gifts. Breathless with excitement, we each found ourselves in receipt of one packet of toilet paper.'[2]

The Japanese had a special enclosure at Shinagawa in which shot-down American airmen were imprisoned. Gunner Mansfield broke into a storeroom, stole some food and then dug a hole under the fence to reach the Americans. He was caught giving them food and almost beaten to death before being tied to a post for over a day.

Some of the POWs in Shinagawa believed that there was an informer in the camp who was passing information to the Japanese, for the enemy had an uncanny knowledge of what was happening in the huts. (The suspect, who was a well-educated British soldier, is now dead.)

Conditions in Aomi camp were little different from those at Shinagawa. At Aomi, which was in the north of Japan, 59 of the 300 POWs died in the first year. The camp had no chaplain, and it fell upon a young officer who had been serving in Singapore in 11 Indian Division to take care of the spiritual needs of the prisoners. The officer, J. P. Burrough, now the Anglican Bishop of Mashonaland, remembers that: 'I suppose I buried more men as a layman than I did during my years in the ordained ministry! The dead were roughly cremated in a kind of brick kiln and the Japanese placed the ashes in small wooden boxes in the sick bay which did nothing to encourage our many sick. But one day the local Buddhist Abbot astonished me by offering to give sanctuary to our ashes. They were reverently placed in his monastery, and after the war I took the ashes to the War Graves Commission in Japan. They are now interred in a beautiful cemetery at Yokohama.' Several urns in other POW camps held the mixed ashes of many allied POWs. These are now at Hodogaya Cemetery and at Jefferson Barracks, Missouri. After the war Japan gave Britain a twenty-five acre plot at Hodogaya for a Commonwealth War Cemetery, which has a beautiful, landscaped memorial park. It contains the dead from Britain, Australia, Canada, India and New Zealand. They fought, suffered and died together, and now they rest together. Japanese frequently visit the cemetery.

One such visitor may have been the little Japanese pastor of the Presbyterian Church who, in swallow-tail coat and striped trousers, arrived in 1943 and conducted a Church of England Communion Service in Aomi camp. 'What the Almighty made of that He alone could decide!' remembers the Bishop of Mashonaland.

'A number of us noticed what appeared to be a wooden cross standing on a distant hillside. Winter came with immensely heavy snowstorms, and the cross disappeared. Most of the prisoners used to look out for the cross anxiously, saying: "As long as it remains on the hillside we are going to be all right." I suppose this was a kind of superstition, but a use of symbolism can frequently be found in Christian circles. When the snow melted, the cross was there, and after the surrender my batman and I, neither of whom were in good physical shape, made an expedition across the hills. In fact it was just a blasted tree which, close at hand, had no appearance of a cross. I brought a small piece of it back with me to England. The Christian faith was something of immeasurable value to men in all the camps in which I lived during the Second World War.'[3]

Corporal H. F. Linge, of the Royal Army Ordnance Corps, captured in Hong Kong, was moved by rail in Japan to Amagasake, near Osaka. At one station he remembers the strange sight of Japanese women and children dressed in brightly coloured kimonos and wooden clogs, watching the prisoners. They showed no sign of animosity although they had been ordered off a train by the guards who had commandeered it.

Linge worked on breaking up pig-iron which was then carried by crane into a furnace. 'It was here that I first experienced the utter despair of total physical exhaustion for eleven hours each day,' he wrote later. 'The work was very heavy indeed. Our Japanese guards in the factory were often former wrestlers, and a Japanese named Verasaki was in charge of us. We respected him as a good man, without rancour or animosity towards us. On one occasion a Japanese who hated POWs refused to allow the prisoners a break. Verasaki and the Japanese came to blows after a violent argument over this. Verasaki won the day, and the POWs had their well-earned break. Not all the Japanese were cruel and unjust. Indeed, I found some to be fair-minded, and as friendly as they dared.'

The exhausting work took its toll on Linge and his weight fell alarmingly. Fortunately a friendly Japanese moved him to a machine shop which made large piston rings. 'I knew nothing whatever about lathes and machines of this kind, but all that was needed was a confident manner which assured passing Japanese that one was fully in command of the situation. During the eighteen months that I worked there, I never turned out anything really useful. My transfer to the machine shop enabled me to survive the war. However, I suffered from malnutrition sores, and the camp medical orderly would squeeze each day about an egg-cupful of pus from one sore on my shoulder. The camp doctor, Surgeon Commander J. A. Page, RNVR, was very able, but badly handicapped by lack of medicines. Some sick were treated locally by acupuncture.'[4]

The Japanese at Nagasaki camp had an effective way of ensuring that an adequate number of POWs was always available for work. Those who were too sick to work received no food; the more sick therefore, the smaller was the allocation of food to the camp. This daily fluctuation in the amount of rations complicated their distribution, and such was the importance of food to the semi-starved prisoners that there was, for example, a roster which determined who should be served soup from the top of the bucket, or from the bottom where a little vegetable matter might rest. The roster also indicated who should receive soup when the ladle was dipped in against the direction of the stir, as opposed to in the same direction. Checkers watched the servers to ensure that the distribution was scrupulously fair. As the shortage of food increased, the Japanese in the factory were themselves reduced to drawing lots for a small piece of fish or a single potato.

Linge was later moved to Takaoka, a small camp in the north-west of Japan, in which there were 1510 Americans who had been captured in the Philippines in 1942. American morale was very low indeed, partly because they had received no news on the progress of the war since their surrender. The British and Americans became great friends, as was the case in other camps. The American POWs had received the full venom of their captors after the US defeats. Of the 26,943 Americans captured then 37% died in captivity.

At Takaoka, Linge made carbons for electrical furnaces. This involved carrying very heavy cans of graphite to a vast vat where the prisoners had to stir a black, obnoxious smelling mass. Such work was damaging to the lungs because of the dust which was inhaled.

CSM E. J. Soden of the Middlesex Regiment, who had survived the *Lisbon Maru* disaster, was ultimately more fortunate. He had been sent to Kobe near Osaka. 'The early days were sad ones as so many died through lack of proper medical treatment,' he remembers. 'We were all paraded in the park opposite our camp for the first funeral, and a proper coffin was provided. Later, when more died, their bodies were just squeezed into an apple barrel. I shall never forget the smell when these poor souls were kept just outside the camp hospital waiting to be collected for cremation. I still get a lump in my throat when I hear the song "Roll out the barrel".

'After a few months we were sent in groups of twenty to work in the docks. It was of paramount importance to steal food, particularly for the sick. When I was unloading from a cold-storage depot, one of the lads hid a large frozen fish between his legs; it was held in place by string. This caused much amusement among the guards who searched him. Feeling the fish they mistook it for his penis, shouting "Oki

Jimpo", meaning "big cock". On another occasion the prisoners at the docks noticed a Jap making a hot bran and oat mash for his horse. He left it to cook, and on his return found the container full of water. His perplexed bewilderment was watched at a discreet distance by the well-satisfied POWs.

'One day I was the leader of a party unloading boxes of oranges,' Soden continues. 'We found a way of removing a panel from one box, and as each man passed he took an orange, replacing it with a stone. If a Japanese approached, someone would shout "shop". However one morning a Jap guard crept round the back of the van, shouted "shop", and watched the panel being quickly replaced. The Jap then took me into the warehouse, and found another box with a loose panel which he pulled aside and explained in Japanese what had been happening, but I played dumb and just took two oranges saying "Arigato", (thank you), upon which he rushed me round to the latrine, telling me to eat them quickly.

'It was always our ambition to smuggle extra food into our camp at Kobe, especially as the officers and the sick received half rations as they did not work. If we were caught we were severely beaten and made to stand outside the guard room for hours.'[5]

While CSM Soden and half the survivors of the *Lisbon Maru* had been sent to Kobe, the other half went to Osaka nearby where dysentery, diphtheria and pneumonia killed many POWs.

Two of the heroes of the *Lisbon Maru* disaster had been Surgeon Lieutenant A. C. Jackson and Staff-Sergeant Ross, Royal Army Medical Corps. Both had managed to keep some of the sick together in the water and on being dragged on board the Japanese rescue ship Jackson operated on Able Seaman T. Eccleston whose leg had gangrene. Jackson only had a ten month old Gillette razor blade, and the wound had to be bound in Chinese newspapers found in the hold since the Japanese would provide no bandages. Nevertheless, Eccleston survived.[6]

Surgeon Lieutenant Jackson commanded the only POW

hospital, which was in the Osaka football stadium and was manned by a volunteer team of eleven Naval ratings and one Royal Marine. 'From October 1942, to July 1944,' reported Jackson to the Admiralty in 1945, 'I endeavoured, against orders, to maintain clinical notes to cover about 700 admissions and 202 deaths. In March 1944, however, my quarters were raided by Japanese officials who confiscated every scrap of paper and arrested my writer, G. H. Bignal, and myself. We were taken to the guard room of Osaka main camp, where we were interrogated all next day. As a result the hospital staff was broken up and the hospital was closed four months later. I was despatched to a "punishment" camp in Kameoka.'[7]

The POWs in Osaka worked in the docks and undertook coolie work in foundries and cement works. They had rather less opportunity to steal than those in Kobe, although on one memorable occasion a group of prisoners went to work in dirty rags and returned that evening in immaculate new uniforms which they had stolen from bales of clothing. Not a single guard appeared to notice that their appearance had changed so remarkably.

In January 1944, the British Camp at Osaka was combined with another which had contained 300 Americans. Also there were Indians in the Merchant Navy, and some Chinese. The Japanese appointed Company Sergeant-Major D. Matheson, Royal Scots, to command the prisoners, and officers were allowed no part in the administration. CSM Matheson ran the camp with courage, fortitude and integrity, in spite of great difficulties.

In Oeyama Camp, on the other hand, discipline had disintegrated despite the presence at one time of forty officers. Sergeant J. H. Harvey of the Royal Army Medical Corps reimposed it by introducing his own brand of violent order. He was short and burly, and had joined the army in 1931.

Sergeant Harvey ruled Oeyama Camp with three other senior Non-commissioned Officers who were feared and hated by some prisoners. Harvey had learnt Japanese and his position was recognised by the Camp Commandant who gave him special privileges. Harvey and his cronies were nicknamed 'The Big Four', and they harshly punished other prisoners. On one occasion, for example, Private U. Frieson of the Winnipeg Grenadiers had twice become hysterical and violent in the camp hospital, and Harvey hit him very hard indeed. The same thing happened a few hours later and Harvey again struck him heavily on the head. Frieson gradually became very quiet and died that evening.

Lance-Bombardier R. W. Hooper witnessed these beatings, and was later threatened with similar treatment. The Japanese had found soya bean paste in the kit of J. Podoski, a Canadian who worked in the cookhouse. Podoski was questioned by the Japanese who passed him over to 'The Big Four' for interrogation. Podoski, to avoid implicating his fellow Canadians, lied that Hooper had stolen the bean paste from the cookhouse and had given it to him. However Hooper denied the story so vehemently that Podoski broke down and admitted his guilt. Sergeant Harvey sentenced Podoski to forty lashes. 'The whole camp was paraded to witness the punishment,' wrote Hooper later. 'I was called upon to administer the sentence with a bamboo rod. I refused and so Sergeant Harvey beat Podoski instead.

'I spent a lot of time in the hospital with dysentery and beri-beri. The end room of the hospital building was set aside for the hopeless cases. On one occasion when I was in it, I miraculously survived, whereas all the other nine occupants were dead the next morning. Sergeant Harvey once got me extra food; there may have been another side to his character.' Harvey's behaviour was investigated after the war.

Gunner P. D. A. Chidell had served in Hong Kong with Hooper. During the fighting Chidell had only one opportunity of firing his rifle – and that was at a fifth columnist and, as he ruefully told his friends, he missed. Chidell had been sent to Nagoya POW camp near Toyama on the west coast of Japan in May 1943, where he worked in a factory making steam engines. 'You could hardly imagine a more cosmopolitan lot of POWs in our barrack room,' he wrote during his captivity. 'I have three French Canadians on one side of me, together with another Canadian born in America of Italian parents. On my other side I have a Yorkshire lorry driver, a Portuguese lad in the corner, three pleasant Cockneys from Middlesex, a Royal Engineer from Shanghai and two Royal Navy seamen. Some spend their spare time making up menus and planning big meals in London. Occasionally we eat the seaweed one sees on the sea-shore at low tide, as there is nothing else than rice. At Narumi they at least gave us grasshoppers which tasted delicious.

'The craving for cigarettes is really pathetic, and men will still sell their food for tobacco although they are already half-starved. I am ashamed to say that some men accept butt ends quite openly from the Japs, and even fight over any butts they find.'

Many of the 376 Canadians sent to Japan on 15 August 1943, were also sent to Nagoya Camp. They worked in mines, foundries, forests and factories without hope of repatriation or release since they could obtain no news of the war. Other Canadians were sent to work in coal mines near Okina camp. Company Sergeant-Major J. Ebdon worked there on night shifts and recorded in his 1944 diary their misery: 'We had eighteen who reported sick with cramps and diarrhoea, but they had to go down the mine just the same to fill trucks, drill and lay rails . . . Tonight had bad accident when the cable broke – four hurt. Bitterly cold, and snow flurries. Still soup and rice for all meals . . .'[8] At another coal mining camp near Ohama, undernourished Japanese miners turned out at midnight in November 1942, to carry the kit of the POWs who arrived to work there alongside them. The local doctor and dentist gave their services, and the villagers treated the POWs as guests. The senior British officer was to say of the camp's Commandant: 'He was the kindest man I have ever known.' Similar treatment was found in a few other small rural camps.[9]

At most camps the issue of mail was extremely infrequent, and few POWs received more than one letter a year. Red Cross parcels or visits from the International Red Cross were so rare that many POWs were unaware that the Red Cross existed. Discipline depended on the attitude of the Camp Commandant. At Camp 17 the Japanese displayed a regulation which read:

> It shall be forbid to plot to kill the Commandant
> (Penalty: Shoot-ted to death and life imprison).
> It shall be forbid to steal of Japanese Army.
> (Penalty: The heavy punish, life not assured).
> All prisoners shall take care of their health.

As 1944 dragged into 1945, life in the camps became tougher as food became scarcer, but morale was boosted by the air raids although many of the camps, particularly in the Tokyo area, were close to military targets.

Meanwhile, on 9 March 1945, the crews of 325 American bombers at Guam, an island in the Pacific, were told: 'You're going to deliver the biggest firecracker the Japanese have ever seen.' The B-29s' bomb-bays were filled with a total of 2000 tons of incendiary bombs. The aircrews received the orders with some apprehension as could only be expected with the knowledge that earlier crews shot down by the Japanese were tried for murder, found guilty and executed. Around Tokyo, the Japanese were reported to have 331 heavy-calibre guns, 307 automatic-firing weapons, 332 fighter aircraft and 105 twin-engined interceptors.

The American pathfinders arrived over Tokyo at midnight. The city was in darkness and the skies were clear of cloud. Flying down-wind, the pathfinders marked the target area with magnesium, napalm and phosphorus, placing their canisters in straight lines across wooden buildings and narrow streets.

Half-an-hour later the main American task force arrived over Tokyo. No fighters scrambled to meet them as the defences were caught totally unawares by the low-level assault. The B-29s began systematically to drop loads of canisters to fuel the growing inferno.

Staff-Sergeant J. Winspear was one of thousands of POWs who vividly recalls the holocaust that night. 'We had earlier watched a solitary B-29 high in the blue sky, and had guessed we would be raided. Night was falling as we trudged back to the camp from work. Suddenly we heard the scream of the air-raid sirens. When the bombing started, there were only a few explosions, but half an hour later we could see what looked like lights on a Christmas tree falling in hundreds of clusters. A dull glow appeared in the sky and a strong wind blew the flames towards us; we could even feel the heat, and it was as bright as day. We listened in our hut to the drone of the heavy bombers and the deep rumbling of the explosions. We waited for the next stick to hit us.'[10]

Fifteen thousand feet above Tokyo, a commentary was radioed back to Guam: 'It's spreading like a prairie fire . . . the blaze must be out of control . . . target completely alight. All Tokyo visible in glare. Total success.'[11] When the last B-29s withdrew after the three-hour raid, about 100,000 were dead and almost half a million more were injured, but not a single POW was hurt. Few US aircraft were lost. Although the raid destroyed 250,000 buildings in an area of about sixteen square miles, Winspear's camp was not destroyed by the spreading fire as it was surrounded by canals.

The following morning the prisoners saw the devastation: 'All the small Japanese houses had become a smouldering mass,' wrote Winspear. 'Their pitiful air-raid shelters were simply holes dug in the ground, covered by a few sheets of galvanised iron. While trying to clear away the damage, we lifted up one sheet and found an entire family crouched down and burnt to death. I called the sentry over and we moved them. The Japanese seemed stunned and made no effort to molest us. Apart from several sadistic guards, life became easier after this raid, probably because the enemy knew the war was lost.

'One day some of us were interviewed individually by English-speaking Jap civilians who were of a better education than any Japanese we had met previously. They asked us to describe our treatment, and implied that the Japanese had no alternative other than to treat us the way they had as the country had been in the hands of people whom decent citizens could not control. This was astounding, and it clearly showed that the war was almost over.'

American bombers devastated other cities, but the POW camps received few casualties due to luck rather than the accuracy of the bombing, although the approximate location of most POW camps was known.

Osaka was a frequent target and, by April 1945, over twenty per cent of the city was in ruins. The camp, which was close to the docks, was destroyed, but there were no POW deaths as the prisoners were out working when the raid took place.

R. J. Wright, a former company clerk in the Middlesex Regiment, later described the bombing at Kobe: 'On 5 June, incendiaries rained down on the camp. Several pierced our ceiling and fire broke out on our floor. The stairs were quickly aflame and the prisoners leaped down them. Outside there was widespread panic and chaos with the Jap staff rushing in all directions. A shelter holding five guards nearly received a direct hit and they came out screaming with their clothes ablaze. Women and children were also dying everywhere. I worked at the pumps with other prisoners, but the thin stream of water from the fire hose was useless and we watched Kobe Camp burn down. Chief Petty Officer Ray was still in the building as he had died the night before.'[12] Possibly at the demand of the Swiss Red Cross, the prisoners at Kobe were moved for greater safety to Maru Yama which was a temporary camp in the hills about five miles away. It had previously been occupied by Australians from Singapore. On the following day some volunteers returned to Kobe to evacuate the sick from Commander Page's hospital which had been severely hit during the bombing. Many patients had been killed. 'Commander Page was famous among the prisoners; countless stories were told of his courage, resourcefulness and devotion to those in his care,' recorded one POW. 'His Naval tunic was shabby, but it still conferred on him that dignity which is so much the hall-mark of the Naval Officer.'[13] The prisoners at Maru Yama and the sick from the hospital were later moved back to Kobe and housed in a school in the Wakayama district.

Ironically, the prisoners were better housed there than the Japanese, for the school was the only building which had survived.

Meanwhile, 7000 miles away in Washington, Brigadier L. R. Groves was deciding the appropriate target for the first use of the atom bomb. General G. C. Marshall, Chief of Staff, had made him responsible for advising on the choice of target in March 1945. The fate of thousands of prisoners depended on Groves's choice.

Kyoto, where there was no significant number of POWs, was not chosen as a target as the city was too historic and of religious importance to the Japanese. Nagasaki was provisionally selected instead. However General C. A. Spaatz, Commander of the Strategic Air Forces, reported that Hiroshima was the only one of four target cities that did not have allied prisoner of war camps, and so Hiroshima was chosen. Presumably the information on where the POWs were located came from Red Cross sources. The decision whether or not to use the atomic bomb to compel Japan to surrender was never in doubt. Churchill and Truman had agreed that it would require 'a miracle of sanity' on the part of Japan's leaders to accept the allies' terms of surrender and thereby prevent the weapon being dropped.

In Hiroshima there were twenty-three American prisoners, all of whom had been captured in recent months when their aircraft were shot down.

At 8.16 a.m., 6 August 1945, the atomic bomb was dropped on Hiroshima. Of the 80,000 Japanese instantly killed or mortally wounded, about one-third were soldiers. Two Americans were said to have been battered to death by their captors and a third was seen, apparently dying, under a bridge.

Two days later, Staff Sergeant J. Winspear, at Shinagawa near Tokyo, remembers seeing: 'A Jap foreman in the factory wearing a large piece of white cloth around his shoulders. He told us about some kind of strange bomb which had dropped somewhere, and that white clothing was some form of protection. The whole place was in a state of total chaos with the Japs running round like wet hens, and all work stopped. On 15 August we saw all the Jap soldiers in the camp gather around a wireless. Amidst a deep hush, we heard a strange voice speaking in such formal and oblique phrases that we could not understand a word. However some of the Japs began to bow and others wept openly. When Emperor Hirohito finished, the interpreter climbed on to a table in our hut and said: "Gentlemen, you are now free. The war is over."

'The prisoners sat in stunned disbelief; then some capered about, wild with joy, while others cried, staring at a treasured photograph of some loved one whom they never expected to see again. The news was overwhelming for Private Dunnell whose will power had sustained him to the end. On knowing that he was free, the emotion was too much and he collapsed and died. Eventually a lorry load of US paratroopers arrived and I met one at the gate. He was a walking arsenal, and the first words he drawled to us were: "OK, Bud, who do you want bumping off?" I replied that he could do what he wished for all I wanted was OUT.'

News of Japan's surrender did not reach the POWs in Nagoya until 22 August. Apart from better food and the distribution of Red Cross parcels, conditions changed little after the surrender and there was no news of the relieving forces until 29 August. 'There was tremendous excitement as American planes came over very low dropping by parachute supplies of excellent food, cigarettes, clothing and newspapers,' wrote Gunner Chiddell in his diary. 'Then we heard a terrible noise and saw a huge column of dust and smoke. We discovered that one aircraft had crashed, while trying to avoid a flagstaff, and killed the pilot which took all the gilt off the gingerbread. On 30 August, we took the plane's radio to try to get some news.

'One of our men named Mears in the Navy died of poison through drinking a mixture of pure alcohol and Castrol which he got off the smashed plane. To think that, having survived almost four years of imprisonment, he should come to such an end!'[14]

Doctor A. J. N. Warrack in the same camp remembers that 'the B-29 food drops were almost as frightening as actual bombs, and we had to dodge cases of bully beef, dropped without a parachute at 500 feet, careering through one wall of a hut and out of the other, scattering largesse as it went. We took to the shelters once more.' Several prisoners were killed in other camps when hit by crates dropped by aircraft.

The arrival of the American relieving forces came almost as an anti-climax for some of the 34,509 prisoners found in Japan. When most Japanese guards heard the Emperor's broadcast they quickly lost their arrogance and hostility.

Some POWs, after the arrival of the Americans, made up bundles of their old shoes, blankets and clothes and went into the countryside in search of the Japanese foremen who had befriended them on their work details. The POWs knew that some foremen had hated the military and monopolistic industrial machine. There was little animosity for the large Japanese companies, household names today, in which the POWs had worked, because they had sought to provide small extra items of food, although the Japanese army resented the inference that the military were not feeding the POWs properly. The ordinary Japanese citizens had shown no antagonism to the prisoners.

According to Admiral Mountbatten's principal Intelligence Officer, there was evidence that some Japanese guards might slaughter their prisoners. Therefore General Chennault in Chungking decided to drop small parachute teams near POW Camps in Manchuria and China as soon as possible after the surrender, in order to bring the prisoners immediate help.

The POWs in Mukden on 14 August had no doubts as to the dangers they faced when the Japanese warned them that a further move was imminent. However the order that haversack rations should be prepared was cancelled, which brought a greater sense of relief to many POWs than any other news during the previous three years.

Next day the Manchurian guards were seething with excitement, and Japanese vehicles could be heard grinding along the roads. The following afternoon POWs saw six American parachutists drop close to the camp. A Japanese unit quickly surrounded the Americans who frantically waved official documents at them. A Japanese officer snatched them away and the Americans were about to be shot when the officer saw from the papers that the Japanese had surrendered.

The POWs were herded away from the camp's gate as they saw 'a strange party of six being escorted into the camp' noted one POW. 'They had white faces, but were clad in queer camouflaged uniforms loaded with fighting equipment. They were hurriedly ushered into the Commandant's office.'

Speculation was intense and several prisoners crept up and peered through the window to see everyone drinking tea around a table. Major R. F. Lamar, an American doctor, was trying to convince the Camp Commandant that the Japanese were now prisoners of the Americans. The Commandant eventually sent for the senior officer of each country represented in camp, and told them that 'there is a temporary pause in hostilities – a sort of armistice.' He added that although they were now free, he would continue to keep his sentries on duty 'for our own safety as the Manchurians would otherwise cut our throats.' The keys of the stores were handed over, and thousands of Red Cross parcels, medicines and undelivered letters were found. Some soldiers dashed out and returned with a cart full of beer.

The heroes were undoubtedly the Americans who had flown from General Wedemeyer's Headquarters in China. Some of them had never parachuted before. The following day a Russian general addressed the allies in Mukden POW camp from a balcony and assured them that he had come all the way from Berlin to liberate them. However some POWs had more interest in the very attractive female staff officer who stood alongside him.

Russian troops arrived in the camp shortly afterwards, and within an hour they paraded the Japanese and made them pile their weapons and swords upon the barrack square. The Russians treated their enemy with humiliation and hostility. 'What I could not stomach,' wrote Brigadier Massy-Beresford later, 'was that the entire camp jeered the

Japanese. I felt that they had only been obeying orders, but my views made me very unpopular and some of my greatest friends would not talk to me for weeks.'[15] Brigadier Wallis noted that: 'A few small-minded men got much satisfaction, I suppose, in ordering Japanese officers to wait on them and even clean their boots.'[16]

The Russians closed down some factories which were then guarded by their soldiers. They looked tough and would talk to nobody.

A Russian female platoon commander was more forthcoming. 'The Russians arranged a dance in Mukden,' remembers an officer, 'and invited our soldiers. There were plenty of Russian servicewomen there, but the only way one could tell their sex was by their skirts, for they were as hideous and as wild as their menfolk. One of our allies was dancing with a Russian "Boadicea" who invited him to move to a secluded place for a spot of "necking". Apparently the necking was not nearly emotional enough to please her, and so she produced a pistol, cocked it, and pointed it below his stomach. The young man took the hint, almost the form of a "shotgun marriage".'[17]

American aircraft dropped supplies to Mukden by parachute and the sick and elderly were evacuated by Dakota. The remainder, including Brigadiers Massy-Beresford and Wallis, were taken by train to Darien where they were able to board two American hospital ships. They sailed to Okinawa and narrowly missed a typhoon. They eventually reached their homes months later by air and sea.

When the Americans arrived at Mukden, they discovered that the Japanese had moved Sir Mark Young, General Wainwright and the other Governors, Generals and Chief Justices to Sian, a small camp 150 miles to the north-east. Major Lamar and Corporal Leith thereupon requisitioned a vehicle and drove to Sian and made contact. Lamar then returned to Mukden to try to arrange with the Japanese authorities for a special train to collect the party. Corporal Leith who spoke Russian and Chinese remained at Sian.

Five days later, on 24 August, thirty Russians appeared at Sian. 'They were dirty and dishevelled,' noted General

Wainwright, 'but the most vigorously healthy soldiers I had seen in years. The Russian Colonel told us: "I'm going to Mukden. If you can provide your own transport and be ready in an hour, I will take you, too."'

The opportunity was too good to miss, and they all set off together. Six hours later Major Lamar arrived with the train, but he failed to find the party who had become completely lost due to inadequate Russian maps.

The British, American and Dutch ex-POWs travelled in three ancient vehicles which became bogged down in swampy ground and had to be dug out. The former prisoners were so weak from malnutrition that only four of them could dig.

The resourcefulness of the Russians surprised everyone. On reaching a large river where the bridge had been destroyed, the Russian colonel drove his jeep over a narrow railway bridge with his wheels straddling the rails. He reached the far side and persuaded everyone to follow him.

The leading vehicle later became so badly stuck in the mud that further progress was impossible. This misfortune took place close to a railway and so everyone waited for a train to appear. Eventually one did so, and the Japanese crew allowed the train to be boarded. They went a hundred yards towards Mukden and then the engine jumped the track. The Russians drove on to Mukden to get another train while everyone settled down for a long wait, during which Private Waller cut Sir Mark Young's hair. They all spent a miserable night in the freezing cold. A second train arrived the following afternoon and a Dutch sergeant, named Exman, who had worked on the railways before the war, drove it into Mukden at 1 a.m. on 27 August, tooting with excitement, his long black hair trailing in the wind. Their arrival greatly relieved Major Lamar who had been searching for them for the last three days.

Later that morning two aircraft flew the VIPs to Chungking. Generals Wainwright and Percival flew on to Yokohama to witness the formal surrender. On 2 September it was received by General MacArthur on board the battleship *Missouri* in Tokyo Bay.

By 1944-5 the news from Japanese newspapers alone made it obvious, even to those prisoners without hidden wireless sets, that the war would soon be won. Except possibly in a few remote camps such as those in Manchuria, it was common knowledge that the allies' landings in Europe had been successful, that in due course allied forces had reached the German frontier, and a few months afterwards that the Rhine had been crossed.

Yet there is no record that this knowledge was ever used by senior officers in any camp to blackmail the Japanese to provide an adequate food diet. It seems extraordinary that there was no confrontation with the most senior Japanese officers on the lines of: 'You must recognise that the war in Europe will soon be over after which the whole allied power will concentrate to smash Japan. Then all war criminals will be brought to justice. If you personally wish to escape this fate, you should immediately ameliorate our harsh conditions.' One can only attribute this remarkable lack of initiative to the debilitating effect of several years of semi-starvation.

The sudden surrender of Japan on 15 August came as a surprise to the British, judging by their inability to re-occupy Hong Kong promptly. In retrospect it seems extraordinary that the arrangements for the liberation of the Colony which would determine its future sovereignty were left void. That Japan would soon be forced to surrender by the dropping of the atomic bomb should have been known to the war cabinet. Yet no plans had been made for the immediate relief of Hong Kong by a British Naval unit. It is not as if the British Government had received no warning of Chinese ambitions to take over Hong Kong. For example on 10 February 1944, Doctor Li Shu-Fan met representatives of the Foreign Office and Colonial Office in London and they discussed the future status of Hong Kong.

Doctor Li Shu-Fan had earlier escaped from Hong Kong, after which he had stayed for four months with Doctor T. V. Soong, a Chinese Government Minister, and during that time he had frequently discussed Hong Kong's future with Chinese Ministers. Li Shu-Fan had told the British officials that the prevalent feeling in China was 'dominated by an intense sense of Nationalism. It was commonly considered that China was entitled to the rendition of Hong Kong. There was indeed an expectation that Great Britain would restore the territory to China as a mark of goodwill.'[1]

A year later, the British Embassy at Chungking warned the Foreign Office: 'There is no doubt that the Chinese after the war will do everything they can to get rid of the remaining foreign colonies on the coast and it is also within their powers, when they think the proper time has come, to make Hong Kong's position very difficult.'[2]

President Roosevelt had hoped that he could persuade the British Government to surrender Hong Kong to the

Chinese, who would then, he believed, turn it into an international free port. The President had apparently been concerned lest the Soviet Union should make use of Britain's presence in Hong Kong as an argument for obtaining a port of their own in China. However President Truman took a more cautious line on Hong Kong's future than had his predecessor, hoping merely that a solution could be found that would satisfy both China and Britain.[3]

When the Japanese surrender became imminent, Chiang Kai-shek emphatically claimed that Hong Kong was in the area in which Japanese forces were to surrender to him as Generalissimo of the China theatre. The British Government told him that the British territory of Hong Kong was not 'within China'. General MacArthur's General Order Number 1 had designated to the Chinese Allied authorities various areas in south-east Asia to whom the local Japanese Commanders were to surrender, but the Order had contained no reference to Hong Kong.

Judging by Chiang Kai-shek's lack of co-operation with the British, his army might get there first, in which case the loss of face to the British would be so great that they would have difficulty in regaining their Colony.

'It is our view,' signalled the Foreign Office to Chungking on 18 August, 'that, irrespective of operational theatres, wherever the sovereign power has sufficient forces available it should resume its authority and accept Japanese surrender in its own territory. Moreover, as a soldier, Chiang Kai-shek will understand that as we were forced to relinquish possession of Hong Kong to the Japanese it is a matter of military honour for us to accept the Japanese surrender there.' This argument was weakened by the fact that, on 18 August, Britain did not have 'sufficient forces' anywhere near Hong Kong. Colonel Ride's BAAG was the nearest British unit which might be able to send small, *ad hoc* groups to the colony, but little had gone well for them after many of their agents had been executed in Hong Kong in 1943, and only one POW, Lieutenant R. Goodwin, had escaped from the Colony since the autumn of 1942.

A planning body called the Civil Administration Unit,

had been set up to move to Hong Kong and run the Colony on its recapture, but the unit was still in London with little prospect of reaching Hong Kong quickly. It was commanded by Mr D. M. MacDougall who had escaped from Hong Kong in December 1941, with the Royal Navy MTB crews. The British Government decided that a message must be smuggled to Mr Gimson. It would tell him to assume the administration of the Hong Kong Government upon his release, although this would initially conflict with MacDougall's role.

The BAAG was told to deliver this message to Mr Gimson and, in the absence of other troops, to provide a token British presence in Hong Kong on the Japanese surrender. On 13 August 1945, the Foreign Office sent to the British Embassy in Chungking a second signal which BAAG was instructed to deliver to Mr Gimson. It read: 'We are endeavouring to secure consent of American Chiefs of Staff to detach British Naval force from British Pacific Fleet to steam for Hong Kong,' and that Gimson should hand over governing authority to the senior British Naval officer on his arrival.

Colonel Ride had these messages passed on to a Chinese agent in Macao who hoped to smuggle them to Gimson in Stanley Internment Camp. This link was uncertain of success as the Foreign Office had banned any contact with Stanley for almost the last two years, for fear of compromising official negotiations which were being made through neutral channels for the repatriation of women and children.

The Foreign Office was warned that delivering the message to Gimson might take a fortnight, and that the agent might be stopped by Chinese Communists. Furthermore the Ambassador in Chungking told the Foreign Office of Colonel Ride's fears that the Americans might meanwhile fly in Chinese officials to accept the formal surrender of the Japanese in Hong Kong. Should this happen the British would have the utmost difficulty in reimposing their authority in the Colony. Colonel Ride's fears in this case proved groundless.

General Carton de Wiart, who was Churchill's representative with Chiang Kai-shek, did not approve of BAAG going to Hong Kong unless General Wedemeyer's agreement was obtained, since Wedemyer had been repeatedly assured that BAAG was not concerned with the restoration of British administration in the Colony.

However on 14 August, Lieutenant-Colonel Wichtrich, US Army, told Colonel Ride that the Americans proposed parachuting a reconnaissance party of six Americans, Colonel Ride and several BAAG officers close to Hong Kong's POW and internee camps. This party would be equipped with radio and would signal the prisoners' requirements which would then be flown in. This was to be done before the Japanese had capitulated. Colonel Ride believed the plan to be foolhardy and suggested that leaflets should be dropped instead. He also mistrusted the motives of the Americans when he noticed that their stores had American flags but not British. He had already been told that the operation would be an American one under command of an American officer.

Colonel Ride later reported to the War Office that: 'It was obvious from the start that anything British in the first re-entry into Hong Kong was to be kept out of the limelight and to the minimum.'[4]

However the Americans' parachuting teams were extremely successful in other places such as Mukden, and the arrival of a handful of Americans in Hong Kong with several BAAG officers would have little bearing on who would eventually own Hong Kong. In any event the British were being less than frank with the Americans who were not told that instructions had already been sent to Gimson in Stanley Internment Camp stating that he was to establish a provisional Government forthwith.[5]

On 17 August the small American team, commanded by Captain C. H. Fenn, United States Marines, left Kunming by air via Canton for Hong Kong. The plan had been modified to land the relieving force by air rather than parachuting them in. Fenn had been working with the Office of Strategic Services gathering intelligence for 14 Air Force in Indo-china before being transferred in July to the Air Ground Air Services.

Captain Fenn had no illusions as to the small contribution which his modest command could make to help the POWs, 'but it would give a great boost to their morale, particularly by assuring them that the war was really won,' he remembers.[6] 'Our scheme to send in teams was too hastily planned to be efficient, and we only had side arms, although we were given a fighter escort which, as I pointed out at the time, would be of no real service and only a provocation to the enemy who could quickly shoot the four or five planes out of the sky. A big effort was made to get clearance with the Japanese, but this was not obtained in the Canton and Hong Kong area. Our intelligence reported that the Kai Tak airfield in Hong Kong was heavily mined except for a strip the Japs were using, the precise location of which we were uncertain. Reports also showed the Japs to be very hostile, aggressive, highly suspicious and sceptical of the sudden reversal from victory to defeat. US planes dropped leaflets on Hong Kong to explain the "facts", but we had no way of knowing whether a single Jap took the "facts" seriously.

'Our DC3 two-engined plane was heavily overloaded with US personnel, Colonel Ride and his team and a mass of relief supplies. It was embarrassing for me, a Marine Corps Captain, although the Commander, to have senior officers along, knowing we might not agree about procedures. Indeed this proved a major flaw in the whole operation, but Colonel Ride insisted upon coming. The weather was terrible – torrential rain and strong winds, and, when flying over the Kwangsi mountains, the pilot had to thread his way between the peaks. It was touch and go, all of us crowding into the aircraft's nose to keep the tail up to maintain altitude. When we circled the airstrip near Canton, we saw Japanese soldiers, but there was no firing and so we landed despite the danger of mines.

'I jumped out with Kwei, my interpreter, as a truckload of Japanese soldiers approached. A Colonel with a hygienic pad over his mouth told us in a very disagreeable fashion that we were all under arrest. Kwei translated to the Colonel the letter General Wedemeyer had given to us which asked for full Japanese co-operation. Meanwhile there was agitation, mainly from the British still on the plane, that we should all take off immediately. Ride was heavily blacklisted by the Japs for his spying activities and his capture would have had disastrous consequences. The BAAG officers should not have come on the mission, and I could not agree to abandon it so precipitously.' Colonel Ride discovered that he had no say in the operation: 'The British were told quite firmly that they were guests in the party,' he wrote later, 'and had no standing nor voice in the decisions that had to be made on the airfield.'

Captain Fenn went to a hut nearby to see Major-General Tomida who commanded the Japanese forces in Canton. Tomida spoke some English, having spent a year in America in 1931, and he was entirely friendly and co-operative. 'But, Tomida explained, the odds were against us, although we had been lucky in finding the one unmined strip on the airfield,' remembers Fenn. 'The Japanese army, he told us, was by no means reconciled to the turn of events, even though they were obeying the Emperor's commands to cease active operations. General Wedemeyer had been too precipitate in sending us, and we would not be allowed to fly on to Hong Kong where antagonism was acute.

'I decided to stay where we were; Colonel Ride was furious and said that I was endangering all their lives to no purpose as we would not be allowed to help the POWs anyway. This outburst had a very unfortunate effect on the surrounding Japanese who sensed a quarrel among the "invading allies", and they menacingly advanced on us with fixed bayonets. I changed my mind about staying, and asked General Tomida if we could leave. The situation had further deteriorated because our fighter escort had been buzzing the airfield in an aggressive fashion. We took off quickly, but we learnt that Nanning, our destination, was under water while Luichow had no lights and it was now approaching midnight. The pilot chose Loling instead. He told me quietly that we would probably have to parachute out over wild mountains as there was insufficient fuel. One tank ran dry, and an engine failed, but he just landed safely.

The Colonel in charge of our fighter escort later came to me with a citation for a decoration for himself already written testifying to his bravery and tenacity in giving us air cover and thus "saving our lives". Because the airforce was so useful to our operations, I had to sign it, and he got his decoration instead of being court-martialled which he deserved for buzzing us against our repeated protests. So ended our attempt to be the first to help Hong Kong's POWs and internees – it was a fiasco.'[7]

Colonel Ride's frustration can be imagined, particularly in view of the uncertainty as to whether his agent in Macao could reach Gimson. For over three years Ride had been endeavouring to maintain Britain's prestige in South China. Now, at the crucial moment, he felt quite helpless, and understandably bitter. Colonel Ride's difficulties may have given the impression that he was not an outstanding person. That this would be an inaccurate assumption can be seen by his subsequent extremely successful career which culminated in a knighthood.

The Americans agreed to British ships leaving the Pacific fleet to liberate Hong Kong. They were commanded by Rear-Admiral C. H. J. Harcourt, and on 29 August they were close to the Colony. A reconnaissance flight of Hellcats took off from the aircraft carrier, HMS *Indomitable*. They met no opposition and so flew low over Kai Tak aerodrome and dropped message bags telling the Japanese Commander to communicate on a particular wireless frequency. He was also told either to send out a Japanese officer to meet Admiral Harcourt, or a British aircraft would bring off the Japanese Commander's representatives. The Hellcats also flew low over the POW camps, and the prisoners could be seen waving frantically.

The Japanese passed some scanty information about mines to the Admiral by wireless, and said that the Japanese Commander, Lieutenant-General Tanaka, was in Canton and so no arrangements could be made for any surrender. Admiral Harcourt replied that he intended to enter Hong Kong and occupy the Naval Dockyard on the following day.

As the afternoon passed, small silent groups of sailors

gathered on some ships' decks. They saw the hills of China take shape out of the heat haze. The fleet was spread over several miles of the light-green water. Ahead five Australian minesweepers steamed in line abreast. On each flank was a group of four submarines in line ahead, their bright camouflage glinting as they caught the sun. Right astern was the Canadian cruiser *Prince Robert*. As they approached, rain swept over the water in a black line; the land became indistinct and the shapes of the ships blurred. There was no sign of life from Hong Kong. Some ships anchored ten miles south of the Colony while the cruisers and aircraft carriers remained further away.

Above the fleet a close air patrol of twelve fighters was kept up all day in case the Japanese attempted suicide attacks on the force.

At 4 p.m. a message was received from the Japanese that a POW, Commander D. H. S. Craven, RN, wished to see Admiral Harcourt. An Avenger with an escort of Hellcats was flown off to collect him, but on landing at Kai Tak it burst a tyre. The Japanese were docile and obliging, and when another Avenger arrived with a spare wheel they eagerly helped to change it.

The Avenger returned to *Indomitable* with not only Commander Craven, but also a Japanese representative of the Foreign Relations Department, Mr Makimura, dressed as an officer complete with samurai sword. Makimura was given detailed instructions on what was required of the Japanese and he was flown off again. By this time, however, the weather had closed in over Hong Kong and the Avenger failed to find either Kai Tak or its way back to *Indomitable* as it was now dark.

The Avenger finally crash-landed in Chinese Communist territory, the only damage being a bent propellor. Chinese soldiers saw the aircraft come down and went to the plane to find out what was happening. To protect Makimura the Chinese were told that he was a prisoner, but a communist handed the pilot a knife saying: 'Here, take this and you can cut his throat.' They failed to understand why the British refused to execute him.

'Meanwhile I had decided to enter harbour at midday the next day,' reported Admiral Harcourt to the Admiralty, 'by which time the minesweepers should have been able to sweep a narrow channel clear of moored mines. The Japanese sent several warnings that the Americans had dropped numerous mines from aircraft in these waters, and Commander Craven informed me that no ships of any size had been in and out of Hong Kong through the Lei Mun pass for some time, so there was a definite risk of mines. I considered, however, that it was an acceptable risk.'[8]

Two weeks before Admiral Harcourt reached Hong Kong, thrilling rumours of Japan's surrender swept through Stanley Internment Camp. F. C. Gimson, the former Colonial Secretary, told the Camp Commandant, who was now Lieutenant Kadowake, that unless there was a formal announcement serious incidents might arise if the guards continued to adopt their usual attitude of arrogance and violence.

Kadowake replied: 'His Majesty the Emperor has taken into consideration the terms of the Potsdam Conference and has ordered the hostilities to cease.' Seeing the bewilderment in Gimson's face, for he had never heard of any such Conference, Kadowake added: 'In other words you've won: we've lost.'

'I suppose I should have been elated at this news,' wrote Gimson later, 'but I wasn't. Victory was always regarded as inevitable. Now it had come, new problems awaited me. Had I then known the wider background against which decisions had to be made, I should have been even more uneasy than I was.'[1]

The following day Colonel Tokunaga, the Commander of all the POW camps in Hong Kong, and Makimura of the Foreign Relations Department visited Gimson. 'I was greeted with effusive handshakes,' Gimson remembers, 'and so I felt it was an opportunity to assert my authority by answering: "As senior officer of the Hong Kong Government, I will take charge of the Administration." However the Japanese said that the future of Hong Kong was not decided and there was no certainty that it would continue to be British. I replied that I was not interested in their opinion, and that I intended to carry out the duties to which I had been appointed by His Majesty's Government.'

Gimson demanded accommodation in Hong Kong for

himself and the Government officials whom he proposed to appoint, and also for use of the wireless station. Gimson's prestige among the Japanese was high, despite almost four years of bitter wrangling with his captors while trying to improve the conditions in the Camp. The Japanese therefore promised to give Gimson what he wanted.

'I returned to my quarters,' he wrote, 'and a knock sounded on the door. A Chinese entered. He proved to be the contact sent by BAAG from Macao with the Foreign Office's messages.[2] He later gave his name as Leung, and he was subsequently to be seen in Hong Kong immaculately dressed in a white silk robe. Leung had the air of making a secret rendezvous. He gave me an account of the international scene. What I learnt convinced me that I should take the oath as Officer administering the Government, and proclaim to the world I had done so.'

Gimson quickly summoned Sir Atholl MacGregor, the former Chief Justice of Hong Kong, who was also an internee. The Oath of Office was administered to Gimson thereby making him the acting Governor of Hong Kong.

Gimson and Leung were then left alone again. 'He asked me if I wanted money,' recalls Gimson, 'and Leung poured from a bag on to a small table golden sovereigns. I took five as a memento rather than for any personal needs. During our internment, money had usually been associated with black market transactions, and the sight of legitimate currency was too much of a shock for me to appreciate its value in a world where food would no longer be supplied as a ration from an alien authority.'

Gimson sent a messenger to the British Consul in Macao, still functioning in the neutral Portuguese territory, with the following note which was transmitted to the Secretary of State for Colonies: 'Have sufficient staff and complete scheme available to set up Civil Administration immediately for a short period without outside assistance. I am taking the Oath as Officer administering the Government. Request immediate advice.'

The Colonial Office sent a reply for Gimson to Macao. It stated that Admiral Harcourt would establish a Military

Administration on his arrival, and that: 'You should then at once comply fully with his instructions. In the meantime I warmly approve your initiative and plans you have made.' However, this reply arrived too late; Gimson's messenger was already returning to Hong Kong. His boat was intercepted by pirates who searched it, but the messenger hid in a pile of dried fish and was not found, although he nearly died of asphyxiation.

Meanwhile, news had reached the POWs in Shamshuipo of the Japanese surrender. On 18 August a flag-raising ceremony took place in the camp. The hymn 'Abide with me' and the National Anthem were sung after which the Union Jack and the White Ensign were hoisted. 'It was the most impressive ceremony I have ever attended,' noted the Canadian, Captain H. L. White. 'Hearts were too full for much singing; many tears were in evidence. I couldn't keep them back. We all realised more than ever before the meaning of Freedom. We also flew the Stars and Stripes and Russian, Dutch, Chinese and Free French flags, all made from coloured rags. Some Indians came over from their camp, and it was very touching to see them greeting their British officers with real big hugs. Some wives with their children arrived from Stanley to meet their husbands. It was so moving, I couldn't watch.'[3]

As the days dragged by, discipline was difficult to maintain and some ex-POWs crept out at night to seek the company of Chinese girls, one of whom was smuggled into the camp. 'They had her in one of the empty huts and there was quite a line up,' recalls one POW. Hundreds of starving Chinese gathered at the camp perimeter with their skinny arms stuck through the fence begging pathetically for food, but the ex-POWs had little to give them.

The frustrations of waiting for liberation were immense, particularly because until 29 August only leaflets were dropped by aircraft which urged them, in General Wedemeyer's name, to stay in the camp.

'What we resented most during our imprisonment was not the bad food, or the cold, or the domineering attitude of the Japanese, although all these were unpleasant,' wrote

Major J. N. Crawford, RCAMC, after the war, 'but what bothered most of us more than anything else was the overcrowding, the complete lack of privacy. Until it is denied you, you can have no idea what a blessing it is to be able to be alone. In camp, we lived cheek by jowl with the same little group, year after year. And under such circumstances, the dearest friend can become hateful.

'On the whole, I do not regret the experience. I think that I learned a lot. I learned what people are like when the cultural surface is rubbed off by the stress of circumstances. I found that some humans are among the nastiest of the Lord's creatures, but I also learned that some are among the finest. I think that perhaps I learned the meaning of tolerance, and that in itself is an education. But I do not wish to repeat the experiment. It is more pleasant in retrospect than it was in reality.'[4]

In many ways the final months at Stanley Internment Camp had been the most worrying, particularly when fourteen internees were killed accidentally by American bombers. After the surrender, before Harcourt's arrival, former Chinese servants visited the internees and some brought little presents of cakes and fruit. 'Most of us collected rice for them,' wrote Mrs Topsy Man in her diary. 'It was really pathetic seeing their joy. I feel that these nightmare experiences, which we have shared with them, have united us with the Chinese more than anything else could have done.'

Another internee, Mrs Mary Goodban, whose son, Nicky, had been born two days before the British surrender, remembers the first British planes from *Indomitable* flying low over the camp giving a special 'victory roll'. 'The children were frightened at first,' she noted, 'because they couldn't understand why, with so much noise, there were no bombs. For the first time in their lives, the children were allowed to ride in lorries, but most were too scared to do so, and they missed the Japanese roll calls. Children had, on the whole, been very content in Stanley, and Nicky regarded it as home, and afterwards he frequently asked me when were we going back there. For the grown-ups, release was much more emotionally overwhelming. We had been cut off for so long that the intense excitement was almost unbearable. There was so much news to hear and so many new developments. We had all become mentally wearier and duller than we had realised, and our emotions had been dead or suppressed for so long that the sudden quickening into life was painful.

'I have often been asked whether I regret those years of internment. My answer is an emphatic "no" because no one who has not lived behind barbed wire can really understand the joy of freedom which we now so often take for granted. Our imprisonment gave us a new understanding and respect for the poor and destitute of every country. It reduced us to a level where race, social standing, position and wealth were of no account beside courage, resourcefulness, kindliness and good humour.'[5]

Shortly after the Japanese surrender, Gimson left Stanley Internment Camp and met the senior British officers in Shamshuipo. They agreed that British civilian authority must be re-established immediately. Gimson requested that two officers be sent into Victoria to liaise with the Japanese Civil Administration which was occupying the building of the former Hong Kong and Shanghai Bank.

Captain D. Heath, Royal Artillery, and Lieutenant I. MacGregor, Royal Scots, were chosen for this task. MacGregor had been ADC to General Maltby before the war. The two young officers were told to meet the Japanese and take over the French Mission as a temporary British Provisional Government Headquarters where they were to hoist the Union Jack. 'And so we made our way by ferry early the next morning to Victoria,' remembers MacGregor. 'We were immediately followed by a large crowd of curious Chinese who had not seen any British troops in Hong Kong since 1941. The Chinese around us were not particularly welcome to us, since our task was supposed to be secret, and the Japanese had still not surrendered in Victoria. Being British, our first thought, despite our important orders, was to find a chemist to buy razors, soap and toothbrushes, and improve our appearance. Having washed and shaved, we walked as fast as possible to the bank accompanied by the ever-increasing crowd. When we were within two hundred yards of it we saw approaching us two fully-armed Japanese military police – one a senior Warrant Officer and the other a Sergeant. They halted five yards from us, staring at us and at our huge crowd of 'camp followers' in disbelief. I saw their hands drop to their gun holsters, and I felt so nervous that sweat trickled down my back. However Duggie Heath did not hesitate; standing face to face with the large Warrant Officer, he said in a voice of controlled menace. "Don't they bloody well teach you in your Army to salute officers when you see them?" For about five seconds, the two Japanese tried to assimilate the changed situation. Then, like puppets on a string, they both sprang to attention and their right hands came slowly up to salute. Duggie walked on with a lazy and contemptuous acknowledgement. I, still feeling like "jelly-legs", in my tattered army shirt and shorts and shabby Glengarry, staggered after him. We must have looked a strange couple, but we received a great cheer from the Chinese.'

At the Hong Kong and Shanghai bank the officers were welcomed by bowing, obsequious Japanese civilian officials, who appeared considerably relieved that the British had arrived first rather than Chinese guerrillas. The Japanese provided transport, food, fuel, blankets, and everything the two officers needed to establish Gimson's temporary Government Headquarters. The Japanese even gave them a Union Jack which was hoisted above the French Mission. 'A symbolic gesture, perhaps, but a very essential one,' remembers MacGregor. 'We had been alarmed to see that every flag flying in Victoria was either the Chinese Nationalist flag or the Stars and Stripes. There was no doubt that General Wedemeyer's and Chiang Kai-shek's agents in Hong Kong had been very active indeed. Within an hour or two of hoisting the Union Jack, others began to appear all over Hong Kong. The British were back.'[6]

The following day Gimson and his officials were driven in an old bus from Stanley to the French Mission. 'This journey,' he wrote later, 'filled our hearts with more emotion than we had previously experienced, and made us appreciate to the full our truly providential survival after the privations of the Japanese. Our route took us through the fishing village of Aberdeen, and my most vivid memory is of the faces of the Chinese there, who, at the noise of the approach of the bus, cast their eyes down to avoid meeting the glances of the Japanese occupants. The faces were slowly raised, and beaming smiles appeared in answer to ours, as our identity was recognised. Days full of incident and anxiety passed as we waited for the British fleet to arrive. Many of my fellow internees left Stanley and started, as far as it was in their power, to resuscitate the peace-time industry and commerce in the Colony.'[7]

Meanwhile the Japanese had recovered from the initial shock of defeat and their morale improved. Their large garrison was still well-armed and fully in control, and Japanese officials told Gimson that they remained responsible for Hong Kong until the official surrender. Moreover, the Japanese argued that the surrender should be made to the Chinese, as Hong Kong lay in the Chinese theatre of war. However they continued to be courteous and co-operative to the skeleton (an appropriate adjective!) Government staff.

On 29 August Gimson was told that the British fleet was approaching, and that the Japanese were refusing to allow a British plane to land at Kai Tak on the excuse that the airfield was under water. Gimson pointed out that this was impossible since it had not rained sufficiently for weeks, and if the Japanese refused to co-operate they would be in serious trouble. The Japanese promptly allowed the Avenger aircraft to land and it collected Commander Craven and Mr Makimura, but, as already related, the plane lost its way and crash-landed in China on its return from *Indomitable*. Gimson did not know what to expect when, at daybreak on 30 August, British aircraft from the carriers flew over Hong Kong in close formation, first as a demonstration and, secondly, to take action in case of enemy hostility.

At 10 a.m. Admiral Harcourt, now in HMS *Swiftsure*, approached the harbour accompanied by minesweepers, cruisers and submarines. A report was received from one of the aircraft that there were almost a hundred small wooden Japanese 'suicide' boats close by which were also heading for the harbour. Aircraft bombed them and air patrols were maintained over the area for the following three days; all the boats were destroyed and the surviving crews rounded up.

Meanwhile, the ships safely negotiated the passage to the harbour at 10 knots, despite the threat of mines. Thousands of Chinese lined the waterfront, and significant Chinese comment was afterwards reported to the Colonial Office: 'The Chinese didn't remark whether the ships were British, American, Russian or Chinese: all they said was "now we will eat".'[8]

On arrival landing parties from *Swiftsure* and *Euryalus* were sent ashore, under Commander W. L. M. Brown, DSC, to seize the Dockyard. Lieutenant MacGregor was waiting to meet them. 'They were a "trigger-happy", tough lot who were only too keen to use their automatic weapons,' he remembers. 'Most of them hadn't yet had a chance of shooting at the Japs, and so they started firing as soon as they saw any. The Japanese had been perfectly quiet until then but, thinking they were going to be wiped out, they returned the fire. I was several times mistaken for a Jap and I frequently missed bursts of fire by flinging myself flat on my stomach. Having survived as a POW, I was not very anxious to be killed by one of my own side. I eventually found Commander Brown and explained that the sound of battle in the Dockyard would certainly excite the Chinese elsewhere who might start attacking the fully-armed Japanese Garrison. Brown therefore climbed to the top of a tower with a megaphone and yelled orders to his men to "take it easy with the shooting".'

Another officer who was in the Dockyard that morning was Lieutenant-Commander R. S. Young. He had been imprisoned in Canton with Boxer, Craven and Haddock. 'Great showers of ashes from Japanese secret documents being burnt close by had drifted through our cell windows in Canton,' he remembers. 'We knew the end must surely be not far off. Shortly afterwards Boxer and Craven were given clean suits and were whisked off to a superb feast with the Japanese 23rd Army Commander and pretty Geisha girls, after which they were returned to our cells and had to put on their old rags again. On the next day, 17 August, we were driven to the station and put on the train to Hong Kong where Colonel Tokunaga met us with lots of bowing. On the day that Admiral Harcourt entered Hong Kong', Young continues, 'we took out to a parting lunch two of our former Stanley guards who had behaved well to us. This little party went off quite well, although the guards left us somewhat dispirited. As I walked back to the Dockyard, I saw British soldiers advancing up the streets in what I took to be house to house fighting style with tommy guns waving this way and that. As all had been perfectly quiet for days, I asked the Lieutenant in charge what he was doing. He said they were re-occupying Hong Kong. I told him to be careful as a few unwarranted shots might easily start the Chinese Communists off, which would cause infinite trouble and clashes.'[9]

Soon afterwards the ominous crackle of sub-machine gun fire was heard, but some mistook the noise for Chinese celebrating with fireworks. In any event there were no Japanese diehards and the landing was unopposed.

The relieving forces were surprised to discover that they were too late; the former internees and POWs had already liberated themselves. For example some internees had worked out a complete scheme for operating the port. Due to their foresight, and energy, they were ready to receive and handle the incoming ships. Another group had produced an edition of the *Morning Post* which was on sale on the day the Fleet arrived.

'Gimson and his gallant band of ex-POWs and internees had already got going,' reported Admiral Harcourt to London, 'and continued to give very good service until some of them literally cracked up, not yet being fit.'

A naval officer met Gimson and took him to *Swiftsure* to meet Admiral Harcourt. They briefly discussed the internees' civil administration which was temporarily governing the Colony. Harcourt explained how he had orders to proclaim a military administration instead. They then went ashore to visit all the camps and hospitals, starting at Stanley.

'On arrival we found all the internees awaiting us,' wrote Harcourt later, 'and we had a most unforgettable welcome. They had refused to hoist the Union Jack until I appeared as they wanted to do it properly. An ex-Naval rating produced a Union Jack which he had hidden in his bedding when Hong Kong was captured. We had a very touching ceremony as the standards of all nationalities in Stanley were hoisted, accompanied by the singing of "God Save the King". In conclusion three cheers were given for the King. The morale in Stanley Camp, as at all other camps that I visited afterwards, was extremely high despite the obvious effects of malnutrition which could be seen in every face. The enthusiasm and cheering was so spontaneous and seemed to express the pent-up feelings of all these years. I shall never forget it. We next visited Shamshuipo which now held all the European POWs, then the camp for Indians, and finally the two POWs' hospitals where I had to go into every ward as they all wanted just to see a British Admiral again. The doctors all said that our visit would do all their patients much more good than the extra food and medical supplies we were able to bring them. One felt no doubt as to the truth of this statement. I hope to start transferring the patients to the hospital ship *Oxfordshire* tomorrow.

'On 31 August, on *Indomitable*, I informed the Japanese Commander that he was to round up his troops and evacuate the Island of Hong Kong,' continues Harcourt. 'He was in a rather truculent mood when he arrived, and introduced the ten officers with him as his "committee". I informed him that I did not deal with committees, that I only dealt with him, and that I should hold him personally responsible for the conduct of his troops. He tried to adopt the attitude that he was negotiating and made complaints. However, my orders that all Japanese were to be evacuated from the Island of Hong Kong to Kowloon by 4 p.m., 1 September, were carried out smoothly and effectively.'

18,000 Japanese troops were gradually disarmed and 4,000 were later placed in Shamshuipo Camp. One Japanese soldier committed harikari with a razor blade and four died of heat exhaustion. Their morale was low, and they reported that they had received no mail for six months.

There were few indications that the Japanese had been determined to put up a stiff fight for Hong Kong. Hills were honeycombed with trenches but the beach defences were practically non-existent. There was no trace of mines, and the only barbed wire was British which had fallen into disrepair. No gun positions were covering landing sites and the main beach at Repulse Bay was completely undefended.

On 1 September, Admiral Harcourt proclaimed the establishment of a Military Government and became the Commander-in-Chief and Head of the Military Administration, Hong Kong. He was impressed that Gimson and his Council already appeared to have the situation well in hand, in spite of the severe shortage of supplies, except for their inability to maintain law and order. To make the civil aspect of the Administration more workable, Harcourt appointed Gimson Lieutenant-Governor, explaining to the British Government that he had done so 'as I feel such an appointment will inspire confidence in the local population'. However Harcourt was promptly told by signal that Gimson's appointment was inconsistent with the proclamation of a Military Government and must be withdrawn. Harcourt therefore cancelled the appointment and explained to the Colonial Office that he had found Gimson's administration to be 'working and felt it necessary to give them every encouragement. Gimson is a most loyal person and is doing wonderfully well, but he and all other internees are very overstrained and should go home as soon as possible.'

C. R. Attlee, now Prime Minister, signalled Gimson, 'I have learned with admiration of the energy and spirit with which you, after your long ordeal in Stanley, first of all took the initiative and have since supported Admiral Harcourt in restoring British administration. I should like you and your civil officers to know the high value I attach to your indomitable courage and splendid service.'

Meanwhile Admiral Harcourt's ships crews entertained the joyous former prisoners. The battleship HMS *Anson*, for example, entertained 1,500 of them on board on 4 September. 'Met the Admiral and had a drink with him,' wrote Captain White in his diary. 'Many of our Canadian boys have changed their minds somewhat about the Limies after today.'

On 7 September, after twenty-four hours non-stop from Madras, a Catalina aircraft put down a weary, unshaven party on the shores of Hong Kong. D. M. MacDougall, now with the rank of Brigadier, and twelve Civil Affairs officers had arrived to run the administrative side of the Hong Kong Government. 'The Admiral met me,' reported MacDougall to the Colonial Office a week later, 'and took me to Government House, hideously rebuilt by the Japanese: entering it is somehow like meeting a hitherto respectable old lady turned painted and wanton with too much rouge and too obviously a lifted face.

'The Colony is seedy and run-down. Apart from that it looks fairly normal on the surface. But nothing really stirs. I was not prepared for the hush that hangs about it. All Far East cities teem, but not Hong Kong. At the moment it carries on, partly from the dying momentum of the Japs: the game is to keep it from stopping altogether.'

Brigadier MacDougall felt that it was confusing to find a former Lieutenant-Governor still virtually in office with an Executive and Legislative Council established by a Proclamation issued the same day and within hours of another which had declared the suspension of civil government. There was great embarrassment all round. 'The internees did wonders – some performed miracles,' wrote the Brigadier, 'but by the time we arrived their small and carefully-hoarded strength was waning. Everything was made ten times more difficult and yet, seeing what they had attempted and in part accomplished, one was proud to be a Hong Kong man. Patience and ingenuity and a bucketful of tact on all sides finally showed a way out. All the internees ought to go home at once: they are doing their health nothing but harm by remaining. We are getting them out as fast as the ships go, which isn't very fast. I'm afraid that, deep down, our arrival was interpreted as a vote of no confidence in themselves.' Such a belief was very natural, but was not the opinion of the British Government which took the view that Gimson in particular had done extraordinarily well. He was rewarded with a knighthood and later became Governor of Singapore.

'It is odd to accustom oneself to a community where words like "jeep" and "D-day" provoked stares of blank incomprehension,' noted MacDougall, 'where one recognised old friends mainly by their voices and where Chinese persisted in bawling like Japanese. The town was dead – deserted streets and shuttered shops: it is beginning to look different now; we can almost feel the city coming alive. Relations with the British armed forces, about which we were warned repeatedly in London, are so far excellent. Admiral Harcourt is a very fine man: he pretends to know completely nothing about colonies or their administration. He refers to the Chinese as "Chinamen" with a fascinating lack of offence and he greets his bewildered visitors of all nationalities by saying "Glad to have you aboard" . . . I have insufficient staff to run a village shop . . . The problems in Hong Kong are of a nightmare variety.'[10]

By 12 September, the Japanese in Hong Kong had still not formally surrendered, and the ceremony arranged for that day had to be postponed because the disagreement between the British and Chinese Governments as to who should take the surrender had still not been resolved. On 30 August, Sir Horace Seymour, the British Ambassador to China, saw Chiang Kai-shek, who stood firm on his position as Commander-in-Chief of the China theatre. Chiang Kai-shek argued that it was unacceptable for a British officer to take Hong Kong's surrender on his behalf. Moreover, Chiang Kai-shek was pressing for certain facilities in Hong Kong, and wanted all the Japanese war material found there. To break the deadlock, Attlee appealed to President Truman for help. Meanwhile, Harcourt signalled the

British Government that the continuous postponements of the surrender ceremony 'are becoming an embarrassment in the Colony, and add to our many problems.'

President Truman replied to Attlee that: 'From the United States' standpoint there is no objection to the surrender of Hong Kong being accepted by a British officer, providing full military co-ordination is effected beforehand by the British with Chiang Kai-shek on operational matters connected with assistance and support to Chinese and American Forces.' This decision satisfied the British who could at last authorise Admiral Harcourt to receive the surrender on behalf of both Britain and China. Chiang Kai-shek, who had never made formal claim to Hong Kong, also appeared satisfied, for he could use the Colony's port to re-deploy his troops prior to his eventually unsuccessful campaign against the Communists. He was also able to obtain the Japanese ships and transport captured in Hong Kong.

On 16 September the formal Japanese surrender took place in Government House. Their representatives, Vice-Admiral Ruitaro Fujeta and Major-General Umetichi Odada, were made to stand behind a small table a few feet from a larger table where Admiral Harcourt, together with Chinese, American and Canadian representatives, took their places. The Japanese then signed the Instrument of Surrender and gave their swords to the Admiral.

After the removal of the Japanese under arrest as POWs, the Union Jack was ceremonially hoisted to the accompaniment of the National Anthem. This was followed by a salute of twenty-one guns from HM ships in the harbour and a fly past of Naval aircraft. In the evening there was an excellent searchlight and fireworks display by the Fleet. The harbour was bright with rockets and star-shells which delighted the Chinese, while the port was choked with the most impressive array of British warships that anyone had ever seen in Hong Kong before.

At the time of Admiral Harcourt's arrival, law and order were maintained by the Japanese who quickly became accustomed to provide such assistance as was asked of them.

After the Japanese departure, looting and organised thieving became widespread. The looters set fire to some buildings which burnt merrily. 3,000 RAF arrived in Hong Kong to keep order, but they had little effect and some troops participated in the looting.[11] It only really died out when there was nothing left to loot.

Gradually everything became deceptively quiet, although there were a number of armed Chinese gangs many of whom had acquired weapons from the Japanese who gave away indiscriminately thousands of small arms before their departure. The Hong Kong Police Special Branch estimated that about 7,000 weapons were in the hands of potential gangsters. However, there was little incentive for armed robbery as most people had sold their jewellery and valuables to buy food during the Japanese occupation, and the Japanese military yen, still the accepted form of currency, was viewed with some suspicion and was not worth stealing.

Peace and stability in Hong Kong was threatened by former anti-Japanese groups such as Triad societies, and also gambling house gangs. One of the most notorious was known as the Chungking gang. It was about 2,000 strong and was led by Sum Chit Sung who had hoped to take control, at least temporarily, of Kowloon and Hong Kong after the Japanese had been overthrown. The gang was believed to have infiltrated into Hong Kong from China in 1943 as an underground organisation to murder Japanese personnel and commit acts of sabotage but in this role they were not very effective. On the Japanese departure, the gang offered to assist preserving law and order. Their offer was accepted and they were allowed to wear arm-bands to indicate their official status, but, instead of preserving law and order, many took to large-scale looting, while others sold their armbands to other gangsters. The gang was therefore broken up with limited success.

The 'Gambling House' group of about 3,000 consisted mainly of Cantonese under the leadership of Wan Tuck Ming, who had been employed by the Japanese to maintain law and order in Hong Kong in return for the lucrative privilege of running the public gaming houses. Wan also offered his services to the British, but his help was refused as he had more armed men than the Hong Kong police. There were reports, without confirmation, that Wan was paid five million yen as a reward for breaking up his gang and taking about forty-five leading gangsters back to China. Only 200 of his gang could be persuaded to hand over their arms to the police, ostensibly for stamping prior to registration, so the operation was only partially successful.

The Triad societies had been involved in exploiting all forms of vice, but one group, the 'Kwantung Peoples Anti-Japanese' force had been active imposing heavy fines on people who had collaborated with the Japanese. They eventually took to selling protection. The police were optimistic that they might leave Hong Kong as their leaders in China ordered them to return there. These instructions were not obeyed as the gang preferred to remain in their comfortable hotels in Kowloon.[12] Finally there were the guerrilla bands north of Hong Kong who had undoubtedly assisted the British in many ways, but who were largely Communist and refused to co-operate with the Nationalist Chungking gang. The Communist group was disbanded in an amicable manner, with some members moving to China.

Considerable problems therefore faced the police force, which was seriously under strength. Their discipline was initially unsatisfactory, and all the pre-war records of the Special Branch were lost.

Chiang Kai-shek's troops passing through Hong Kong created a feeling of uncertainty among the local people, as the troops fostered a rumour that Hong Kong was to be returned to China.

The Hong Kong Government's relationship with China quickly became strained because the Colony had imposed a policy of restricting entry of Chinese into Hong Kong. It is not without interest that this policy continues to be imposed today. In 1945 this step was taken because of the lack of supplies, and caused considerable resentment in China, despite the presence of Sir Chan Chak, KBE, the one-legged Admiral who had led the Royal Naval MTB party to freedom. Chan Chak had received a knighthood for his services to the British and had become the Mayor of Canton, but he was overshadowed by the Commander of South China, General Chang Fa Kwei, who did not like the British and regarded it as an insult that 'honest Chinese merchants' should be refused entry. 'Nothing which Hong Kong does will be right in the eyes of this disappointed and ambitious war-lord', MacDougall reported to the Colonial Office. However, there was no hostility between Chiang Kai-shek's troops and those in Hong Kong, although at least one newspaper believed otherwise. A French Canadian publication, *La Patrie*, had earlier reported that no Canadians would 'fight Chinese who are trying to liberate Hong Kong they feel to be theirs'.

Within two months of Admiral Harcourt's arrival, the relief supplies reaching Hong Kong had amounted to only one shipment of rice, about ten days' consumption, and one shipload of coal diverted from Naval stocks. 'For the rest, the Hong Kong Administration has had to depend on its own efforts to beg, borrow or steal stocks of essential foodstuffs, wherever they could be found in what appears to be a hostile and unfriendly world,' MacDougall reported. 'In general the Colony has kept one jump ahead of a breakdown. For firewood she burns the wood of floors and doors; when there is no coal, a skeleton supply of power is pumped from warships; when rice and meat stocks drop almost to a vanishing point, another cargo is somehow spirited from elsewhere at ruinous prices.' One officer responsible for immigration had to be detached from the police force, already 85% under strength, and sent to Borneo to purchase firewood. Another had to leave the hard-pressed Secretariat to go to Shanghai to buy coal.

The Prison Service was so weak that four months after the liberation it contained only two European officers, despite an establishment of thirty-eight. Garbage and refuse had been allowed to accumulate in heaps during the Japanese occupation, and half a century of painstaking anti-malarial work had been undone by four years of neglect.

The problems facing Hong Kong by the end of 1945 were

still of a nightmare variety. Eighty per cent of the population showed signs of malnutrition and the food situation was still precarious. Hospitals and clinics were pitifully inadequate. The legacy of gangsterism left by the Japanese had not been eliminated. Finally there was the political chaos to the north where new assertive nationalism and growing antagonism between Communists and Nationalists caused many anxieties.

But overall the situation in Hong Kong was satisfactory compared to the chaos which reigned in the Dutch East Indies and in French Indo-China. In Hong Kong disease and unrest had been contained, law and order to a great extent prevailed, the currency was re-established, the shops were open, and the harbour waited to handle cargo ships rather than war ships.

The cheerfulness and resilience of the Chinese were, from the beginning, Hong Kong's most notable asset. At no time after the Japanese departure was there any lack of confidence that the colony had a golden future.

Some Japanese guards in Hong Kong were cruel, unpredictable, and indifferent to the POWs' welfare. The Japanese Military Police used torture extremely seldom on POWs, and only when strong evidence existed of BAAG's spying activities, as in the case of Major G. Bird, GM, who suffered the 'water treatment'. They made no serious attempt to indoctrinate the POWs to their viewpoint either in Hong Kong or Japan, and their propaganda was clumsy and ineffective, although the Japanese did persuade many Indians to change their loyalties.

After World War II the Chinese Communists perfected their indoctrination methods against the Chinese Nationalists. Their techniques and 'thought reform' programmes, which were set up all over China immediately after the Communist takeover, were based on old Chinese and Russian methods.

The Chinese in the Korean War (1950–1953) used this process of *Szuhsiang kai-tsao*, translated as ideological remoulding or 'brain washing', with devastating effect. United Nations POWs were put through extreme physical hardship and subjected to chronic pressures to give up their existing loyalties and to collaborate. The 'water treatment' torture was not unusual.

From a psychological point of view 'brain washing' has been called a 'recurring cycle of fear, relief and new fear'. Some UN prisoners were kept in fear of death, torture or starvation while their beliefs were systematically distorted by controlling the information they received. The conditions of stress and deprivation wore away their physical stamina and mental orientation until the captors' description of 'truth' was accepted.

As a result of these techniques, against which the POWs had received no training or forewarning, about 12% of the

British and American POWs in Korea co-operated wholeheartedly with their enemy, even to the extent of signing propaganda statements which they themselves believed to be untrue. Twenty-one Americans chose to remain in North Korea after the war.

The Korean War confirmed that the stamina and toughness of the individual's resistance in captivity depended largely upon whether he had learnt to live hard before capture. 38% of the Americans and 15% of the British died in captivity. Whereas not one Turkish POW died, although several hundred had been captured, for they were better able to withstand prolonged hardships, and Turkey was not a prime propaganda target. The Chinese concentrated their efforts against some Americans which partly accounts for the higher proportion of their deaths.

The Chinese Communists systematically set out to break the spirit of the prisoners. In Korea, and Vietnam too, medical attention, food and mail were used as instruments of pressure to destroy the will of the POWs. Even the Japanese did not treat their prisoners with such deliberate inhumanity.

In Vietnam (1962–1975) US POWs were often chained in cells in solitary confinement. Communication was not allowed between cells, but some POWs had been taught a modified morse code before their capture with which they could tap out messages in the same way that those imprisoned in Hong Kong's Stanley prison had communicated almost thirty years earlier. Some POWs in Vietnam also communicated by a form of deaf and dumb language when, for example, sweeping up leaves in the prison compound.

Rice was the POWs' staple diet in both Hong Kong and Vietnam, but in the latter case it was usually more adequate although seldom ample. The prevalent diseases in both cases were similar – malnutrition, dysentery and beri-beri, although the Americans did not have any known deaths from diphtheria. On the other hand they faced interrogation at the hands of the Vietcong and North Vietnamese – a horrifying experience designed not so much to gain useful military information but, as had been the case in Korea, to 'break' the prisoner and win his co-operation for propaganda purposes. Interrogators were more than willing to use physical abuse and psychological terror against prisoners as a matter of policy.

Some American POWs were seriously maltreated by civilians while being moved from one prison to another, whereas ordinary Japanese in World War II had usually shown no animosity. 591 US prisoners in Vietnam were eventually returned by their captors and only 74 are known to have died in captivity, but 1,400 Americans are still unaccounted for. Sadly we must presume that no information will ever be forthcoming as to how they were killed or died. A comparison between the behaviour of POWs during any campaign during the last fifty years can be misleading because the POWs were subjected to very different pressures from their diverse captors. Nor should the Chinese Communists, North Vietnamese, Vietcong or Japanese be especially criticised, for about 45% of the Germans imprisoned in Soviet camps and 60% of the Russians captured by the Germans died in captivity.

How did POWs survive? One American pilot shot down in Vietnam explained later: 'Without training in resistance before my capture, I would certainly have died, not just resisted, but died. I was manacled to a concrete "box", exhausted with hunger, and sick. I was dying. Suddenly it struck me that I had been taught in the classroom before my capture precisely how I now felt. I started to resist, just as I had been taught, initially simply by flexing my muscles within the confines of my "box", and by mentally "rebuilding" my self-respect.'

No such training had been given before World War II or Korea. As a result some POWs sunk into a deep depression, became apathetic, refused unpalatable food and virtually chose death. Those prisoners who lived, in whichever war, often cite the essentials for survival as pride, devotion to a faith, determination, and above all discipline, whether imposed from above or self-discipline.

There is an interesting example from the experiences in an

Other Ranks POW camp in Germany towards the end of World War II when communications had largely broken down resulting in insufficient food for POWs. A soldier captured at Arnhem recorded that:

'The British and the Canadians stood the imprisonment the best, and the Americans the worst in conditions in which discipline was essential for survival. The British and Canadians were lucky that they had RSM J. Lord, without doubt one of the best Regimental Sergeant-Majors the Guards or the British Army has ever produced. He created order out of chaos, gave us back our self-respect, improving conditions. There is no doubt that without this fine soldier there would have been far more British graves in Stalag XIB.'[1]

The return of the ex-POWs and internees to their families and homes was a traumatic experience. About 1,000 left Hong Kong on *Empress of Australia* on 17 September. 'We steamed into Manila Bay; past numerous sunken ships,' remembers Major Colquhoun. 'Manila had been bombed out of recognition, but at the dock an American band and cheering people met us. We were absolutely delighted with the American repatriation system. The meals were meticulously prepared in the big transit camp in the middle of nowhere. I asked one farmer's boy from Wisconsin what had brought him to the Philippines to act as house-mother to a bunch of Limey POWs. He replied that volunteers had been called for a Far East assignment where tact and discretion would be required. One day he said to us: "do you guys have a singer called Gracie Fields? Yeah? Well, just walk over the hill and you'll see she's there." I didn't believe him, but in a deep hollow we found her in a long frock with a grand piano, and her accompanist in a dinner jacket.'[1] Almost 8,000 watched her perform under the stars in the flicker of the spotlight. She gave great pleasure to many in the strangest of places.

The American hospitality in Manila astounded some British ex-POWs. 'We were issued,' remembers F. Linge, 'with forty cigarettes, five cigars and two cans of beer a day – untold wealth to men who had lived so sparsely for so long. When an American sergeant discovered we were lining up for a second free chocolate bar, he issued each man a whole box of them. The Americans could not do too much to make our transition to civilianisation as pleasant as possible. We eventually embarked on HMS *Implacable* where everything was done to help us. We disembarked at Vancouver where we received a most enthusiastic welcome.'

Major Colquhoun was less fortunate for he was crowded

on board a small US Liberty ship which was already full of American 'vets'. 'I was mildly astonished,' he noted, 'that so many veterinary officers should have been involved in a conflict in which horses were virtually unknown. I put this down to just another example of the Yanks leaving nothing to chance, until I learned that anyone with more than a year's service in the Pacific Theatre was a "veteran". We disembarked at Esquimalt, near Vancouver, on the Canadian Pacific coast where the scenery was lovely and the people were kind. We were accommodated in what had been the local golf club over which a Union Jack flew, and there was a waiter in a white jacket with a tray under his arm. We were penniless and adjourned to a grassy knoll where we sat in the sunshine under the pines while nice Canadian ladies plied us with tea and amiable conversation, and sewed on our campaign medals. It had never occurred to me that I was entitled to any medal, let alone three. I had been mildly apprehensive that there might have been trouble over our signing, admittedly under duress, the Japanese undertaking not to escape.'

CSM Winspear and other survivors from the *Lisbon Maru* were also bound for Canada. He had been taken aboard the hospital ship *Benevolence* in Tokyo Bay where he was scrubbed, scraped, deloused, disinfected and shaved all over before being given a US seaman's outfit. By now he had only two possessions – a small silver teaspoon which he had found in a ruined house in Japan, and an American propaganda leaflet dropped by a B-29, which showed Belsen inmates on Germany's surrender. Winspear was transferred with others to HMS *Speaker*. Several of the crew were sent below to help the ex-POWs with their kit. 'Some of the men of the *Speaker* were dressed like us,' remembers Winspear, 'and one Able Seaman from Yorkshire who was carrying my kit was mistaken for an ex-POW by a ship's officer who patted him on the shoulder and said: "Don't worry any more my friend, we'll soon put you right!" The startled Able Seaman replied: 'I'm glad to hear that, sir, for I've been with the ship for eighteen months.'[2]

Winspear and other ex-POWs saw the Japanese sign the

surrender on USS *Missouri*, after which they were assembled on the flight deck of the carrier. She steamed slowly round the great battleships, cruisers and destroyers of the Pacific Fleet, every space being manned by sailors who cheered the POWs enthusiastically.

'This first welcome was the best and the most heart-warming of all those we were to receive on our long journey home,' remembers Doctor Warrack. Some returned to England via Canada on USS *Gosper*, with many Canadians from Hong Kong. They were accommodated by Princess Patricia's Light Infantry in Victoria, British Columbia, and had a marvellous time before travelling for four days by train across Canada. The scenery was beautiful and Canadian hospitality overwhelming. They passed through the Rockies by night and whenever they stopped, whatever the hour, however isolated the outpost, local residents were waiting at the station to give them hot coffee, chocolate and fruit. On arrival at Halifax, Nova Scotia, they boarded the *Ile de France*.

Great was the excitement when it was announced that a Royal Army Pay Corps team was about to pay the British. Equally great was the dismay when the 'team' turned out to be a bespectacled Lance-Corporal with insufficient funds to pay more than a platoon, let alone a couple of thousand restless and frustrated ex-POWs.

The food on board was good, but there was no love for the Captain of the *Ile de France* who refused to let them smoke below decks, and there were notices everywhere telling the ex-POWs not to steal the towels. They retaliated by numbering in Japanese during the ship's boat drills, and released several men serving sentences from the ship's cells.

On arrival at Southampton in late October there was great disappointment, for the quayside was virtually empty and the ex-POWs felt let down after the warmth of American and Canadian hospitality. Apparently the public had been advised not to come to the docks to meet them. Mail was delivered at Southampton, and one soldier vividly recalls the bitter shock of opening the first letter he had received from his wife for three and a half years. It told him that their marriage was at an end. Several other wives had fallen in love with other men. Some returned to their husbands for a few months to help them recover, before marrying their boyfriends.

From Southampton a number of ex-POWs were sent straight off to a resettlement camp for three days, although their families were waiting for them at Waterloo Station. However, CSM Winspear and others travelled direct to London and found that cars awaited them. A uniformed chauffeur employed by the Duke of Grafton's son drove Winspear through devastated, bombed-out East London to his sister's home at Dagenham. Thereafter, Winspear remembers, disillusionment set in. 'We had been given a ration card which entitled us to double rations for six weeks, and we had to apply for them on the same form as a pregnant woman. One of the form's questions was: "How long were you confined?" I put down 1,324 days. I got the double ration, but a sour note crept in when the manager of the local Co-op would not accept my coupons. From that moment, I knew that I was back home.'

Another ex-POW who arrived at Waterloo station was Lieutenant-Commander Young. 'I saw a taxi draw up which I tried to enter, but a gruff policeman said, "Can't you see there's a queue? These people have been waiting for an hour or more. Go to the bottom end." Quite exhausted, I sat on my suitcase and replied: "I have been waiting four years." The couple who had just got into the taxi must have realised who the thin, forlorn creature was, and they invited me in, and fed me on the way with biscuits and tea from a thermos. I had earlier flown back via Kunming, Calcutta, Karachi and Cairo, and so I was one of the first POWs to reach England where I was a little surprised to find out how bitter the feeling was against the Japanese; to my mind everything that had happened was a clash of Western and Eastern civilianisation and culture.'[3] This view is not typical, and many ex-POWs from Hong Kong still to this day feel a deep bitterness towards the Japanese.

Lieutenant MacGregor also flew back from Kunming, in

a converted RAF Halifax bomber. 'A US pilot,' he recalls, 'told us cheerfully that the last three planes had crashed. The bomber was desperately overloaded and there was only room for us in the tail. It was bitterly cold and without oxygen we were soon all but unconscious; the pilot came back to see how we were, and had to rush back to his co-pilot to report that we were all blue and possibly dead. Although the weather was appalling, the pilot had to fly several thousand feet lower to revive us. In Suez I was told by an Intelligence Officer that the Japanese had been planning to murder us in Hong Kong on 13 September, had the surrender not taken place. I and about five others had already heard this from a trustworthy Formosan Corporal before we were released from Shamshuipo. The Corporal had told us that we were to have been crammed into a basement nearby and blown sky-high. Anyhow the atomic bomb saved our lives.'

Major Colquhoun was sent to a Rehabilitation Centre with some other Royal Artillery officers. 'The Centre was in a stately home in Kent, and after changing for dinner we descended to the ante-room where there was a roaring fire, waiters with silver trays and a genuine, pompous full Colonel in scarlet mess-kit, medals and spurs. The whole idea was to re-create the atmosphere of a pre-war Regimental Guest Night. After dinner and the Royal Toast, the Colonel made a speech in which he told us that he was in a position to guarantee us an appropriate posting of our choice, and that if any of us had any psychological problems, a highly qualified psychoanalyst on his staff could help. "Just give your name to the waiter, who will be coming round now," said the Colonel.

'All this high-grade flannel had induced in me a mood of careless abandon, so I gave my name to the waiter. A few minutes later I was ushered into a cosy room where I expected to be questioned on a couch and encouraged to think about sex. Instead, over a decanter of Cockburn '98 port and a brace of Churchillian cigars, an elderly man listened to my story. "My advice to you, old boy," he told me, "is that you should go to Ireland for a holiday; their steaks are excellent and their Guinness is good, too. You do

248

the paying, but I could probably wangle you a couple of weeks leave." So much for the psychoanalysis. Next day I told the qualified career planner that I would like to be posted to a Field Artillery unit in the south of England. "Excellent, old boy," he replied, "would Southampton suit you? Good! Consider it done." We shook hands warmly. A week later a War Office letter arrived, posting me to an Anti-aircraft battery in the far north of England.'

Private Waller, the former batman to Sir Mark Young, was another soldier who was left in no doubt that he was in the Army. He had sailed from Halifax on the *Ile de France* and eventually reached an Infantry Depot at Amersham where he was told that he should remain until he had been 'processed'. 'I had already been processed at Okinawa, Manila and Halifax and I had had enough. And so I went absent without leave,' he remembers. However, eventually he returned to the Depot where: 'Everyone thought us prisoners of the Japs were all a bit bonkers, and so we were given plenty of understanding, and I was quickly discharged and a Major drove me to the station.'[4]

Sir Mark Young and Major-General Maltby had been among the first British prisoners of the Japanese to reach England by plane, via Calcutta, on 5 September. Sir Mark had immediately visited Waller's son at school and given him a mouth organ. During the war Mrs Waller, who never knew for certain that her husband was still alive, received food parcels from Lady Young. Sir Mark never fully recovered his health as was the case also with some regular soldiers who, to their bitter disappointment, were too ill to continue their service careers.

Lance-Bombardier R. W. Hooper was found to have TB in both lungs due to the after effects of beri-beri, and he was told that he had six months to live. CSM Winspear was eventually sent to a commissioning board, but was discharged as being medically unfit for further service.

Was this typical? Were many of the ex-POWs of the Japanese permanently affected by their imprisonment, and more so than their compatriots who were imprisoned by the Germans in Europe? Were some of the British and Canadian wives and children of the Far East POWs seriously affected? The answer to all these questions is 'yes'.

A study of Canadian POWs showed that one year after repatriation they were frequently encountering such problems as poor vision, nausea, restlessness, irritability and insomnia. A follow-up study fifteen years later showed that their sight was still damaged[5]. Between 1945 and 1956 over 500 former British POWs were found to have the same symptoms. An American study revealed that ex-POWs of the Japanese had a mortality rate during the first two years following liberation over double that of other veterans of comparable age. Another study of Canadian ex-POWs arrived at similar findings[6]. Prisoners captured in Europe, on the other hand, showed no such trends because they were incomparably better treated. The principal cause of death among the POWs from the Pacific was tuberculosis which occurred about five times more frequently than the national average.

The social effects on the returned POWs were as profound as the physical and psychological damage. Higher rates of unemployment and inability to adapt to work among the former Canadian POWs were recorded. The repatriated POWs of all nationalities faced changes in their personalities and sense of values, and discrepancies in expectations of both husband and wife seriously affected many marriages.

It has been suggested that two measures which might have helped counter disturbed family adjustments would have been comprehensive programmes especially designed to support the returning POWs, and the provision of social workers to assist the families to prepare for the return of their husbands. Insufficient was done for the ex-POWs from Hong Kong and Japan and their dependents suffered accordingly. This was also the case for the United Nations POWs who had fought in Korea.[7] On the other hand at the close of the French Indo-China war, the French wisely sent specialists to Vietnam to support their returning POWs. More recently in Israel, to help families re-adjust, former Israeli POWs were successfully used as informal 'care-givers' for the dependents of men who were still kept prisoner.

Studies on the effects on children of the absent father indicate evidence of an over-protective, emotionally-neglected mother and a depressed, aggressive or alienated child. The POWs' heightened irritability, chronic fatigue and sometimes emotional instability during their years of captivity made it difficult for them to re-adjust to the traditional role of father on their repatriation.[8]

Those ex-POWs from Hong Kong and Japan who expected special treatment were quickly disillusioned, for some initially received a rotten deal. 'Pacific pay', for example, had been authorised for 1,625 Canadians who had trained in America but were never sent to the Pacific whereas, such was the miserliness of the Canadian Government, that the Canadians who had spent almost four years in prison camps in the Far East were told that they would receive the 'Pacific pay' only from the time the Regulation was passed – six months before the end of the war.[9] They therefore received a derisory $50, although Canada was holding fifteen million dollars in assets seized from the Japanese and Germans. The United States Government, on the other hand, used the assets it had seized to pay compensation to US ex-POWs who had been forced to work during imprisonment.[10]

In 1946 the Canadian ex-POWs formed the Hong Kong Veterans Association to campaign for a fair deal. By 1951 many of them were on partial disability pensions ranging up to 47% unless totally disabled such as the blind. The Canadian Government refused pensions in excess of 47% lest they would be liable to pension the widow of an ex-POW. Yet in 1964 a Government Commission carried out a two-year survey of the problems of war veterans. 100 of those who had been imprisoned in Hong Kong and who had brothers, were examined, as were the brothers who had been elsewhere during the war. The survey showed that the former had suffered significantly more than the latter and more than other ex-POWs, and so the Hong Kong Veterans Association bombarded all Members of Parliament in Canada with letters, submitted briefs to the Pension Commission, lobbied and pressured for what they believed they should have. As a result of their efforts over thirty-five years, the Canadian Government gradually became the most generous.[11] Today the majority of Canadians who fought in Hong Kong have qualified for a total of 100% combined disability pension and POW compensation – almost £280 a month for a single man and £350 for the married. Nobody is receiving less than 50%, therefore on the death of an ex-POW his widow automatically receives a pension. The American ex-POW Association is trying to obtain similar compensation. The Canadian disability pensioner at present receives a substantially greater benefit than his American counterpart.

The British who were imprisoned in Hong Kong receive no special pension unless they can prove disability. Mr Hooper, who survived TB and can now do light work, receives a 60% pension of £150 a month, while Mr Winspear who is totally disabled receives over £500 per month. He recently won a competition for old soldiers who would like to make a sentimental journey to somewhere he had served during the war. Winspear chose Tokyo and Nagasaki and the sites of the former POW camps. Wherever he went he received the warmest hospitality from the Japanese. This is not unusual, and many other former POWs who have visited Japan have received nothing but kindness.

About twenty-five years earlier Mr Winspear had received compensation from the Japanese which was paid to the British POWs who had been imprisoned. The funds came from the Japanese assets in Britain seized during the war and from the eventual sale of the Burma-Siam railway. The total sum amounted to about £80 for each POW or widow.

When some ex-POWs in England and Canada had started to pick up the threads of their former lives their evidence against the Japanese who had allegedly committed atrocities in Hong Kong was required. British and Indian supposed traitors, and those who were believed to have collaborated with the enemy were also placed on trial.

The trials started in Hong Kong in 1946. Inouye Kanao, the vicious Canadian-born guard, had been responsible for many deaths. He was found guilty and condemned to death but it was then decided that since he was Canadian, treason was a more appropriate charge and so he was re-tried on that count. He argued that he had renounced his Canadian citizenship after the Japanese surrender and so owed no allegiance to the Crown. However he was again found guilty and was hanged in Stanley Gaol in August 1947.

Two other Japanese who faced the death penalty were Colonel Tokunaga Isao, the overall commander of all Hong Kong's camps, and Captain Saito Shunkichi, the camps' medical officer. The charges against them included killing Canadian and British POWs.

Major J. N. Crawford, the senior Canadian medical officer, told the Court that of 128 Canadian deaths from diphtheria, 101 would not have died had the Japanese provided the serum. It was stated by Warrant Officer F. W. J. Lewis that £30,000 worth of British medicines and surgical instruments were in the Colony when it was captured, but that they were deliberately withheld. Had throat swabbing been done earlier, many of the lives lost would never have been in jeopardy. 'The death of every man who died of diphtheria because of failure to ensure segregation, or the lack of serum, was directly Saito's responsibility, no less than if he had grasped the man by the throat and choked him to death,' declared Major

Puddicombe, KC. The prosecution also stated that slappings and beatings were almost daily occurrences; collective punishments were forbidden by International Law, yet they had been inflicted on POWs. Four Canadian and five British POWs as well as countless Chinese civilians had been executed without trial, although this was illegal both under the International Code and Japanese Regulations. Red Cross parcels and milk for sick POWs were pilfered by the Japanese; men dying on bare floors were hidden from the Red Cross who were inspecting the POW camps, and unfit men were made to work for the Japanese.

The Japanese Counsel for the defence, Fujita Tetsuo and Hasegawa Yukichi, found several British POWs who were prepared to give evidence in favour of Tokunaga and Saito. Major C. R. Boxer called Warrant Officer Lewis's evidence about a beating by Saito, 'a tissue of lies', and Major J. Smith of the Volunteers wrote to the Court about the kindness Tokunaga had shown him.

The defence maintained that diphtheria serum was not available in time to save patients. Saito told the Court that there were only three cases of cholera among the POWs due to his efforts, whereas 1,700 Chinese died of it in Hong Kong. He blamed the high proportion of Canadian deaths from diphtheria on inevitable overcrowding, inadequate sanitary discipline, and the poor knowledge of the POW doctors who, Saito argued, were responsible for the diagnosis and treatment of their men. Japanese slapping was explained away as being 'a sort of training – an everyday affair in the Japanese army – more of a reminder than a punishment.'[1]

Tokunaga claimed that he had been given, rather than stolen, Red Cross parcels, and that collective punishments had been ordered by Isogai, the Governor-General. During the trial Tokunaga occasionally showed his impatience and irritation at being questioned, and he claimed that he was so hungry in Stanley gaol that he sometimes had to eat grass. He felt that he had done his best for the POWs, and that he had been ridiculed by Japanese officers of other units for doing so; Japan had been fighting a bitter war and the POWs were disgraced by surrender whereas, he maintained,

Japanese 'women and children find it better to die than become a POW'. He added that he felt he deserved a medal. However, the evidence was so overwhelming that the hangman's noose was considered appropriate. The trial lasted almost two months and finished on 13 February 1947. Colonel Tokunaga was found guilty of eight charges out of ten, and Captain Saito of four charges. Three other guards were also convicted of mistreating POWs. The Court took about an hour and a half to consider their sentences.

Before they were passed, Tokunaga said that he was sorry his subordinates must be given sentences since they had worked hard and carried out their duties towards the POWs with the best intent. As far as he was concerned, he had said his prayers to atone for his crimes.

The President, Lieutenant-Colonel R. C. Laming, in the presence of a large number of ex-POWs, told Tokunaga that he was guilty of being concerned with the killing of Canadian and British POWs under his charge, while Saito was responsible for inhumane treatment to POWs, causing death to some and suffering to others. Both were sentenced to death by hanging. Tokunaga and Saito received their sentences stoically, displaying no emotion. The three guards were sentenced to between one and three years' imprisonment.

Despite the enormity of Tokunaga and Saito's crimes, their death sentences were commuted to life and twenty years' imprisonment respectively. One is left with the impression that the courts-martial in Hong Kong were far more lenient than they should have been. The British have never been good haters. The severity of the sentences at other trials appeared to depend upon where they were held. Those tried in Hong Kong were fortunate. Major-General Tanaka Ryozaburo whose Regiment was among the first to land on Hong Kong Island received only twenty years' imprisonment although the court was satisfied that: 'The whole route of this man's battalion was littered with the corpses of murdered men who had been bayoneted and shot.' Among the few executed in Hong Kong were Colonels Noma and Kanagawa who had commanded the Military

Police in Hong Kong. They had been responsible for many callous murders during interrogations. They never discovered the name of a particular individual who smuggled medicines and money to the POWs, doctors and internees, for he was no other than a Japanese guard named Kyoshi Watanabe. He had frequently risked his life also in passing messages between POWs and their families in Stanley camp. Tragically his entire family was killed in Hiroshima. A few other Japanese surreptitiously helped POWs both in Hong Kong and in Japan.

Among Japanese who were tried in Japan were Hong Kong's two Governors. Isogai received a life sentence and his successor, Lieutenant-General Tanaka, was executed. Meanwhile those responsible for the overall policy of callously neglecting POWs were sought, but Lieutenant-General Uemura, the chief supervisor of POWs in Tokyo's War Ministry committed suicide, as did Hamada, his deputy.

Mamoru Shigemitsu had been the pre-war Japanese Ambassador in London where he had been universally respected, but as Foreign Minister in Tokyo during the last two years of the war he had failed to press for investigations into the conditions and treatment of POWs, despite receiving protest after protest which went unanswered or were only answered after months of unexplained delay. Shigemitsu was sentenced to seven years' imprisonment and served barely two. Mr Justice Pal, the Indian member of the Tribunal, announced that Shigemitsu should have been acquitted, but it was felt by some that the Indian's findings were not based on evidence but influenced by political considerations.

About 400 Indian soldiers captured in Hong Kong are believed to have joined the pro-Japanese Indian National Army. Overall, 40,000 Indians from all theatres had been gathered in Burma for an invasion of their homeland, though it is fair to say that many had so enlisted in order to obtain better food and conditions. According to two Indian writers 6,000 INA fought in the ranks of the Japanese Army at Imphal and Kohima against their own countrymen.

Their goal was India's independence. There is much strong evidence that their fighting amounted to no more than a token gesture. When the war ended the British in India decided that those who had joined the INA to wage war against British India should be dismissed from the Army and sentenced to imprisonment, while those who had been misled or yielded to pressure should be dismissed with forty days paid leave. At the same time those who had committed atrocities were to face the due process of law. From a purely legal point of view all who had joined the INA were guilty of treason and liable to the death penalty but behind the law there were other considerations. The INA prisoners had become symbols of India fighting for independence and so were treated as heroes. The trials dramatized and gave visible form to the old conception of Empire versus Indian Independence.

Several of those who had sided with the Japanese in Hong Kong had treated with brutality their compatriots who were loyal to the British; however they were saved by the fast-developing political situation. Congress whipped up public opinion, using the INA trials to gain an electoral advantage and increase the pressure on Britain for independence. The Royal Indian Navy mutinied, and many Indian Army officers supported the popular demand for the release of INA officers. 'All courts-martial were later quashed for political consideration,' recalls a British officer from Hong Kong then serving in the Indian Army. 'Later senior ranks who had been dismissed without pension were not only reinstated but promoted in the new Indian and Pakistan armies. Imagine the bitterness of the loyal who had suffered so much!' Viewed through different eyes, the pro-Japanese Indians had marched as soldiers with Delhi as their objective where they were eventually to arrive as prisoners. However, as prisoners they had sparked off revolt in India, and the impact of their trials contributed to strengthening Indian nationalism.

The trials of British servicemen who were alleged to have co-operated with the Japanese were less controversial. It came as no surprise to the POWs from Shamshuipo that one of their officers, Major Cecil Boon, Royal Army Service Corps, faced a general court-martial on eleven charges, one of which was assisting the enemy. The trial took place in London in August 1946. Evidence was given by former prisoners that he was too obsequious to the Japanese, that he informed on them and helped the Japanese find wireless sets and tunnels for escape. Boon was alleged to have said to other prisoners: 'We must do as the Japanese tell us. We are officers of the Japanese Army now. I don't regard myself as a British officer, but as part of the Japanese staff. I owe no allegiance to the King.' The prosecution called forty witnesses and there was no ex-POW to give evidence for the defence.

A full Colonel presided, with five other officers as members of the court. Major Boon, who had been under close arrest since the end of the war, was not at his best, and his conviction seemed probable. However it soon became evident that the desperate years of imprisonment had made the witnesses' memories unreliable and their testimony in part contradictory. Some of the witnesses broke under formidable cross-examination.

'I think,' wrote one of the defending counsel later, 'that it does great credit to the court-martial system and to the fairness and common sense of the officers in the Court that ... after appalling initial prejudice against him, the Major was acquitted.' Boon appeared half-stunned by the proceedings and his acquittal, and was scarcely able to enjoy the celebrations at the Savoy Grill afterwards. In the absence of legal aid he had to pay his entire defence costs, a considerable sum.

Sergeant J. H. Harvey, Royal Army Medical Corps, faced thirty charges, including that of the manslaughter in Oeyama POW Camp of Private U. Frieson of the Winnipeg Grenadiers. It was also alleged that in 1944 he had rounded up men too sick almost to totter, let alone work, and had sent them to the mines to please the Japanese. Harvey was arrested in Canada while about to board the *Ile De France* for England with other ex-POWs. British, American and Canadian troops gave evidence against him at his trial in

Winnipeg, and told how he had beaten them for misdemeanours such as stealing from Japanese custody Red Cross parcels, cigarettes, wood and coal. Under cross-examination witnesses agreed that Harvey had nursed them when they were sick, scrounged food for them and kept them alive.

Harvey admitted that he had given Frieson sharp slaps after which he had died, but only because the medical officer, he said, had decided that Frieson had hysteria and, in the complete absence of medical facilities, he could not have known that Frieson had a disease of the brain. On the other charges Harvey argued that the strong stole and ate while the frail starved and died. There was only one effective punishment for stealing, and that was physical punishment. He said that he prevented thieving and stopped starving prisoners from bargaining away their handful of rice for a cigarette, thereby saving many lives. As for sending sick prisoners to work, Harvey told of his agonising decision in bargaining with the Japanese Camp Commandant to release Red Cross parcels if Harvey made up the labour force, which could be done only by making some sick work. He therefore gained precious extra food, although some suffered. It was not disputed that deaths in camp had dropped dramatically under his regime. There were plenty of witnesses for the defence and as the trial progressed Harvey was treated with warmth, whereas, at the beginning, he had been regarded as an English traitor who had curried favour with the Japanese by thrashing Canadian troops.

Harvey was acquitted of manslaughter but was found guilty on six of the thirty charges. He was moved for sentencing to England on the *Queen Mary*, locked in a cell once more. On arrival fate took an unexpected turn. He was told that the verdict of guilty had been quashed, and instead he had been mentioned in despatches for his conduct in the POW camp. After eleven months of allied imprisonment, he was honoured for exactly the same deeds for which he had been court-martialled. Harvey was later commissioned and reached the rank of Major in the Royal Army Medical Corps.

While the Indians, Major Boon and Sergeant Harvey were facing trials for co-operating with the enemy, suspected collaborators were being held in custody in Hong Kong. They were charged with specific offences under English law such as treason or breach of the Defence Regulations.

There were complaints from many Chinese in Hong Kong in the immediate post war months that persons whose names used to figure prominently at Japanese functions now figured equally prominently at British functions. MacDougall reported to the Colonial Office, within two months of his arrival: 'The most serious (and from the point of view of our pre-war system, the most damning) factor is that there seem to be no new Chinese of the younger generation anxious to shoulder the responsibility for public affairs. I have been unable to find candidates anxious to contest the local leadership of the established order.'[2]

While some of the most prominent Chinese of the 'established order' were believed to have collaborated, 'few substantial citizens of the Colony escaped contact with the occupying forces: consequently few are free from the besmirchment of rumour and whisper,' it was reported to the Colonial Office. 'The result has been hideously embarrassing. Much of the business of conducting local affairs has in times past been conducted through various committees of Chinese: those who served on these committees occupied at least nominal positions of responsibility under the Japanese: it seems certain that a proportion of them behaved very badly.'

On Admiral Harcourt's orders Sir Robert Kotewall was told by MacDougall that he was to withdraw from public life immediately and await investigation. A British officer recalls: 'I was under strict orders not to admit him to a Council meeting and it was a terrible moment in my life to have to tell Sir Robert that he could not come in, for I had dined many times in his house before the war.' However, as related earlier, several British, who had been leading members of the Hong Kong Government before the war, announced that Sir Robert had been formally asked by them in January 1942, to co-operate with the Japanese and thereby to do whatever was possible for the Chinese community. He was to some extent vindicated after the war, but the subject remains controversial to this day.

Newspaper reports indicate that fifty-four Europeans, Eurasians, Indians, and Chinese were found guilty of collaborating with the Japanese, but few influential Chinese were among them. This was recognised by one jury in November 1946, which, after finding a European stock-broker guilty, added a rider to their verdict that it was inconsistent with British justice that one collaborator should be punished when so many others escaped unpunished. Five collaborators were hanged, but most of the others served relatively short periods of imprisonment. Hong Kong was too pre-occupied in looking forward, and in consolidating its initial advantage over neighbouring countries, to attach much importance to these trials.

The Hong Kong Administration had no choice other than to rely upon the Government's pre-war Chinese advisers as so few new figures had emerged at that time. However, there was in the air a genuine, if vague, desire for something new. 'Hong Kong will not meekly acquiesce in an attempted resuscitation of the worn-out governmental machine which let us down so badly in 1941,' stated one Hong Kong newspaper editorial. 'In view of all the noble utterances concerning the new World Order, there has been some feeling of disillusionment.' Presumably the editorial was referring to the Atlantic Charter.

Preaching at the Cathedral on Armistice Day 1945, the Bishop of Victoria, the Rt Rev. R. O. Hall, touched upon the same subject. After reference to the heavy losses of the men who had defended Hong Kong so gallantly, he said: 'Under God we dare not stay in Hong Kong unless it is our purpose to build here, as part of the great Pacific civilisation of the future, a city in which truth and freedom and justice are not tainted by national pride or racial fear.'

On 30 April 1946, Sir Mark Young the first post-war Governor of Hong Kong arrived in the Colony. The King had reappointed him as he had shown such outstanding leadership during the battle for Hong Kong and later as a prisoner of war. It caused great gratification to all who knew him that Sir Mark should return.

On the following morning the White Ensign of Vice-Admiral Sir Cecil Harcourt over Government House was run down, the Union Jack being raised in its place.

The dark period of tyranny and oppression under Japan's flag of the Rising Sun had gone. Disillusionment vanished and racial problems did not materialise. The resilience and optimism of Hong Kong's inhabitants ensured that a golden future lay ahead.

Those who fought for the Colony and those who endured the wretched years of occupation could scarcely have dreamed of Hong Kong's post-war years of prosperity while violence and misery ravaged neighbouring countries in South-East Asia.

Thousands had fought and died in Hong Kong to restore freedom to mankind. 'At the going down of the sun and in the morning we will remember them.'[3]

Acknowledgements and Sources

During five years of research for *At the Going Down of the Sun* I had the privilege to be in touch with several hundred men and women who took part in the events described. Many of them lent me their reminiscences, diaries and letters written during or shortly after the war, and I have been extremely fortunate in being able to meet most of them. I remain very conscious of the generosity and helpfulness of the following in particular who contributed to this book and answered many queries for the chapter indicated:

Chapter:

2. Cdr G. H. Gandy, Lt-Cdr J. H. Yorath
3. C. B. J. Stewart, Brig. C. R. Templer, DSO
4. Mrs G. A. Goodban, Mrs. C. M. M. Man
5. Tom Forsyth, Capt. H. L. White
6. Arthur Alsey, P. D. A. Chidell, E. H. Field, J. D. A. Gray, Maj.-Gen. Kampta Prasad, MC, Roger Lamble, John Monro, MC, Lt-Col. M. E. E. Truscott
7. A. G. Atkinson, Cdr J. C. Boldero, DSC, A. R. Colquhoun
8. Brig. J. H. Price, OBE, MC, R. D. Scriven
9. J. A. Ford, MC, the late Sir Lindsay Ride, CBE
10. The late G. V. Bird, GM, TD, J. L. Flynn, J. R. Harris, D. Hunter, R. S. Young
11. Major and Mrs Charles Forrester, Lao Wei-Ching, Leo d'Almada E. Castro, CBE, G. S. Zimmern
12. G. C. Hamilton, CBE, Bob Parkinson, Alf Taylor
13. Brig. T. H. Massy-Beresford, DSO, MC, John Waller, Brig. C. Wallis
14. G. P. Adams, R. W. Hooper, H. F. Linge, J. P. Burrough, The Bishop of Mashonaland, E. J. Soden, A. J. N. Warrack, MBE, J. Winspear, H. R. Yates
15. Charles Fenn
16. Iain MacGregor
18. John R. Stroud

I should like to acknowledge the helpfulness and efficiency of the archivists of the Public Records Offices in Hong Kong and London where I was able to obtain access to extensive, unpublished material. I have also been most fortunate in obtaining much new information from the Department of History, NDHQ Ottawa, and from archives in America and India. In Hong Kong I was able to study the World War II records in possession of the Hong Kong and Shanghai Bank, Royal Hong Kong Police, Jardine Matheson and the Bishop of Hong Kong. Juliet Cornwall's patient research on my behalf in the Colony solved several riddles.

In England special thanks are due to the staff of the Imperial War Museum, Ministry of Defence Library, Royal Naval Historical Branch and the Royal United Services Institute. Mrs D. C. Snowdon very kindly gave me access to the numerous unpublished papers of her father, Sir Franklin Gimson, and Colonel B. A. Fargus, OBE, Royal Scots, was among the most helpful Regimental Secretaries.

Of the many who helped me in Canada I must single out Neil Bardal, Grant S. Garneau, whose thesis, *The Royal Rifles of Canada*, proved invaluable, and Brereton Greenhous, the senior Historian National Defence Headquarters.

I must also acknowledge the patience and good humour of my wife, Clare, who continued to bring me black coffee at strange hours while 'following the drum' in Hong Kong, Canada and England. Finally, I owe a great deal to my father, Sir Martin Lindsay of Dowhill Bt, CBE, DSO, who commented on all the drafts, made invaluable suggestions, and endeavoured to improve my literacy. One of his telegrams to me read: 'Sentences much too short. Terribly lazy. Much Love Father'!

OLIVER LINDSAY

Brookwood House,
Brookwood,
Surrey

References

Abbreviations: ADM Admiralty Files
                CO   Colonial Office Files
                FO   Foreign Office Files
                IWA Interview with the Author
                LTA Letter to the Author
                PRO Public Records Office, Kew, London
                WO   War Office Files

Location of Material: Unless indicated otherwise all ADM, CO, FO and WO documents are in the PRO, and all reports, diaries, letters, and reminiscences are in the possession of the author.

1 THE FALL OF HONG KONG
1. Kirby, *The War Against Japan*, Vol. I, p. 146
2. For a full description of the Hong Kong Campaign, see *The Lasting Honour*, Hamish Hamilton, 1978, Sphere Books, 1980
3. CO 129 590/25
4. Fortress HQ War Diary, p. 29

2 THE GREAT ESCAPE
1. Reminiscences of Lt-Cdr G. H. Gandy
2. Report by Cdr H. M. Montague 16.1.42. RN Historical Branch, Empress State Building, MOD, London
3. Capt. F. Guest, *Escape from the Bloodied Sun*, 1956
4. Kirby, *The War Against Japan*, Vol. II, p. 95

3 SOME CORNER OF A FOREIGN FIELD
1. Loose Minute 29.5.42 CO 129 590/25 HN 00152
2. Report by Ride, Ibid.
3. Dr Li Shu-fan, *Hong Kong Surgeon* NY, 1964 p. 103
4. LTA
5. CO 129 59L Pt 1 X/N 00265 p. 9
6. CO 119 590/25 HN 00152 p.5

4 STANLEY CIVILIAN INTERNMENT CAMP
1. CO 980 59 HN 00493 p. 9
2. Report GHQ India 21.7.42 CO 980/53
3. Unless indicated otherwise, all Gimson's Quotations are from

his *Personal Impressions as Recorded in a Diary*, See also CO 980 192 HN 00745

4. Letter to Lord Moyne 8.11.41, CO 129 590/18 HN 00152
5. Letter 23.7.42 written by W. Floyd Carman, D 98053 HN 00493, PRO
6. CO 980 59 HN 00495, p. 13

5 THE CANADIANS AT NORTH POINT
1. G. S. Garneau, Thesis, *Royal Rifles of Canada*, p. 251
2. Churchill, *The Grand Alliance*, 1950, p. 177
3. File S 8873 National Defence HQ, Dept of History, Ottawa
4. Sir Lyman Duff, *Report.on the Canadian Expeditionary Force to the Crown Colony of Hong Kong*, Ottawa, 1942
5. IWA
6. Capt. H. L. White, POW Diary, p. 8
7. Report to Admiralty RN Historical Branch
8. Capt. E. L. Hurd, Diary quoted in Garneau's Thesis

6 SHAMSHUIPO CAMP
1. CO 980 59 HN 00493
2. Luncheon Address, Canadian Memorial Association Annual Meeting, Winnipeg 26.6.47
3. Evidence at Saito's Trial 17.1.47
4. *Manitoba Medical Review* Feb. 1946, p. 63–68 and *Canadian Medical Association Journal*, 1947, p. 1–4
5. LTA
6. IWA
7. LTA

7 ARGYLE STREET OFFICERS' POW CAMP
1. CO 980 155 HN 00745, p. 10
2. CO 980 54 HN 00649
3. FO 916 761 HN 00649
4. WO 208 3486 HN 04176

8 OPERATIONS TOP SECRET
1. IWA
2. WO 203 129 HN 00745
3. WO 208 3260 HN 04176
4. Young, *China and the Helping Hand*, p. 418
5. ADM 199 1286 HN 00493
6. Report by Capt. Valentine to CO HKVDC
7. WO 208 3260 HN 04176

8. Details obtained from National Archives, Govt of India, New Delhi
9. Ghosh, *The Indian National Army*, 1969, p. 55
10. J. A. D. Morrison's account in Hong Kong and Shanghai Bank archives
11. Sir P. S. Selwyn-Clarke, *Footprints*, p. 71

9 DISASTER
1. IWA
2. Information obtained from captured Japanese documents CO 980 62 HN 00265
3. IWA
4. Statement by W. J. Anderson, PRO Archives Hong Kong CR 7676/45
5. Report by Maj. C. R. Boxer 26.8.45

10 INTERROGATION
1. Report to Admiralty 1945. RN Historical Branch
2. LTA
3. IWA and report Sept. 1945

11 JAPAN'S NEW ORDER
1. K. Mattock, *The Story of Government House*, p. 87, HK Government Information Services 1978
2. *South China Morning Post* 4.6.50
3. CO 129 591/4 HN 00035
4. CO 980 59 HN 00493
5. Report by Father Meyer Jan. 42–Aug. 45
6. Report INDIA/1296 CO 980 54 HN 00649
7. CO 980 61 NN 00265, p. 7
8. CO 980 53 HN 00493, p. 6
9. CO 129 591/4 HN 0035
10. Bishop of Hong Kong's Newsletter 10.12.45
11. LTA
12. Kweilin Intelligence Summary No. 28 CO 980 60 HN 00265
13. Sir P. S. Selwyn-Clarke, *Footprints*, p. 83
14. FO 916 453
15. Loose Minute 16.1.43 FO 916 769 HN 00649
16. FO 916 761 HN 00649
17. CO 980/61
18. Account of Sir F. C. Gimson, p. 9
19. FO 916 735 HN 00649
20. CO 129/589/18

21. CO 980 52 HN 00265
22. Ibid. Telegram to FO No. 177 27.2.42
23. Russell, *The Knights of Bushido*, 1958, p. 63

12 ORDEAL AT SEA
 1. IWA
 2. G. C. Hamilton, *The Sinking of the Lisbon Maru*, p. 4, Green
    Pagoda Press, Hong Kong, 1966
 3. IWA
 4. Article in *The Thistle* (Regimental Journal of the Royal Scots)
    April 1946
 5. RN Archives Adm 199 1286 HN 00493, p. 188
 6. IWA
 7. LTA
 8. Report 29.12.42, British Embassy Kukong to Foreign Office
    CO 980 67 HN 00649

13 CHANGI TO MANCHURIA
 1. BAAG report 21.11.44 CO 129 591/4 HN 0035
 2. IWA
 3. J. A. White, *The United States Marines in North China*, p. 50, 1974
 4. Ibid., p. 50
 5. CO 980/63
 6. Ibid.
 7. CO 129 590/25 HN 00152
 8. Evidence of Brig. Blackburn, IMT, Far East Proceedings,
    p.547
 9. Letter 11.11.42
10. IWA
11. Wainwright, *General Wainwright's Story*, p. 206, 1970
12. Interview with Brig. C. Wallis

14 THE DECLINE OF THE RISING SUN
 1. LTA
 2. Doctor A. J. N. Warrack's Reminiscences, p. 14
 3. LTA
 4. LTA
 5. LTA
 6. LTA from W. Parkinson
 7. Adm 199 1286 HN 00493, p. 188
 8. MS Group 30, E 328 Public Archives of Canada
 9. G. P. Adams, *Destination Japan*, p. 21. Printed privately. 139
    Banks Rd., Sandbanks, Poole, Dorset, 1980

10. J. Winspear's Reminiscences, p. 11
11. *The (US) Army Air Forces in World War Two,* Vol. 5, 1952
12. Wright, *I was a Hell Camp Prisoner,* p. 114
13. Ibid., p. 117
14. P. D. A. Chidell's Diary, p. 62
15. IWA
16. IWA
17. Brig. T. Massy-Beresford, Reminiscences, Ch. 30, p. 6

15 THE FUTURE SOVEREIGNTY OF HONG KONG
1. CO 129 591/4 HN 00035
2. Letter 21.2.45 to FO 203 2/342145
3. *Foreign Relations of the United States,* 1945, VII, p. 120
4. WO 208 3260 HN 04176, p. 109
5. Signal No. 835, 14.8.45 Ibid.
6. IWA
7. IWA and Captain Fenn's Official report Sept. 1945
8. C in C Hong Kong's report 5/67/3 CO 129 591/18 HN 00152

16 FREEDOM
1. Sir F. C. Gimson's Reminiscences
2. F. W. Shaftain's Reminiscences, RHK Police records
3. Captain H. L. White's diary
4. *Manitoba Medical Review,* Vol. 26, No. 2 Feb. 1946, p. 63–68
5. Mrs M. H. Goodban's Reminiscences, p. 4
6. IWA
7. Sir F. C. Gimson's Reminiscences, p. 7
8. D. M. MacDougall report to G. E. J. Gent 7.11.48
9. IWA
10. D. M. MacDougall's reports dated 15.9.45, 7.11.45 and 5.12.45 to Sir George Gater, Colonial Office, are on files CO 129 594/6, CO 129 591/20 and CO 129 594/6 respectively
11. CO 129/592/5
12. CO 129/592/6 HN 00182. Also CO 129/595/9

17 SURVIVAL
1. James Sims, *Arnhem Spearhead,* 1979

18 REHABILITATION
1. IWA
2. LTA
3. IWA
4. IWA

5. J. T. Baird, *Canadian Medical Services Journal*, 12/485–93
6. J. D. Hermann Report to the Minister of Veteran Affairs Ottawa 1973
7. P. J. Metres, *Family Separation & Reunion*, p. 147–56 US Government Publication
8. J. Sigal. Paper presented at Annual Meeting of Canadian Psychiatric Association, Ottawa 1974
9. *Star Weekly*, Toronto 28.8.65
10. *Macleans Magazine*, July 1968
11. *Township Sun*, Autumn 1975, p. 63

19 RETRIBUTION
1. See Hong Kong Newspaper articles in particular *South China Morning Post* during the trials
2. Letter 7.11.45, CO 129 591/20 HN 00152
3. 'Poems For the Fallen' by Laurence Binyon

Bibliography

(Other books are referred to in References)

G. B. Endacott, Alan Birch, *Hong Kong Eclipse*, Oxford University Press, 1978

Ralph Goodwin, *Passport to Eternity*, Arthur Barker, 1954

K. K. Ghosh, *The Indian National Army*, Meenakshi, India, 1969

S. Woodburn Kirby, *The War Against Japan*, 5 vols., HM Stationery Office, 1957

Lord Russell of Liverpool, *Knights of Bushido*, Cassell & Co., 1958

Christopher Thorne, *Allies of a Kind*, Hamish Hamilton, 1978

General J. M. Wainwright, *General Wainwright's Story*, Greenwood Press, USA, 1970

Robert J. Wright, *I was a Hell Camp Prisoner*, Brown, Watson Ltd, 1963

Arthur N. Young, *China and the Helping Hand 1937–1945*, Harvard University Press, USA, 1963

Index

273

275